I'll Never Tell

Odyssey of a Rock & Roll Priest

I'll Never Tell

Odyssey of a Rock & Roll Priest

By Monsignor Harry G. Schlitt

Foreword by Kevin Starr

Edited by Cindy Arch

SHRP

Sand Hill Review Press

Published by Sand Hill Review Press
www.sandhillreviewpress.com
P.O. Box 1275, San Mateo, CA 94401
(415) 297-3571

Library of Congress Control Number: 2016940036
Memoir
Christian

ISBN: 978-1-937818-45-6

Graphics by Backspace Ink

Photos from the private collection of Msgr. Harry G. Schlitt except "Clyde and Harry setting out for St. Louis" used with permission from the *Southeast Missourian,* photo credit G.D. Fronabarger; and "Father Harry teaching at the minor seminary" used with permission from the *The Mirror*/Diocese of Springfield-Cape Girardeau.

SHRP
Sand Hill Review Press

for Jan

who saved my life more than once

Father Harry, like Odysseus,
traveled on epic journeys,
faced many temptations, obstacles and tests.
He was between a rock and a hard
place far too often, failed,
displayed weakness, but always
returned to his Church.

Foreword

Monsignor Harry Schlitt is a survivor from that tsunami of more than 40,000 priests who left the ministry in the aftermath of Vatican II. In this vividly expressive memoir, Monsignor Schlitt relates the stories of priest friends who made this painful decision. He does so in a spirit of understanding and fraternity and with a kind of wide-eyed wonderment that—thanks to the grace of God, he believes—he himself was not swept up in this exodus. Innumerable lay people who have benefited from Monsignor Schlitt's priestly ministries are likewise grateful that he remained active in the vocation that has defined his life.

I'll Never Tell is written with panache, unpretentiousness, and love of the people by a Missouri lad from a hardscrabble background who barely into his teenage years knew that he wanted to be a Catholic, and even more, a Catholic priest, although at the time he had little idea of what exactly that meant. It took decades for him to find out and to adjust to the fact that priesthood—however diversified in expression, however successful in outcome—involved a high level of sacrifice that would never come easily.

Only a diocesan or secular priest could write *I'll Never Tell;* for these are the priests whom the Church requires to throw themselves headlong into the service of the people, to read the signs of the time, to be in the world but not of it, to animate themselves with a non-self-conscious piety emphasizing priestly service to others along with the acceptance of people's faults as well as their own faults.

The diocesan or secular priesthood of the Roman Catholic Church represents the cutting edge of the Church's pastoral ministry as far as preaching, counseling, and the administration of the sacraments are concerned. In apostolic times, the apostles created bishops to guide and govern the church and deacons to serve its administrative and practical needs. Towards the conclusion of the apostolic era or somewhat later, bishops shared a significant portion of their priestly identity with presbyters (priests) representing the bishop in rural areas. As Christianity further urbanized, so too did the presbyterate, and the priesthood emerged as a fully established tier of Holy Orders whose primary responsibility was the spiritual care of the people in all their complexity and challenges as they journeyed through life. Diocesan priests were until recently called secular priests— from the Latin *saeculum*, meaning in time, in the world— because they were of the world, not leaving it but serving its spiritual needs. Over the centuries, the Roman Catholic Church developed an array of religious orders that since the Counter Reformation became increasingly clericalized. But the freestanding diocesan or secular priest, loyal to his bishop, taking no vows but promising celibacy, became the norm for parish life.

A graduate of the North American College in Rome (the West Point of American priestly training), Father Harry, as he was then known, created a unique ministry as a rock & roll priest, the continuing star of the television and/or radio format the God Squad. Two contending forces converged in Father Harry: his Roman education, preparing him for an elite career in the Church, and his rock & roll self, keeping him in environments that were decidedly non-ecclesiastical. Ordained in the early 1960s during the Second Vatican Council, Father Harry assumed priests would have permission to marry within five years. He turned out to be wrong. In this candid memoir, Monsignor Schlitt deals with the friendships and associations he formed over the years with female colleagues. In his younger days, he looked like a rock star and, it can be surmised, faced a rock star's temptations. Yet he prevailed in his calling. In his later years, moreover, he experienced great success and satisfaction as a pastor of an established parish. Appointed the chief operating officer of the Archdiocese of San Francisco, he was named a domestic prelate (with the title monsignor) by Pope Benedict XVI.

Here is a memoir about Catholicism, the priesthood, and a search for New Age ministries, such as hitting the bars on

Chestnut Street in San Francisco, where Father Harry ministered to a ragtag congregation of high-born and low, respectable and not so respectable, believers and those wishing they could believe, whom he befriended and counseled. All this outreach occurred within the matrix of a lifelong commitment to continue in the priesthood as the best way of making sense of his own life and being of service to others.

This is an engaging, sometimes a slyly humorous book, sometimes a book illumined by lightning bolts of religious insight. It is the real McCoy, expressive of the contradictions and confluences of our era, and it possesses a particularly American point of view: not only in its depictions of a boyhood enlivened by conversion and vocation almost simultaneously, followed by a journey from simple beginnings to the splendors of Rome, followed by a half-century of priestly ministry orthodox in content but frequently unorthodox in style: all this told matter-of-factly and frequently with a playful irony downplaying self-absorption.

What turbulent times we Catholics, lay and clerical alike, have lived in this past half century! How remote seems the triumphalism of an earlier era. And yet, how enduring seems the Church that carries through time Christ's promise that He would be with us for all days. That He knew each of us. That even the hairs of our head are numbered. In the complexities and contradictions of who we are—who we really are, what we dream of, what we hope and fear, what delusions motivate us—we struggle towards a better self while remaining grateful for our individuality. Like Father Harry, we struggle to live out our lives in a spirit of self-acceptance, faith, hope, and charity.

Kevin Starr
California State Librarian Emeritus

Prologue

I have been one of those fortunate people who has really never had any insurmountable crisis and, therefore, have managed to remain happy most of my life.

It was 1968 when I wrote those words. I was a new young priest, fresh from Rome, teaching Preparation for Marriage to teenage Catholic girls in the Ozarks and working as a disc jockey for a rock & roll radio station on Route 66. Filled with the Holy Spirit and great love of the Vatican, the pope and the Church, I was eager to change the world.

I was a pioneer in the media ministry frontier opened by the Second Vatican Council. *I'll Never Tell* was my weekly call-in show for teens. It was a first of its kind and a big sensation. I mixed clips from *Billboard* hits with upbeat non-denominational messages centering on the inevitable problems of youth. The phone would light up with calls from kids drawn by the music as well as the desire to be heard. It was a public yet anonymous confessional of the airwaves with a Top Ten soundtrack. They knew their parents weren't listening and I was.

I was influenced by teenagers who trusted me and taught me how important it was to talk about it. Communication and relating in person were big then, unlike today where we all have private devices with pictures to share our thoughts and plans. I was impressed with how much I could do using the tools of mass media. I lived and loved rock & roll music and found a way to use it on the radio and television. *I'll Never Tell* launched a career that I'm grateful to say has lasted to this day.

In fifty years as a priest and a broadcaster, I've had the remarkable good fortune to walk among the likes of Saint Pope John XXIII, James Brown and Joan Crawford. I've shared the stage with Bob Hope, the screen with Michael Douglas, shared the bill with the James Gang, the pulpit with the cast of *Godspell* and the altar with Fulton Sheen. I've lived in world capitals— Rome, New York, San Francisco—but I came from a small town in Missouri (never really grew up there) on the banks of the Mississippi River. It was a town made up of dirt and animal farmers trying to adjust to sidewalks, pavement and quasi-city politics.

At age fourteen I left home for seminary training. My Catholic family was very supportive except for my sister who read the daily schedule and decided I wouldn't last a week. Of course, I didn't know all that it would entail. I thought I would be married within five years of my ordination in 1964. The Second Vatican Council was that breath of fresh air that we all needed for the Church.

It's important you know that I saw the change and am looking forward to going back to where we were going fifty years ago. Pope Francis has renewed my hope and trust in the Vatican and is beginning to open the treasure chest of the Church, not filled with gold, frankincense and myrrh but rather with a rich tradition of helping those who cannot help themselves, of reaching out to those who might have made bad choices along the way and given them a new lease on life in their present relationships.

After fifty years, not a lot has changed. We now have married priests but they are all from other Christian denominations. For us Romans, celibacy rules! I'm sure it will change the minute I begin to croak. Someone will rattle on about how the first pope, Peter, was such a good man and how much he loved his mother-in-law. I'll die with a smile on my face.

Part I

Formation

O Lord, you have probed me and you know me:
you know when I sit and when I stand;
you understand my thoughts from afar.

Psalms 139:1-2

If God can work through me, he can work through
anyone.

Francis of Assisi

1. Life on the Mississippi

It was the third of June, 1939, and the heat and humidity both were in the 80s. Our little red brick house was stifling when I took my first breath. As I emerged from the womb onto the kitchen table, the air became even more liquid. My pee-pee exploded all over the birth attendant, my cousin Marvine, who delighted in telling that story until the day she died. Missouri people, at least the ones in my family, were like that. Years later when I was ordained as a Catholic priest, Marvine laid claim to being my first baptism. Oblivious to the embarrassment it would cause me, she related the story during the banquet at the Holiday Inn that followed my first solemn Mass in my hometown. All hope for a dignified celebration hee-hawed right out the window.

My beautiful mother doted on me. At the urging of my aunt Armella, she even entered me in a contest when I was two. Few in the family were surprised and none expressed it when I was proclaimed "Prettiest Baby in Cape Girardeau." After all, I had inherited my mother's looks.

I was my parents' last child. My brothers and sister were already in school by the time I was born, so I was the baby to all of them. During the war years I remember quite well my family giving up their sugar on breakfast cereal, to give to me, because I had such a sweet tooth at that age. I was the first in our family to attend a kindergarten and there I distinguished myself for being a bit of an extrovert. I had the main part in a play put on for the parents. I got a lot of attention from my family, although sometimes the boys treated me more like a puppy. They taught me to swim by standing on opposite sides of the river and coaxing me across. As soon as I would reach one bank, I was tossed back in toward the other brother. It was an exhausting

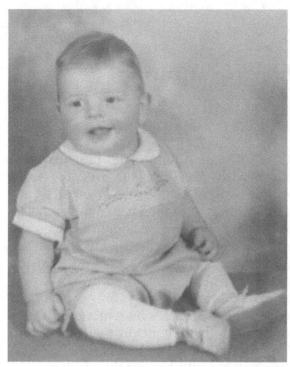

Baby Harry

process and my little legs finally gave out. Charlie was talking to a buddy and didn't notice me going under. Johnny dove in and pulled me up sputtering and gasping. They never talked about what happened, but both were proud that I'd learned to swim.

Hot summer days in southern Missouri often went right on into the night. There was very little shade for shelter in the daytime and at night it seemed even hotter because what might have been a breeze disappeared. Shortly after supper Dad would inform the family that he was going for beers. Mom would decline the generous offer as she rarely had a beer, wine or any spirits. The older kids preferred their own friends, so Dad would take me. We'd walk the six blocks to Broadway to settle on a stool where the floor was covered with peanut shells, stale beer and popcorn that you dipped out of the machine with a coffee can from Folgers.

You couldn't beat Jones' Walk-In for down home atmosphere. There was no music, no entertainment, no particular draw except the idea of a beer oasis in the sweltering Midwestern Sahara. Of course, I got the four-ounce root beer that was served in a frosty mug just like the big beers guys like my dad had. I can still recall going back to the popcorn machine with my Folgers coffee can for a refill. It was free and salty so you could drink that much more. What a treat for a kid who was five or six or seven. No one asked me to leave the room or give up my stool for someone who was going to purchase a beer for a quarter knowing my root beer cost a nickel. If I had been older, I'm sure I would have developed calluses on my elbows those hot summer nights.

"Let's have another, Jonesy!" was the refrain up and down the bar. Dad would never have more than three beers but by then my little tummy was stretched like a camel tent in the desert wind. Two root beers and multiple coffee cans of popcorn made for lots of activity on those hot summer nights.

On other nights he would say after dinner, "Son, get in the truck. I'm going to buy you some candy." We would stop at a drive-in liquor store whose approach was in an alley with the window on the passenger side. So I would hand the money to the man for a pint of peppermint Schnapps and a package of Sen-Sen, a black licorice kind of hard seed that was supposed to hide the smell of alcohol. After the purchase we would drive a bit by the Mississippi River with the windows rolled down. My dad would have a swig now and again and I would suck on the little black "candies." What a guy, my dad!

Today, we have all kinds of descriptions of people who are in various states of intoxication from alcohol. There are stories about people and from people who are working hard to overcome the disease. When I was a kid, I never knew if my dad was an alcoholic or not. I would say not, but he did enjoy his drink. I remember a few times when Mother suffered because of his staying too long at the saloon after work. He never drank that much at home. It was only after Dad died that my cousin Theon, just back from the Korean War and living in our basement, was the first to make a public case of it. He discovered an empty bottle here and an empty bottle there stuck in the rafters. He was searching for a place to hide his own empties and the rafters were full. Mom pretended she didn't know. For a guy who worked as hard as Bill Schlitt, this was little recompense.

My dad owned a garage. He was a mechanic all his life and a good one. His shop was filled with old farm vehicles that every stubborn German in southern Missouri refused to take to a professional because they were holding on to the first dollar they ever made and also because, as fixer-uppers, they knew that a piece of baling wire and an old rag could hold anything together. (Duct tape wasn't around yet.)

My dad used to say, "Man doesn't bring anything, can't expect anything." Years later studying in Rome, I was surprised to come across a Latin proverb, *"Ex nihilo nihil fit,"* that echoed my dad's wisdom. "Out of nothing comes nothing."

Dad had some really great expressions. Not sure I should relate them, but I know he's in heaven and wouldn't want me to hold back. One was a simple description I always looked forward to because it made me laugh. It had to do with someone who might have been hit by the ugly stick during life.

Bill Schlitt

"My butt would make that guy a good Sunday face," Dad would say.

Sunday was an important day in our family and we always put on our best when it came time to go to church. It only seemed natural for Dad to know how important a Sunday face was to a person.

Then there was a guy who used to walk by the garage who was short in stature. That is, vertically challenged. He was a pal of my dad's. After he had passed by and only his rear was showing, Dad would remark, "Oughtta sue the city."

"What for?" I would say.

"For building the sidewalk so close to his butt."

Then he would light up another Lucky Strike, cough a few times, and return to that dirty, greasy, smelly, unhealthy work that was his livelihood.

There was another man who walked by the garage every day on his way to the saloon. Dad called him Horse Piss Hank. Hank was quite proud of his identity. When questioned why the strange handle, he would launch into a ten-minute tirade about how his father could make real beer, beer that you could taste, beer that would lighten your spirits, beer that was filling and fulfilling. "All of this stuff they sell at the saloon is only horse piss." Most people in town knew his name and that his father went out of business shortly before prohibition ended.

Nicknames were not uncommon in those days in Missouri. They were usually descriptive but not always kind. In grade school it was "Peach" for the girls and "Fuzz" for the boys. Today fuzz is a moniker for law enforcement. Some people have fuzz busters in their cars to alert them when the Highway Patrol might be in the neighborhood. I present this as a sidebar just to show how names, even nicks, can be taken way out of context and leave us searching for a deeper meaning to life and who we are. Here's how I got my nickname.

So I'm in the General Garage. That was the name of the shop my father owned and operated and where my brothers worked. A big truck rolled in with carburetor problems. It was loaded with freshly picked peaches from the nearby orchards on their way to market. Barefoot, no shirt and in my little short pants, I climbed up the back of the truck and launched myself into this pile of ripe fruit. I don't know how much I ate or how long I ate but sleep came over me. I awoke suddenly on the highway headed across the Mississippi River for Illinois.

Immediately, I began crying and screaming for help. The driver of the truck was so pleased that his engine was running again and he wouldn't be late for his cargo to be unloaded. It was a steamy summer day and fortunately his windows were down and he heard my screams. As the truck rumbled off the asphalt to a dusty stop, I could see a pickup truck in the distance roaring toward us with the bright sign on the top, "General Garage." The screaming subsided, the tears dried up and little Harry, aka Peach Fuzz, climbed out of the truck and jumped into the pickup eager to return to the safety of his family.

All the way back, I scratched and scratched and drove my nails into every piece of exposed flesh. The itching was fierce and prolonged. There was no spray or comforting aloe to remove the ever-present fuzz from the peaches that had invaded every part of the skinny skin that I had at that time. I could get no relief except from my two older brothers scolding me for getting into some strange man's truck.

Fortunately I was safe, and more importantly, they actually missed me and instinctively knew I must be among the fuzzy confines of the peaches. Back in the garage they hosed me off and then soaped me and hosed me off again.

To my brothers, I was lost. For me, it was a frightening ride for a little kid in a truck headed for who knows where. We all feel lost at one time or another. We need to find a place, our place, a place in life. When we find it, we can rejoice with the widow who swept her floor until she found the coin, or the Alzheimer's patient who discovered his glasses in the fridge, or when you finally got to the bottom of your purse and, yes, there were your keys.

Peach Fuzz discovered at the age of five that his big brothers Charlie and Johnny really did love him, missed him and no matter how much they laughed about calling him Peach Fuzz they knew he was worth the rescue.

Some Sundays in the summertime, Dad would drive with Mother and me to visit the country relatives a few miles away in New Hamburg.

"Keep the noise outside," my dad would say.

It was my own high-pitched teeny voice annoying my father. It was coming from the backseat of that old Dodge we had and so, with the windows wide open, I would oblige Dad and stick out my head. I took to the air chattering on like a talk show host describing the barns, the fields, the other cars whizzing by— makes, models, colors and, more than once, the year they were made. After all, I was the son of an auto mechanic and it was impressive to know these things. I never thought it would come in handy on a radio show decades later when the tape failed or the record didn't start at the right time and you had to vamp. Interesting word for maintaining sound or noise when the prospect of dead air was just unacceptable. Dad would simply want my noise outside.

"And lock the door so you don't fall out," he'd add. "We don't want to lose you."

A lifelong Gemini, my inner broadcaster had signed on and

"Father Harry" was hot on his heels.

I was in the second grade when I took my first holy communion. I still have a picture of our group on the steps of St. Mary's Cathedral after the ceremony. We boys were all dolled up in our white suits and white shoes. The girls had little veils and cute little white dresses. These could be handed down from child to child in large families. We were given a prayer book for children and a rosary, black for the boys, white for the girls. I honestly believe that this was the first serious recognition that I had of my faith and especially my belief that Jesus was present in the bread that I took on my tongue and swallowed.

Sister Mary Christy taught me about Jesus in the Eucharist. She did a good job because even today when I take communion I remind myself that it is, "My Lord and my God," the words she taught me to say when I was seven. God would be part of me and I would be carrying the Savior who carried the world. It was that deep and real for me. Sister Christy made it last.

I think my habit of going to Mass in the morning throughout grade school was motivated by the sacrament every bit as much as it was by the doughnuts and milk that we got for a dime after it was over. There are five-dollar definitions but simply put a sacrament is a sign, instituted by Jesus Christ, to make us holy. The *matter* for the sacrament was bread and wine. The *form* was the same words I've said over and over for the past fifty years as a priest, "This is my body. This is my blood. Do this in memory of me."

My early childhood in elementary school was filled with, "Oh, isn't he cute! He's the little brother of John and Charlie Schlitt." They were star pupils and athletes in high school by then, but many of my teachers had also taught them. My only crisis in grade school was to discover that someone did not like me. I think one of the few times I have ever cried in my life was to find out that I was not the most popular boy on the playground. I used to spend hours worrying about this and trying to remedy situations where I was ill at ease with someone.

Back to that little red brick house where I was born. It's now an accountant's office owned by Charlie Joe Herbst. He and I became friends in the first grade at St. Mary's and went to school together for eight years until I left for the seminary. As a boy he raised rabbits in his backyard and when the great tornado of 1949 hit Cape Girardeau, it wiped out his entire rabbitry. I recall going around the neighborhood the next morning with buddies from school picking up dead rabbits. We built a huge fire in Charlie Joe's yard and burned their furry little corpses. It was one of the saddest experiences I had up to that point in my life. Since all the guys were Catholic, we offered a prayer. I led. Charlie Joe was devastated, but his family was safe with only minor damage to their home.

That tornado was one of the most brutal storms Southeast Missouri ever endured. It killed twenty-three people and over 100 more were injured. There was no warning. It struck just before seven o'clock on a Saturday evening in late May. We were lucky my dad was home from work. He didn't like the way the sky looked and the stillness was unsettling. Dad ushered us into the basement, all except my brother Charlie. He was home on leave from the Army and out in his little green Ford looking for his buddy Jake. As the twister approached, the storm intensified. The gullywash of rain and the roar of the wind and the hail beating against the glass were truly frightening. The whole family was concerned about my brother but no one said anything. Suddenly the basement door flew open and there was Charlie. He never found his pal.

After three days, everyone except my brother had given up. "Old Jake is too mean to die from a little wind," he persisted.

Workers dug into Jake's basement, piled high with bricks and covered with boards, dirt and debris. Much to the surprise of the whole community—and to the pride of my brother—they found the young man alive. Jake became a legend in that little town.

Cape Girardeau was defined by the legendary Mississippi flowing at its side. A rock promontory at a bend in the river sixty miles below St. Louis enticed an explorer named Jean Baptiste de Girardot to establish a trading post there in 1733. Meriwether Lewis explored the area seventy years later and wrote about "temperate, laborious and honest" Germans. That would describe my ancestors, who arrived via steamboat from New

Orleans in the mid-1800s. The weather, the people and the economy all flowed from that river.

I had a lot of freedom as a boy in Cape, except when it came to Donny Werner. He was the Lutheran neighbor kid my mom didn't want me playing with because of his religion. My religion was that strict. On Saturdays I used to ride my bike out Perry Road to see my friend John Pickens. He was tall and skinny and predictably nicknamed Slim. I didn't realize how poor his family was at the time. All I knew was that they had goats and goats were kind of cute if they didn't attack you, nor if you had to smell them. They were all over the yard and into almost everything. The yard had all kinds of trash available and we would tinker with

"I promise to do my best..."
Harry the Cub Scout

old throw-away stuff. You couldn't really break anything, it had been broken before and had time to rust, rot and become even more of an eyesore. I was a kid. I didn't notice.

John and I joined the Boy Scouts together. We got merit badges together and camped together. The first time I ever went away from home by myself was to Camp Don Bosco. Of course, it was a Catholic camp somewhere near St. Louis and John Pickens was with me (thanks to Dad and Mother). There were tents and sleeping bags and crafts, horseback riding and swimming. They had a pool. After I said good-by to my parents and the beginning jitters left me, John and I shlepped off to make ourselves known, popular, cool (not a word that was used by me or any of my peers in the day). Being away from home for the first time is supposed to be frightening. I took to it like a fish to water. After a couple of days there, I thought I had died and gone to heaven.

My parents came from a long line of Catholics. They fostered my faith with daily devotions, nightly prayers and Sunday Mass. They introduced me to the concept of heaven and hell at a tender age. I had no doubt about my desired destination, but was not as clear about the route. All that changed when I was ten. A Maryknoll priest came to our fifth-grade classroom one day and showed us a filmstrip about missionaries helping people in Africa. Afterward he challenged us to do something for others. I'll never forget his opening statement:

"If you want to help someone, be a priest. You don't have to go out looking to do good, it comes to you."

I wanted to be able to help people when I grew up. I was told that if I helped other people I would go to heaven. Serving people would give me the pass I needed for eternal life.

I nurtured this idea in the back of my mind for the remaining years in grammar school. I never told my teachers for fear of getting that extra pat on the head, which would make me unpopular with my fellow schoolmates.

I followed the advice of Father John Martin, Maryknoll Missionary. In my fifty years of priesthood, I have always found it to be true.

I suppose it works for many vocations but in the priesthood, it's a done deal. I'm not talking about confessions or counseling. I'm talking about all kinds of questions that come to a priest on an everyday basis, like:

"Father, is there a hell?"

"Where will I go when I die?"

"Will I make her pregnant by being naked?"

"If God loves us, how could He send us to hell?"

"Is it wrong to put my mother in an old folks' home?"

"Why would God allow a tsunami if He is all merciful?"

I could fill a couple more pages with examples of questions

that come to me from friends, family, strangers, people who see you in a black suit and a Roman collar and remark how comfortable they feel sitting next to you on an airplane. Or how uneasy. The opposite is also true. There are people who get nervous when a guy is in a black suit with a collar.

I've often told the story of how the plane would begin to wiggle and then go up and down and it was obvious that we were in some strong winds. The captain would say buckle up and we'll try another altitude. A really frightened flight attendant would notice my Roman collar and ask if I were a priest.

"Yes," said I, "but a nervous one at this time."

"Could you do something religious?" she pleaded.

So I told her to empty the peanut basket and have a seat and I would take up a collection. The story still works for me and most people who hear it.

I have a small plaque on my wall awarded to me by one of my nephews, which reads "Champion Fronabarger Award for Successful Crappie Fishing in Texas." Fronabarger was a professional photographer who worked for the Cape Girardeau newspaper. Mr. Fron's claim to fame was to fish close to anyone who was catching fish. As soon as the person would bring in the fish, Fronabarger would be ready with his pole and bait and drop in on the exact spot where the person just brought in a fish. My dad made him famous among fishermen by yelling at anyone practicing this greedy form of fishing, "Hey, you're doing a fronabarger on me."

There are lots of fishermen around who pull the old fronabarger routine. I guess that's why I have an award on my wall.

There is certainly nothing wrong with wanting to be successful. All of us are eager to follow in the footsteps of someone who has found the right spot, or as they say in some fishing families the honey hole, where you are not only expected to get a bite but to catch fish. To remove ourselves from fishing, there are other kinds of sure things, honey holes if you will, that come to us in life. We only have to watch TV or listen to the radio and the answer is there for everyone. We should all be perfect if only we would follow this advice. We'd manage to have everything we've ever wanted (but didn't need) and everything we needed (but didn't know could be had).

I didn't fronabarger anyone in my choice to become a priest. But along the way, I've seen a number of people waiting in the wings hoping for the success of the person on stage so that they too could follow in their footsteps. Even though I felt that calling after watching the film in the fifth grade, it took lots of people along the way to show good examples for me to know that success breeds success.

Come follow me.

Jesus' disciple Matthew didn't have anyone showing him the way but he heard a call and responded accordingly.

2. Baby Priest

I HAD NEVER HEARD of anything like it. Music Appreciation class. For a fourteen-year-old boy wanting to be a priest, thinking that he'll be practicing the sacraments, saying Mass, forgiving sins and marrying people, this was way out of line. It was not at all what I expected from the seminary.

The class was taught by Father Mike McHugh who was young, enthusiastic about his musical knowledge and ability, and looked at the likes of me as a real challenge. To think that he could take a boy from the sticks whose Hit Parade consisted of Little Jimmy Dickens warbling "Taters never did taste good with chicken on the plate" and teach him to appreciate all kinds of movements in classical strings—without lyrics! Impossible, but worth the challenge.

It could not have been more than the second or third class when, after concluding his remarks about Rachmaninoff and before placing the needle on a 331/3 rpm disc, Father Mike startled us.

"Boys, you may smoke in this class."

It was in the auditorium and there were ashtrays about, but freshmen in high school being invited to smoke? Today we would have used the expression, "I wonder what Father Mike is smoking!"

We were 114 strong, divided into three groups. There were day-hops and boarders. Our Group C was about fifty-fifty, guys who went home every night to their families and those of us who lived there. Johnny Grimes was sitting next to me. He was a very smart kid who was also a good athlete and a fun guy to be around.

Father Mike: "Those of you who have never smoked might want to give it a try."

Man, if my mother knew this was being encouraged in the seminary I would have been yanked even though my dad was a chain-smoker all his life.

Father Mike: "If you need a cigarette, borrow one from a buddy."

Johnny Grimes was the man. He had a pack of Viceroys. We all lit up. I didn't see anyone in the class without a fag. That's what cigarettes were called back then. Once the auditorium was flooded with smoke and several of us were coughing and spewing saliva that we didn't know we had, we heard the scratch of the needle as it was removed from the LP.

Father Mike: "OK boys, take note. Some of you are coughing and trying hard to breathe normally. Others are not sure what to do. Still others are embarrassed or thinking that your parents would never allow you to do this at home."

"Have you guys noticed me? I cough a lot and never seem to have a clear throat, even though I teach music and so like to sing. Look at my fingers. They're almost yellow. Note my teeth and how they are stained with nicotine. My breath is always smoker's breath. I urge you boys, before you become men, to give up the smokes before they become habitual. You could become like me. I'm not proud that I smoke. I'm not even happy about it. But I have to do it. It's a bad habit."

Slowly I watched the smoke spiraling from my Viceroy with the filtered tip and the long stately white stem. I put it out. Johnny Grimes is laughing at me.

That was my first, last and final attempt at smoking. I never learned to smoke cigarettes (nor appreciate classical music).

Now and again, people will ask who the most influential person in my life was. For me, that would depend on the time I was influenced. As a student in secondary school, it had to be DJ Ryan.

Father Don Ryan was a young Vincentian priest from Chicago who had sparse red hair, mostly freckles and a dome. He was a wonderful basketball player and came to the gym at odd times to shoot around with me. Sports were and always will be an integral part of my life. Basketball was king. I had been voted most valuable player in Cape in the eighth grade. Thanks to a good coach and my older brothers who both played very well, I was inspired to overshadow them with my roundball skills. Actually, I was pretty good as a freshman but went downhill after that as I never grew to be any taller than five feet eleven inches. I could dunk a softball and a volleyball but never could get the orange ball over the rim. Father DJ, as we called him, admired my athletic ability and my country boy honesty. He was a special friend of mine, and also my superior and model. I was flattered that he felt he could share his time with me and enjoy the competition of shooting a roundball at a hoop above us both.

Most of my classmates were from St. Louis and I was teased at great lengths because of my accent. I was unaccustomed to the styles in clothing and the latest fads in music and thus began my new life as a zero personality. I compensated rapidly by becoming the best athlete in the class. I made the varsity teams as a freshman both in baseball and track. In basketball I played as a regular. I soon became a hero and my classmates overlooked my country ways.

Seminarians, cousins and future monsignors Phil Bucher and Harry

Father DJ introduced me to my first fancy restaurant with tablecloths and mystifying pieces of cutlery and taught me how to be nice to those who waited on us. Menus were a new addition to my way of life. What I had learned as a busboy at the Sunny Hill Dairy did not apply to an eating establishment with starters, soups or salads, entrees and dessert. I can still see the place with all the dark wood, with pewter plates and cups, and the never completed question, "What would you like?"

I had no idea as the names were not fried chicken, fried this and fried that, followed by something else fried. From an early age until I entered the seminary, I was hardly aware of any other form of food. Now to be fair to my mother and family, there were other foods but not that I liked or wanted. I wander!

Father DJ ushered me into manhood by removing as many of the rough edges from a country boy as he could and replacing them with simple courtesy and manners that I had not fully grasped at home.

I had only been at St. Louis Preparatory Seminary for two months when my dad, at the age of fifty, was diagnosed with lung cancer. He'd long been a true believer in L.S.M.F.T. (Lucky Strike Means Fine Tobacco). And his years working as a mechanic without ventilation, especially in the winter months when it was cold and the garage door could not be opened, were an oncologist's nightmare. There was no opportunity to filter out the carbon monoxide from all the other fumes permeating the cold winter air. There was little choice. You either kept the heat from the coal-burning stove and the hot engines in, or opened the doors so your fingers would freeze and you couldn't handle the tools you needed to repair cars. It was a brutal occupation.

As a mechanic, he cured me of any desire to follow in his footsteps. Night after night, I had watched him scrubbing his hands with gasoline to remove the grease and grime, only to smell like gasoline as he sat down at the table to spread the jam Mom had made and eat the fried pork skins or the grease off the cooked pork loin that had been in the pot most of the afternoon.

I played dumb in that garage for so many years. Believe me, it wasn't that difficult. I searched for hours for left-handed wrenches and kinds of hammers that never existed. I broke off so many spark plug heads that it cost my dad for me to work in his garage. When the idea and the call of priesthood came along, I didn't have to think long or hard about what I would do in life or how I would spend it. I knew it would not be in the car repair business.

Bill had exploratory surgery in November of 1953 at Barnes Hospital in St. Louis, not far from the seminary. Father DJ took me there to see him. The surgeons opened him up, saw the disease and said he might live six weeks to six months. It was unknown to me at the time that a person could die that way. I thought they could always cut something out or replace something, just like this man did in his garage work for so many years. A freshman in high school with a small-town knowledge of medicine could not be expected to fully grasp such dire consequences.

Seminarians were not allowed to leave during the school year (except for the day-hops who lived at home). Father DJ had obtained special permission for me to see my dad at Barnes and twice more in Cape on weekends that spring, but those were extraordinary occasions. I went home in February for my uncle Leo's funeral. He was my dad's last brother. As a seminarian, the family considered me almost a priest and I was asked to lead the prayers. I was so nervous I skipped part of the Hail Mary. It happened not once or twice but over a couple of decades of the beads. Some of my relatives remarked that it was the fastest rosary they had ever recited at a wake. I was already a hero for my brevity in prayer.

In March, I went home when my dad's last sister, Coletta, died. It seemed like every time I went home there was a funeral. I remember my dad sitting silently in a chair, waiting. There was nothing more to do.

Father DJ was close to Sister Bertha who was the Daughter of Charity in charge of the nursing school at nearby DePaul Hospital. My sister, Della, was in training there. Because my dad was suffering from cancer of the lung and was given only a short time to live, Sister Bertha made sure that the little boy from the country would have some perks that he might not expect. In June when I turned fifteen, a large birthday cake with my name on it appeared at the table in the seminary.

The twelve guys I had to share it with were in awe as I knew no one in St. Louis except, of course, Sister Bertha who made sure that Father DJ would get the cake to me and allow me to celebrate with my freshmen classmates.

I completed my first year at the seminary and returned home to Cape for the last months of my dad's life. I always felt good about him in those dying days of summer. We used to pray the rosary and the prayers to the Sacred Heart of Jesus every day. He still referred to me as *ach du kleine engel* (oh you little angel).

His parents had been first-generation Americans and he was the youngest of their seven children. All of them were musically inclined. They sang and played tunes late into the night. Dad played the fiddle and the harmonica and whistled quite well, especially when the fish were sleeping and I was complaining about flies and mosquitoes, itchy weeds and one soda for the entire day. I don't remember him singing very much, but then his life was so short.

I only had my dad for fifteen years, but he made a wonderful impression on me. He probably drank too much but I never noticed. He was hard working with no formal schooling beyond the eighth grade, but he was bright and could figure things out on his own.

My most horrifying experience was waking up to him screaming, "Hit me! Hit me, I can't breathe! Knock me out!"

I was skinny and weak and not able to make a fist big enough to do the trick. My mother said to run down the block and get my older brother. He was big and strong and could knock Dad senseless. My father was choking on the liquid wrath that his lungs were producing and it would stick in his throat so that he could not get his breath. After watching him beat his head to no avail against the headboard, my brother reared back and punched him in the face. He fell from the wood to the mattress and there he lie. It only took a few seconds and he spit up the blockage and once again could breathe. His eyes were watering and tearful and he rubbed his jaw and thanked my brother for a successful blow.

Bill drew his last labored breath at six o'clock on a Sunday evening at St. Francis Hospital. It was August 22, 1954, and the Catholic feast day of the Immaculate Heart of Mary. His parents and all of his brothers and sisters were already dead. My mother and two of his sisters-in-law were present when he passed.

I had been at the hospital most of that day but I was fifteen and feeling restless. That afternoon I talked my mother out of twenty-five cents to go see *Francis Joins the WACS*. It starred Donald O'Connor and a talking mule. The price at that time was ten cents for admission and some kind of strange tax was added to make it fourteen cents. After viewing this very funny but pointless movie, I returned to the hospital to find my father's bed empty and my mother in the hall weeping. I was much too young to comprehend what had just happened. No more difficulty in breathing. No more pain. No more wondering when and where and what will be after I'm gone. His death was an answer to our prayers but as his little angel, it hit me hard.

Father DJ was present at my dad's funeral and was always there for me when I had no clue of what might be happening. I respected him more than I knew how to love him or even appreciate all that he was able to do for me as a young kid.

Having to decide whether I should then remain home with mother or go back to school was not a tough decision as one of my father's dying wishes was for me to become a priest. Noble though I was in making the offer to remain with my mother, neither she nor the others in the family would hear of it. It was at this point that I decided to make the best of my life.

Two weeks later, I returned to the seminary and began my sophomore year. It was a relief to be back among my classmates and teachers but I was sad to leave my mother alone. She was fifty years old and for the first time Theckla Schlitt was living by herself. Both my brothers were married and my sister was in her last year of nursing school. Not one to give way to her emotions, my mother kept busy volunteering at St. Mary's, babysitting for the grandchildren and keeping the books for the General Garage, which my brother John had taken over that summer. I didn't see Mother again until Christmas.

The prevailing wisdom at the seminary was that separation from the outside world minimized temptations and kept teenage boys focused on their vocation. Reading material was restricted, visitors were not permitted, not even family, and seminarians were not allowed to talk to "externs" meaning people from the outside. The emphasis was on the internal community where we had the priesthood in common. The model was drawn from Jesus and his apostles and, like the Twelve, we recognized our privilege and the corresponding responsibilities. It was our duty to prayerfully and honestly discern whether our calling was true. Illusions or false hopes didn't do anybody any favors and could be harmful to ourselves, our classmates and the Church. The priests who were our teachers and advisors became like family.

During this time, I became very friendly with the dean of students. I recall lying to him once then the next day apologizing. This sign of genuine country honesty was something he hadn't witnessed very often. It hurt me, but it did so much to affect me that I will never forget it. I started to excel, except academically where I was a solid B-, and was elected president of the student body.

Father John Martin, M.M., who first opened my eyes to becoming a Catholic priest when I was ten, came to the seminary on a regular basis. For a while before he was assigned to Rome, he was my confessor. Confession, or the Sacrament of Reconciliation, was a weekly activity for me all through my seminary training. It was a means of grace and a reliable measure as to how you were progressing in your spiritual life. It was also a relief of conscience from the terrible temptations of the flesh.

I didn't have a driver's license, I had never been on a date and I had never been kissed, but I was becoming a young man. In many ways, I was still a baby when I left home. By going directly from elementary school to living full-time in the seminary, I never had the chance to experience girls.

There was a little pink pamphlet that had all the answers about sex. The guys and I referred to it as *Modern Youth and Plumbing* but the real title was *Modern Youth and Chastity*. It was written by a religious man, who could prove on a blackboard to a class of sophomore high school students that kissing was a mortal sin. That pamphlet was very influential in my own life. I wasn't sure what it all meant, but reading about it was exciting and in more ways than you could imagine.

The seminary by its very nature was a fortress against all sexual activity, but defense against our imaginations proved more of a challenge. When the church at the neighboring parish was damaged by fire, the pastor and his congregation used the chapel at the seminary for Sunday morning Mass. We were relegated to our dormitories during the service, but by twelve o'clock the crowd had dispersed. Noon was one of the three times daily that we gathered in the chapel for the Angelus, a devotional prayer commemorating the incarnation of Jesus. We never saw any parishioners, let alone any females, but as soon as we entered the chapel we walked headlong into the unmistakable evidence that they had been there. The scent of perfume pervaded the small building and our senses went wild. Impulses were transmitted directly to the part of our brains dealing with emotion. We were completely unprepared. It was erotic.

We fell to our knees and the bell tolled the first notes of the Angelus. The priest recited the verse:

The Angel of the Lord declared unto Mary.

We gave the response:

And she conceived of the Holy Spirit.

Together we prayed the Hail Mary. The bell tolled again and the second verse rang out:

Behold the handmaid of the Lord.

And we responded with the words of the Virgin:

Be it done unto me according to your word.

The prayers dropped from our lips. We prayed fervently to be made worthy of the promises of Christ. The bells began to peal. The fragrance was relentless.

I didn't feel guilty. I never thought there could be a sin from the sense of smell. It wasn't sin. But it was exciting! I felt a lift from the all-male environment that constituted my daily surroundings. That heady perfume brought some femininity to the cold stone pillars of a dark chapel, occupied ninety-nine percent of the time by praying males.

Desires were and always will be with young men—regardless if they are in the confines of a chapel—and others who are striving to be perfect and follow the rules of *Modern Youth and Plumbing.*

I think the only sexual permission was the nocturnal emission. The wet dream, as it's called, was perfectly all right for Catholic boys. And if you woke up following or during it was OK, as long as you didn't take pleasure in it. I can't imagine anyone putting this in writing and calling it moral theology. When you reach the age of seventy-five, it all seems so silly. But what we are is where we came from and it's good to go back and see how we arrived at our judgments today.

The introduction of "nocturnal pollution" is not meant to be racy or sexy or catchy, but informative and helpful to the few young people who might feel that the weight of the world is upon them because of how they view their own struggle with being chaste and sexually healthy.

It's no secret that plenty of little pink pamphlets and those who espouse them are out there. On the other hand, there are too few who offer common sense and encouragement to deal with the reality of what is and the desires that come to people who are growing both emotionally and physically.

In my high school seminary, there were roughly 300 young men living communally and we all had dreams and goals of one day serving God as priests. But there were bound to be a few bumps along the way. Reality grabbed me one night after lights out, in the form of the guy one bunk over. I was half asleep and he caught me completely off-guard but my instincts kicked in. I pushed his hand away and told him to cut it out and asked him what he thought he was doing. I was out of my bunk in a wink and immediately found the dorm monitor. I was quickly and quietly re-located to a different bed across the dorm room. I was more distressed for my classmate than for myself. I knew who I was, but he was struggling.

Shortly after my birthday, I returned home for the summer. It felt good to be back with my family and I was looking forward to swimming, baseball and seeing my teenage pals. Our long-time parish pastor, Monsignor Marion Forst, had been the one to steer me toward the archdiocesan seminary in St. Louis. (The Vincentians had a seminary right there in Cape, a block from my dad's garage, but they never sought me out.) He had kept up with my progress. My mother loved Forst. He would come for dinner. He was the kind of priest who got along well with women.

His associate pastor at St. Mary's, Father Jake Duffner, watched over me and helped me safeguard my vocation. At his suggestion I joined the parish Legion of Mary and kept busy with "spiritual works of mercy" like visiting the sick. It was good training for a priest-in-the-making. Generosity, humility and a willingness to serve others were attributes any successful priest would need. Plus, Father Duffner let me use his car.

My mother also nurtured my spiritual development. We went to Mass together every Sunday, the first Friday of the month and on holy days of obligation. Tuesday evenings she and I regularly attended devotions to Our Lady of Perpetual Help. In fact, I almost had the prayers memorized. While the Angelus commemorated the conception of God the Son, the prayers of this devotion were pleas from wretched sinners for succor. In the company of the fallen I begged Mother Mary for recourse to her in all attacks of hell. One Tuesday after devotions, I met Flickers.

My first impression of her was that she was about the most beautiful woman I'd ever seen. She was a country girl with one of those mellifluous voices that accompanies the simplicity of the back country. My brother Charlie called her "Flickers" because she had these great big beautiful eyes with long lashes. Her eyes sparkled and were dimmed only by natural lashes so long-stemmed that one could almost feel the breeze when they fluttered. I can still see her blush as my brother teased her about anything just to see those eyes flicker. She pitched for her softball team, excelled in school and, although Baptist, was a leader in her church. She attended devotions with her fiancé, Charles, and his parents, for whom she was converting to Catholicism.

Flickers' picture was in the Sunday paper the day after her wedding. There were three other brides, but her photo was the largest and she was top and center. She looked like Elizabeth Taylor in *Father of the Bride*. Her flowers were long-stemmed and exotic, her bodice was described as "snugly shaped." She was the epitome of marital love and a true madonna.

About the same time girls were becoming attractive to me, I became an object of fascination for them. I think it first began when several high school girls suddenly joined the Legion of Mary. And they were all cuties. I couldn't swear by it, but I think it was because of me. Father Duffner was sure of it. He said I was a great "draw" for the growth of teen spiritualism in Cape Girardeau.

I had always been athletic and that summer I played

baseball for the Fire Department. I recall making the All Star team and batting .275. Most of the All Stars were batting .400 or more. But I could catch, play the outfield and was good for morale and team unity. Girls came out to Capaha Park in groups, paying their nickels for long blue Frostee Pops or Drumsticks and cheering us on. The Legion of Mary was always well represented. One night we lost a squeaker to Schiff's Shoes. Despite the defeat, I'd had a spectacular game. For one reason or another, as soon as I walked off the field, I was surrounded by girls. Fresh and cute and smiling, they encircled me.

I was flattered and enjoyed the attention, but I told them I had to leave. I didn't even know what hard to get was, but at an early age I was practicing what I was later to preach. Then it was like playing with fire to be surrounded by such pulchritude and not be tempted to go any further. (Pulchritude is the kind of word our teachers at the seminary would use when speaking about beauty and temptation.)

When I was in southern Missouri during vacation from the seminary, I would pass most of my time on the Mississippi River. The river winds its way down from St. Louis and tries to free itself from the chemical and waste deposits coming from the city's factories and meat-packing plants and the million people living there. In early summer it was brutally brown and full of mud and who knows what else. I'm sure the catfish loved it.

My official start to the summer was to leap off the boat with a single slalom ski and go underwater. I would surface with a mouthful of the Mississippi and spit it in the air with the same expression, "I'll glow in the dark if we stay till evening," or "Oh boy, same chocolate flavor as last year!"

The river began as a clear and honest stream in Minnesota. But by the time it had made its way to Cape it changed from a straight-on stream to a gurgling gang of muddy water filled with logs and brush from the spring thaw and the early rains, to a complete whirling dervish of a monster. One never wanted to mess around with Mother Nature in the form of Mississippi mud.

When I came up from the water and gave the sign to hit it, all was forgotten and forgiven. There were no lakes or rivers nearby and this body of water was in my backyard. You couldn't really swim in it unless you went off the channel to one of the inlets. The main body was a beast and not to be taken lightly.

Now above the water, in cars and vans and sometimes on bicycles, all the young people gathered along the bank to spoon and make goo-goo eyes at each other as the sky lit up the river and gave it a sparkle as it surged around Cape Rock. It was also here that Trail of Tears State Park was established as a memorial to the Cherokee who had crossed from Illinois to Missouri over the frozen Mississippi, exiled from their homes in the warm South to the Plains states of the West after gold was found on their tribal lands. Many of them perished on this forced march, thus the name.

I water skied just about every day in the summer because my brother and I would leave the General Garage after work and motor down to the diversion channel (a big ditch) and check the trotlines we had put out for catfish. I would ski down and back with my old water skis that were nicked and beaten from hitting sticks and logs while skiing the Mississippi. It wasn't easy especially in the early summer when the river was still on the rise from the thaw of the ice and snow all the way up to Minnesota. It was all I had for summer skiing. I couldn't be too choosy.

One summer when I had just turned eighteen, a marine shop burned to the ground with several boats sitting on trailers in the showroom. Two weeks after the fire, a salvage group from Chicago came in and held a sale. All you had to do was bid. I took my savings from the Farmers Bank (all $600) and my brother John OK'd the purchase by telling me the motor was in fine shape and was worth the price. The underside, which is most important in the water, was not a bit damaged. So I got boat, motor and trailer for the price of my life's savings.

The boat was fiberglass and, taking a page from Tom Sawyer, I soon had all my buddies sanding and refinishing the seats. It was not long before we were set for the summer. On weekends, it was a regular thing to hit the river both Saturdays and Sundays for more muddy, murky, thrills on the cheap boards I got them to throw in with the boat.

Six o'clock on Sunday morning, be at the Honkers Boat Club dock 'cuz we're all cruising for St. Louis at six a.m. sharp.

I had no intention of really making the 127-mile trip on skis, but one by one other guys from the Honkers Club reeled me in.

"I'll give you five if you make it all the way non-stop." The next guy wagered ten. When it was up to forty bucks, I made up my mind to do it. Clyde Wallis, a radiator repairman and veteran of Korea, was also aiming to ski with me. It was after 8:30 that morning before we finally got underway. We averaged about twenty miles per hour and without a stop it was quite grueling. I joked and laughed, ate and drank, and contributed in a timely manner to the pollution already present in the mighty Mississloppy.

When everyone stopped at Chester to go ashore and stretch and do their duty to God and nature, I stayed in the water attached to my skis and held on to the rope. It was part of the deal, after all, that I go the whole way on skis without stopping. I'm not sure how long we were there, but all the boats (three or four) gassed up and then we were ready for the completion of the trip.

It started to rain but nothing could dampen my spirits. After about five hours on the water, we rounded one big bend and I could see the skyline of St. Louis. We went under the Jefferson Barracks Bridge and I thought, "I'm home free. I should make it now. The forty big ones are mine."

Little did I realize that the Mississippi meandered back and forth for another twenty-five miles before you actually got to the downtown banks of old bricks that made up what is now the famous Gaslight Landing. That last leg took two hours. The waves and constant slapping of the boards on the water had numbed my feet. I could see they were almost white and I felt nothing, but nothing! They were like frozen Popsicles in the rubber boots attached to two hard boards that just kept flopping as the day wore on.

About three-thirty that afternoon, we finally arrived and I landed. The boys paid up and pictures were taken. The *Southeast Missourian* ran a front-page story about our record-setting trip with a big picture of Clyde and me as we left Cape.

The photo made its way to the St. Louis paper with a story about the *Guinness Book of World Records* and the longest non-stop ski on the Mississippi River. I never saw the article but was told of it many times, especially after someone else (much younger) had gone twelve hours non-stop.

Clyde and Harry setting out for St. Louis

The problem wasn't the record or not, it was the reception I received a week later when I returned to the seminary to begin college. I hardly had my bags unpacked when the rector called me to his office. He reprimanded me for this feat of waterworks that he could not exactly spell out, except to say it brought undo attention to myself and therefore I would be on probation until December.

Maybe it was the page one photo in swimming trunks. Or maybe it was too much like walking on water. One more flagrant breaking of the rules and I would be water skiing for a living and not for fun or for forty bucks.

Fortunately the rector, Father Riley, was a client of mine. Seminarians weren't allowed to hold outside jobs so to assist with my tuition and books I cut hair at the seminary for fifty cents a head. It was very helpful to give him a really good haircut and then say, "Oh no, Father, no money please. It's on the house." (At least until December.)

Except for that incident, my first year in college was not very exciting. They'd built a new high school to accommodate the boom in vocations and the smaller college was re-located to the old high school. I had already completed four years in the same building with the same classrooms, dining room, recreational areas and most of all the same group of guys. Still, it was good to be with old friends again.

Floyd and I had hit it off in the first year of high school because we had so much in common. We loved basketball. We had both committed ourselves to the priesthood when we were thirteen. We were both of German descent and from a cultural background that was thrifty. The difference was that his family was in the city and mine in the country. I had a lot to learn from this guy and I dare say he benefited from hanging around with me.

Floyd and I spent a lot of time together. When I was class president, he was vice president. When he was athletic director, I was his assistant. We studied, worked, played and enjoyed one another's company. When I came to the seminary to cut hair during Christmas or summer breaks, I spent many nights at his home in South St. Louis as a welcome guest and, even more, as a part of his family. He was there when my father died and I was there when his father passed.

First-year college did bring in some new blood to the seminary as graduates from Catholic high schools came aboard. Teachers and parents were still encouraging young men to pursue philosophy and theology in order to serve our Catholic churches. Charlie was a tall handsome young man with a slow southern drawl that fooled no one. He was bright as a beacon and a wonderful athlete. We found ourselves in the gym shooting hoops on his second day. He had more height and more muscle but was not as fast. Boy, did we have fun playing basketball and enjoying the same dream of serving God by serving His people. Roundball was only a distraction from the reason we were there, but sports gave us an outlet for all that youthful energy.

Many of the new guys were skilled at soccer. Almost all the Catholic kids in St. Louis played. It was a booming sport among the Catholic Youth Organizations and high schools but completely unknown to me before the seminary. In soccer, my size was no longer a disadvantage and my agility and overall athleticism served me well. I excelled at the new game and was excited to be part of a great team.

While my high school education had been pretty standard, my course of study in college was focused entirely on philosophy—knowing how you know. This provided the groundwork for later graduate school studies in theology. The Catholic Church has trained its priests in pretty much the same way for nearly a millennium. Central to the teachings are the works of 13th-century theologian and philosopher Thomas Aquinas.

As I stare at these four big blue books on my shelf, the *Summa Theologica* of Saint Thomas Aquinas, I can't help but think they would have been a good boost for a little person who needed to sit up closer at the dinner table. They would have been that much more useful than they have been for me. Of course, I was fortunate enough to have teachers and professors who could read the Latin, understand the context and translate to a mere mortal what it comprised.

Thomas reached the apex of Middle Age thought, which still exists with force today. It helped fuel the fire of my philosophical and theological background that has guided me well through years of mind improvement based on good sound logic. Thomas would never claim me, but he was a mentor for those of us who felt that his thinking and writing were much more than the "straw" that he claimed it amounted to.

Jeremiah the prophet proclaimed loudly to the Lord that he was too young to take on the tasks that were his by Divine decree. As a college student, I had no choice. It was the *Summa Theologica* if I were to continue my studies for the priesthood.

Philosophy and logic brought only a new vocabulary. It was still work to study and you had to do it in a methodical fashion. There were tests and exams, but more importantly papers to write, which required some time in the library and researching from other texts besides the ones you had for a class. All of this was mind expansion without even knowing it was happening.

Philosophy accounts for most of our thinking, but we never

fully realize or appreciate that we are philosophizing when we come up with new ideas and ways to do things. All of us think we are logical, but until we see the working dynamic of that logic—in practice not just in theory—we would never know whether our reasoning is valid or faulty.

3. Coming of Age

WHEN THE DIOCESE OF ST. LOUIS was erected in 1826 by the Bishop of Louisiana, it encompassed all of the U.S. west of the Mississippi, except Louisiana, plus half of Illinois. It was the largest in America. With deep Catholic roots and a legacy of offshoot dioceses, it was nicknamed "Rome of the West." Because Cardinal Glennon College was the archdiocesan seminary, my classroom education was bolstered by encounters with key leaders of the American Catholic Church.

The first cardinal I ever knew was an archbishop at the time. During my eight years in the seminary, the future Cardinal Joseph Ritter was the Archbishop of St. Louis. He came there often and as a class officer I was regularly assigned to greet him and escort him around the grounds. He was a gentle man with a great smile and a Midwestern brand of sincerity that we all look for but seldom find in leaders whether in the Church, the government or our hometown.

A liberal for his time, Archbishop Ritter ended racial segregation in the Catholic schools and hospitals of the St. Louis archdiocese, seventeen years before the Civil Rights Act became federal law. He had done the same thing while bishop of Indianapolis in 1938, inciting the Ku Klux Klan to burn crosses in front of his cathedral. In St. Louis, over 700 white Catholics from twenty-three different parishes threatened to sue him for violating state law. Archbishop Ritter threatened them with excommunication and said that all souls were equal under God.

Seminarians learned from the examples set by elders and priests as much as from the classroom. I once broke a bone in my left hand after making a catch in a football game. It was my guiding hand for my roundball jump shot and it was the same bone that basketball great Bob Pettit had broken. He was my idol. A player named Loscutoff crashed into him and knocked him into the second row of seats and Pettit broke his hand. It didn't seem to bother the tall, lean, handsome man from Louisiana who was such a star in the NBA. He had a cast put on and was able to overcome the handicap, scoring twenty-eight points in that year's All-Star Game and leading the St. Louis Hawks to the NBA finals against the Boston Celtics. And I sported the same injury and the same badge of courage made out of plaster of Paris.

I was so proud of that cast. It was an exact replica of Bob Pettit's. Father DJ had taken me to the doctor and I knew that he had told him to fit a cast just like the one that Mr. Pettit had so I could brag about it in the gym with the guys. My shot was hindered, but I continued to play. Don Ryan would smile at the swishing sound from the ball striking just net and shake his head.

Father DJ not only mentored me, he became very close to my family. When Della married Peter Darling, he officiated at their wedding ceremony. When my baby nephew died in a tragic accident, Father DJ was there to console my brother and sister-in-law.

Charlie and Mary had four children in their first four years of marriage. They had become good friends with Flickers and Charles. Both had large families and people thought twice about inviting them to dinner. John and Betty were parents to six. My brothers and their wives were inseparable in their early days of raising families. They helped each other in any way they could so that they would both be successful.

On Saturday nights the Schlitts would get together and play pinochle (a game I never learned). One weekend just before Christmas, Charlie and Mary had gone to John and Betty's to play cards. A babysitter was with my eldest brother's kids. She didn't see the baby climb up on the kitchen counter, open the cabinet door and find a bottle of aspirin. This was before childproof caps were invented. Bobby swallowed little fistfuls of the pills. He turned blue and they rushed him to the hospital. They pumped his stomach and at five o'clock the next morning the doctor told the anguished parents they thought the boy was going to live.

My sister-in-law went to the early Sunday Mass and prayed so hard in thanksgiving to God that her son was saved. It was a bitter twenty-three degrees when she left the church and the sky was overcast. She went home and arrived to the ringing of the telephone. It was the hospital and they said little Bobby had died.

Mary began to curse God and screamed that it was all a hoax. She was raging and out of control. What mother wouldn't be after losing her baby boy? He had lived just one year, eleven months and ten days. They buried the child two weeks before Christmas and his birthday. The notice of the baby's death was on the same page of the newspaper as the announcement of the birth of Charles and Flickers' latest son.

It took time and some good counseling from Father DJ, who helped Mary find peace with what had occurred. She became more spiritual than she had ever been and was a daily communicant. She and Charlie became active in a renewal group called Cursillo de Cristiandad. *Cursillo* means a short course; *Cristiandad*, Christianity. I've been a part of it both as a chaplain and as a participant. Over the years it has brought thousands of people to a greater relationship with God.

A year after Bobby died, Mary gave birth to a baby girl; ten months later, it was twin boys.

Training for the priesthood entailed pastoral, intellectual, spiritual and human formation. One of the components of spiritual formation is celibacy. During my junior year in college I was able to be completely chaste for one whole year. I was told that this would be a good way to ascertain whether or not I had a true vocation to the priesthood. It was murder, especially in the summer when I didn't have the same order of daily routine and the protection of the seminary (defined as a hot house for seedlings to grow).

I recall a rather skinny young woman who used to clean the faculty rooms on the second floor. We would spot her now and again racing down the hall with mops and brooms anxious to enclose herself in the safety of the room she was cleaning. In a kind way, and never to her or even behind her back, she was referred to as Turnpike Tessie, the "sure cure for concupiscence."

It was a long year and I was twenty, but when I completed

that period I felt that I was now worthy of continuing my pursuit of the priesthood. Inner feelings of self-satisfaction and pride celebrated alongside each other. Little did I know that a year free from self-abuse would not change the libido nor the desires that I would carry the rest of my life. Nor would I ever be "cured" of what I was taught to be both unnatural and mortally sinful.

The human formation aspect of priestly training required many things from a seminarian, among them physical fitness, the ability to communicate, the capacity to relate to others and living a public life. Some things we come by naturally.

My mother's grandfather was the personification of these traits and I am glad to have had him as an ancestor. Michael Dirnberger was a famous character in southern Missouri and larger than life. He was born in Bavaria, Germany, in 1835 and came to America in 1844 with his brother and his parents. Mike's first job was carrying the mail from New Madrid, Missouri, to Cape Girardeau. He was fifteen years old but a wonderful horseman and apparently one of the fastest riders in the county. When he died, the *Scott County Kicker* reported this about him:

> "Mr. Dirnberger was, perhaps, the most widely known German of the county. He was a lover of fast horses and, in his younger days quite active in politics. Some twenty-five years ago he and Uncle Jim Walker arranged a horse-race from New Madrid to Benton in which Billy Moore, who rode Mr. Dirnberger's horse, lost the road and therefore the race."

My aunt Armella recounts the story this way: "Billy was so far ahead that as he was passing the local saloon, just a dirt road from the finish line, Mike was so proud he hauled him in to celebrate his victory only to discover after a couple of steins that the other rider was kicking up the dust in front of the saloon to ultimately finish before Billy."

Mike's son Andrew had twelve children, among them

Armella and my mother, Theckla Louise Dirnberger. Theckla is not a common name. I have discovered that it's German for Theresa. Most of the family referred to her as Teck or Tay. She was born on October 9, 1903, and died on August 15, 1960, just before my final year in the seminary. Like my father, she too died on a Marian feast day, the Assumption of Our Lady into heaven. And like my father, she died from cancer.

Theckla knew about cancer and the pain that it could cause. Unlike her husband, Bill, she did not smoke nor drink nor work in a noxious fume-filled building. But she lived with secondhand smoke for the twenty-six years she was married to Bill. She had complained about back pain for a long time and tried all kinds of cures. Finally X-rays revealed that the spinal column had been eaten away and nerves were exposed. The diagnosis was metastatic reticulum cell sarcoma.

She did all the treatments available. There was no radiation or chemotherapy that could help. She too was given a period of time to live. By then the word terminal was familiar in our family. My sister, Della Darling, brought her two toddlers and came for several weeks to help Armella and me care for Mother.

Theckla entered the same hospital as Bill had six years earlier and essentially followed the same pattern in preparation for death. She lingered in a coma for the summer months. She had a long time to prepare for the afterlife and I shared that preparation with her. The Franciscan sisters who ran the hospital could not have been more loving to our family. I would stay the night and go to the five-thirty Mass every morning in the hospital chapel, then say good-by to my mother and go home and sleep for a few hours.

I was given all the attention and concern for what I was doing, but at the same time I began to look for every excuse to play. I think I was wishing she would pass on so I could play ball and boat and water ski. That summer was supposed to have been the peak of my career as a water skier. I had been awarded a number of trophies already and had my own ski school and this was to be my big year for entering some of the national tournaments. I had to stay with my mother and none of that was possible.

August 15 was a Monday. By this time my sister, who was

expecting her third child, had returned home. In their last exchange, Mother had told Della not to come back for the funeral. My brothers had their jobs. Their wives had the children. My aunt and I were keeping the deathwatch. Theckla had not opened her eyes nor said anything for two weeks. I remember that morning as I prayed very pointedly to God to release my mother from her coma and take her to paradise where she could sing with the angels and once again play the piano with great joy. We celebrated the fourth Glorious Mystery, the Assumption of Mary, when the Mother of God was raised into heaven body and soul.

After Mass, I had breakfast and went to her room one more time before going home. My mother lay there motionless with only those dying gasps to acknowledge that she was teetering on the edge of life. I whispered in her ear that perhaps Jesus would take her on this day as he had taken his own mother. In a sublime moment of grace, Mother opened her eyes and looked at me.

"Maybe God will take me today," she said. Then those luminous eyes closed for the last time and she slipped back into the coma.

Theckla Dirnberger Schlitt

I left the hospital in the new Ford that she'd hardly ever gotten to drive. My brothers had bought it for her when she could no longer park the old '49 Chrysler with Fluid Drive that had been the red apple of my father's eye. It was a tank compared to our cars today. I parked in the driveway thinking that I might have to leave in a rush to return to the hospital. It was two o'clock when the call awakened me to say Theckla had returned to the Lord in whom she put so much trust.

To me, a twenty-one-year-old kid with very little life experience, it was a blessing from God and a favor to my mother that at last peace had come to her battered body and she would now join the angels and saints in proclaiming glory to God.

So the month of August holds special meaning for me when I have the privilege as a priest to offer the sacrifice of the Mass for Bill and Theckla. I thank the Mother of God for taking them on two Marian feast days.

Anniversaries, even of death, are good for nothing more than to recall what happened, to teach us all something. The Latin words *annus,* meaning year, and *versare,* meaning to turn, are such simple explanations for what happens in time as the days turn to years and gather like ripples on the water into decades and a lifetime.

4. Omega and Alpha

THE MOST IMPORTANT THING in the world to me is life after death—eternal salvation, consumption of death and what will be. It's not sad nor hurtful but part of reality.

After seeing death firsthand with my parents, I had a jumpstart on people who were dealing with death. I loved but didn't know how much I loved. They were providers more than people I loved. I never was able to say, "Dad, I love you."

Mother was always there and loved me and prayed for me, but in all my life I never once heard her say, "I love you." It was a Teutonic, Germanic thing where we did not say nor talk about love, but rather just lived without the touchy-feely Italian way of showing deep and close and personal things.

After her death, I had remorse about the time I had spent with my buddies instead of being at the hospital. My sister and brothers had families and obligations. I was the guy with time on my hands who should have been bed-side with my mother.

I had lots of support from classmates and guys I knew. I handled the situation, but I didn't handle anything. It made me even more popular. But it just "happened." I had no choice as to what was going on.

Most priests have a personal devotion to Mary. Catholic catechism says devotion to the Blessed Virgin is intrinsic to Christian worship. She enjoys an integral and important place in the history of salvation. I took comfort when my dad died on a Marian feast day. After Mother died on the Assumption, I took that as a personal sign. It played a significant part in my vocation and what I was to do as a priest.

My last year in the seminary was a whirlwind. Out of the blue, my bishop, Charles Helmsing, wrote me and asked if I would like to study in Rome. He was the head of the newly created Diocese of Springfield-Cape Girardeau and needed some of its seminarians to be trained for future leadership roles. There were seven in our class from the diocese and two of us were selected. Two guys from the St. Louis archdiocese were also invited (but not my buddy Floyd). I've enclosed the bishop's letter just for perusal so that you could see the kind of appointments that young men received in those days:

> *Feb. 10, 1961*
> *Dear Harry,*
> *This is just an exploratory note and I want you to consider it with absolute liberty. In answering you may discuss the matter with your spiritual director and any of the Seminary authorities, as well as with your closest relatives. In these consultations, I would suggest that you ask that the matter be kept confidential.*
>
> *I am considering sending a student or two to the North American College in Rome for the study of Sacred Theology. Since you will be ready for the course next fall, I would like your reaction to the idea of going to Rome.*
>
> *I repeat, I want you to be absolutely free in answering. Your reply will in no way jeopardize your position in the Diocese in the future nor will it necessarily mean that I will choose you for the Roman course of studies.*
>
> *May I look for a reply at least by Easter?*
>
> *Meanwhile, I pray that every grace and success may be yours in the important phase of your seminary training that you are completing this spring.*
> > *Sincerely yours in Christ,*
> > *Most Reverend Charles H. Helmsing, D.D.*
> > *Bishop of Springfield-Cape Girardeau*

Naturally, I responded with the greatest surprise and humility but all along I had felt that this was going to happen to me. There was something similar to female intuition that reigned in my heart for so long a time; the announcement was only an inevitable conclusion.

After four years of philosophy and before commitment to the major seminary for the final four years of study, my pal Charlie decided his goals in life were not the same as mine. With great sadness, I bid him good-by. He was returning to his hometown and I was off to Rome to study.

Charlie would have been successful in whatever he did. And he was! I see signs with his name and logo all over California as his company has grown from the small auto parts store his grandfather started into a major corporation with more than 4,000 stores across the country.

Father Don Ryan returned to Chicago before I graduated from the seminary. I didn't know the circumstances, but some years later I heard from credible sources that he left the priesthood and married. There are so many like him who do so much for small children and teenagers and they go unthanked and unremembered. That's why I believe it is so important to write about people like DJ Ryan.

When Bishop Helmsing extended the offer to me to attend the North American College, he never mentioned getting there. He also failed to tell me that I would not be getting back for at least four years. I had no means to support my studies in Europe. My parents had not been wealthy and they were both gone. Either fate or the Holy Spirit stepped in. A devout Catholic couple had heard about me from our family doctor. He had told them that my parents were dead and my sister and brothers were all raising young families. The Ohrmans had no children of their own and were very comfortable financially. They had a philanthropic interest in furthering Catholic education, especially where it would have a great impact.

Mrs. Ohrman decided to take me under her wing and sponsor my education in Rome. She bought my books, paid my tuition and sent checks to cover my living expenses. Whatever was required, she provided. Without her patronage, my life would have been completely different.

In the middle of May I graduated from Cardinal Glennon College. When I started high school there had been 114 guys in my class. About forty of us (but not Johnny Grimes) made it all the way through the minor seminary. I received my Bachelor of Arts in Philosophy during an evening Mass of Thanksgiving. I don't remember any of my family being there. The next day I packed up and left the place that had been my home for eight years.

I lived in the basement of my brother Charlie's house for that last summer in Cape. He was thrilled when I got the appointment to study in Rome. Charlie had been my mentor as I was growing up. He seemed to know a lot about everything and not too much about anything. I liked that about him. Spending those three short months watching his family grow did a lot for my own growth and development. I worked both in Charlie's office and a little bit in the garage with Johnny. About all I could do that was not harmful to the mechanic's realm was sweep the floor. So I did.

Charlie was the boss of his own company and I had fun answering the telephone and talking like I knew as much as he did. I sold State Farm Insurance for him. When I say that in the singular, I mean it. I sold one policy the entire summer and it was to a friend of mine who left the seminary and bought a car. I was so proud that day.

When it came time for lunch, I used to get on the phone and call my two sisters-in-law. Both of them cooked big "dinners" since the main meal was at noon and my brothers both went home for it. I would ask one and then the other what they were having and depending on my taste (such a spoiled kid) I would accept the invitation and go to that home. I never missed a meal, and a good one, all summer. When you're cooking for six children or nine children you would have to prepare a lot and you'd know leftovers would be scarce, but Betty and Mary always managed to have enough for one more. Both of these women were exceptional cooks and they could really "put on the dog."

My brothers nor my sister could have done any better than the spouses they married and lived with all their lives. It was and still is a hidden joy of mine to know how successful they were as family people. You can say what you want about religion or the gift of faith, but when it comes to individuals making it happen on a daily basis, usually there is a connection to God or a relationship with the Divine. Neither of my sisters-in-law nor my brother-in-law, Pete, was Catholic when they began dating my siblings. It was almost a *"sine qua non"* in our family that if you were going to consider marriage you chose a person who had the same faith. "Without which no deal" is the translation of the Latin phrase. But it didn't seem to matter with the Schlitts. The in-laws all converted to Catholicism.

I recall coming home one noon when my sister-in-law was pregnant with the twins. One of her boys had put sand in his little sister's diaper. The baby was wailing so loudly the leaves were falling from the trees. Mary was trying to hide behind an oak as she was so big and could not run to catch the little monster. I was so happy to round him up for her so she could give him "what for." That's what we called a spanking and it was still do-able in those days. We both laughed so hard and the little guy had no idea how funny the situation was, but he never put sand in his little sister's diaper again. He ended up joining the Marines. That was the beginning of a whole new kind of discipline. Oorah!

I had one little window to look out that summer and it gave me just enough light to know it was day and I had to get up and go to work. I recall telling my sister-in-law how good it was to sleep in, on occasion, in the summer. She looked at me and LOL—laughed out loud! She had been pregnant for the past six or seven years and forgotten what it was like. There were always little ones who were up early or hurting and wanting attention. She had ten babies in all. This is how she handled the question of who was her favorite. "It's always the one who is hurting the most at a given time."

I've never forgotten that lesson and have tried to make it part of my priestly encouragement both to myself and others.

While my brothers raised their families in one Cape, my sister was raising hers in quite another. Peter Darling's mother had owned a home on Martha's Vineyard since 1941. Pete had summered on the island since he was five and passed on that heritage to his family.

My first trip to Martha's Vineyard was in the summer of 1961, just before I was to leave for my studies in Rome. I think

Pat Boone was singing love songs. Except for Bobby Darin, he was my favorite crooner. And some guy with blond hair and blue eyes dominated the movie scene with a romance set on a tobacco farm in the South. That's what I remember hearing and reading about between runs to the beach and running on the beach, swimming in the ocean, riding the waves, paddling on Chilmark Pond and digging up clams with my toes from its muddy waters.

Being on the East Coast was a new experience, different from any I had ever had before. After all, I was a country kid from southern Missouri who had yet to see any part of the world where they didn't speak the same way or eat similar food. Seminary living did not provide much in the way of the unfamiliar. No mind-boggling happenings or heart-churning emotions, whether from people or culture or food or life in general. Seeing how people lived on an island off the coast of Massachusetts was as novel as the idea of living on another continent.

Martha's Vineyard normally has a population of about 17,000, but bursts to over 100,000 in the summertime. Presidents vacation there and of course the Kennedy compound is famous. Numerous other celebs come and go year after year. That in itself makes it an expensive place to live. My brother-in-law's stepmother was a year-round resident, which made her special. The flora which she tended so delicately would not be outdone by many others. She was recognized on the island as one of the best in her field, or rather, garden. She would eagerly quiz me on rudimentary European geography and it was as if she were speaking to me in a foreign tongue. I felt inadequate in so many conversations with her, but also knew she had no idea who Stan Musial was.

It would not be right to spend all these words on Martha's Vineyard without mentioning that there is great fishing on and around the island and off the beaches. One of the neighbors took me out in his small dinghy off the coast of Gay Head. As the waves beat us up on all sides I was knocked to my knees with pole in hand and was hit by a huge striper, which I was able to land. My fishing mate, who was skunked, complained to the family that I had fallen to my knees in prayerful pursuit of the

Lord's blessing in order to catch such a magnificent fish. It weighed over forty pounds and at that time was by far the largest fish I had ever seen or caught.

I wouldn't be seeing my sister for four years so it felt good just being together. Although she was closest to me in age, Della and I had never really spent much time with each other. Growing up, Peach Fuzz preferred tagging along with his brothers. When I was nine and she was just fourteen Della began working part-time at St. Francis Hospital, already focused on a career in nursing. Like most teens, she wasn't around home as much. We were ships passing in the night. When we were both studying in St. Louis, we saw each other a few times but we never were heart-to-heart types.

In those dwindling days after I had returned to Missouri and before I left for Rome, two momentous events transpired.

Our pastor at St. Mary's was the diocesan head of the Propagation of Faith, a missionary society of the Catholic Church. The national director was Bishop Fulton J. Sheen and, improbably, a month before I was scheduled to leave he came to Cape Girardeau.

Every Catholic priest who has spent any time in media work over the past fifty years often thinks about Bishop Sheen. He had one of the top television shows in the country and a weekly audience of 30 million viewers. He had a clever way of teaching Catholicism and converted thousands of people to the faith with his show called *Life Is Worth Living*, for which he won an Emmy—defeating Edward R. Murrow, Lucille Ball and Arthur Godfrey for the title of Most Outstanding Television Personality.

He had a couple of things going for him, which I believe assisted him in his great success as a broadcaster and as a priest. He was able to identify a common enemy of good and that was Communism. He likened it to the devil lurking about like a lion seeking one whom he might devour. It was a time in the history of our country when the common thought was how bad Communism was and how its ideas could threaten the safety and well-being of every American. He didn't have to proselytize the Catholic faith. He merely said the devil/Communism was its opponent and we all needed to do something to overcome it.

The good bishop came to the rectory where I was staying for

those final weeks. It was a Sunday afternoon and his talk was to be that evening. The doorbell rang about three o'clock and before I could get to the door another man did, and there stood Bishop Fulton Sheen. He had those piercing steel grey eyes that could penetrate a bank vault. He must have had the man in conversation for fifteen minutes when the man asked me if I could go to the kitchen and make him (the bum) a sandwich. I was so impressed I did everything in double time.

Later that evening at dinner with the great man, out of jealousy or envy, one of the young priests began challenging statements that Sheen had made at the table. I was quiet and humble and ashamed that a man of such stature should have to undergo a pop quiz from a young guy who couldn't hold a candle to the accomplishments of the renowned priest and communicator.

The next morning Bishop Sheen celebrated Mass and I had the privilege of serving. I don't suppose I have to add anything to these little snippets to convince you that, yes, like many other priests who dabbled in media, I was influenced by what Bishop Sheen had done. He was always letting us know that he spent an hour before the Blessed Sacrament every day. All did not come to him because of who he was, but with much prayer and quiet time. It's no secret that I could not affect the world like him, but it is the truth that I've had many opportunities to make my mark as a believing preacher of the Word who only wants to do good.

I just read some statistics recently where they are no longer circumcising most male babies. According to the *New York Times*, in the 1980s about 80% of baby boys were circumcised but in this decade only about one-third have their foreskins removed. When Britain's baby Prince George was born, a will-they-or-won't-they story in the *Telegraph* said just 3.8% of infant boys there go under the knife. It was very surprising to me because of what happened when I was about to go to Rome to study theology.

I was twenty-two years old and my doctor felt that at that late date I should be circumcised. He became concerned that my living in Europe might make me susceptible to strange diseases or whatever. He was not a Catholic and I don't think he understood how deeply committed I was to becoming a priest. For whatever reason, not important today, I agreed to do it.

It was September and I was to leave for Rome the following month. My brother John felt that this was a great sacrifice (he knew more than me) so he took me to St. Louis the day before the procedure to see the Cardinals play baseball. It was hot and steamy and I'm sure we had more than our share of Budweiser products and peanuts to curb thirst and appetite.

I was supposed to be at the hospital around 5:00 p.m. to check in. I arrived at 7:00 p.m. and they were not too happy. I put on the proverbial nothing gown with the back open . . . you know what I'm talking about. I was ordered to take the pills they gave me to clean out my system. It worked. It really worked. I raced across the hall and the insides of me began to exit from whatever orifice they could find. I spent over an hour cleaning the bathroom because I was so embarrassed by the huge mess that I made. I knew many of the people who worked in that hospital because of my time spent there with my mother.

To add fuel to the fire, a male nurse arrived with shaving cream and a large blade and informed me that he was assigned to shave my pubic area in preparation for the surgery the next morning.

"OK," I said, "whatever is necessary."

It happened on schedule and there I was lying with a tent over my private parts, knowing that in the little town where I lived there would be an announcement in the newspaper of those "At the Hospitals." Sure, all my buddies would know and would be eager to visit and laugh. But the worst was the nuns who had taught me in grade school and were so proud of me having been selected to study in Rome. Here they came the next day, wanting to know what was going on. "Oh," I said. "Male surgery. Not to worry."

Did I mention that it was extremely embarrassing? Certainly not a badge of courage that you could brag about if you had a cast on your hand or a bandage on your head with a fife and drum announcing your coming. And very, very painful. It was awful! I wouldn't wish it on anyone. I guess the Israelites had other ways of looking at it that are beyond my comprehension. I'll find out why Dr. Ritter thought it was so important when I see him in heaven. I'm sure he'll have a better explanation than the one I've given or the one given by the rabbi before he snips little kids in the temple. It was a difficult few weeks as I had to learn to walk with a wide-open stance because everything was so tender. It felt like the Pontiac commercial years ago when the wide body was such a huge success. It curtailed my swimming and boating activities for the remainder of the summer and my pals were eager to invite me everywhere just so they could whisper behind my back that I had had a very delicate surgery.

I don't smoke cigars. Never liked them, they didn't like me. But one evening late that summer I sat in the swing on the porch outside my brother's home puffing on a stick of ugliness thinking the whole world was great. I was thinking about so many beautiful experiences that I had had living with my brothers and I knew that the fall would see me leaving my home for Europe and four years in Rome. As I raised my beer for a wash down of the cigar taste, I heard the squeak of the swing as I went back and forth. All of a sudden it was annoying. Oh my, I thought, it isn't a perfect world. Even with all the great things going on in my life this little squeak is annoying me. It's been that way my whole life. I have had so much good fortune with family, friends, relationships, callings and culture, yet just about every time I begin to think it's all perfect a little squeak shows its ugly face and brings me back to reality.

In October of 1961, I boarded the SS *Cristoforo Colombo* in New York headed for Naples, Italy. I had never been to New York, never been at sea and never had seen such a huge ship. While waiting in line to board, I met fellow seminarians Wayne Ressler from Iowa and James Kogler from New York. Kogler immediately spotted two country boys, both of whom had been on the Mississippi River in small jon boats and thought they were great sailors. After making a few smart remarks about shoes and hayseeds, Jim offered to host us with his family in a room aboard the ship where relatives were allowed to send off their loved ones. Wayne and I were welcomed with open arms and made to feel at home with Clare and Carl Kogler. Once the hugs and kisses were over, Jim's parents hit the plank for the New York docks and the ship sailed out of the harbor.

Mal de mer was never a concern for me as I had been in boats on lakes and rivers most of my life. The sea was another story. I now had graduated from champagne at the Koglers' bon voyage party to a mixed drink from the retro bar, that is, the one in the rear. Not really knowing much about drinking, except the difference between 3.2% "Sunday" beer and 5% beer, I ordered a Tom Collins. Hanging on to the rail of the *Colombo*, whose sister ship had been the doomed *Andrea Doria*, I witnessed a major storm with huge waves and a driving rain. I would have been frightened but didn't really have that much sense to be.

I was praising God for the immense power of the seas as they banged against the sides of the huge vessel. I should have been more concerned when the crew began putting up ropes around the deck, asking passengers to hold on when walking and suggesting that we return to our cabins. So I slugged down my second Tom Collins and began following the ropes to the stairwell. I had no idea where I was going but knew that I was a true sailor. My stomach was strong and there was no sense of the seasickness that I had noted from several other passengers as they tried to navigate the stairs with both hands on the rails.

So, as nature would have it, the great sailor of rivers was now controlled by the god of the seas. Every step I took down, I was met by three steps coming up. This must have lasted at least half an hour as I could not find my cabin. Stumbling down the corridors noting the small receptacles on the side where sick passengers were tossing their cookies (if not their Tom Collinses) right and left, I finally found my cabin. I pushed open the door only to discover that my roommate was flat on his back moaning about the ups and downs of the sea and begging God to take him before he had to endure any more. I smiled and had barely said hello when lo and behold the mal of the mer hit me broadside. Yes, the Missouri Huck Finn had met his match. I hit the head with great gusto and was not able to get out of bed for the next two days. By that time the seas were calm, my roommate was up and about eating and drinking and bragging about how he had out-sailed his partner from Missouri.

As my new friend Jim said when we landed in Naples, "Man, look at all the foreign cars!"

5. Ciao Roma!

THE PONTIFICAL NORTH AMERICAN COLLEGE is up the hill from the Vatican, near the Tiber River. From the roof you can see all the way to the Spanish Steps, as well as most of ancient Rome. It's one of the best views of the Eternal City. People come from all over to see it. The college was founded about a hundred years before I got there when Pope Pius IX thought it would be a good idea if some of the seminarians in the U.S. came to Rome for their theological formation. Where better to impart the tradition and universality of the Church? Bishops nominated candidates for admission, as happened in my case, with an eye toward grooming future "executives" for the American Church. If you wanted to be an officer in the military you went to West Point or the Naval Academy, for priests it was the North American College.

In the European system of education, colleges are often divided into national groups where the same language is spoken. We lived and played and prayed at the NAC, but we went to class at the Gregorian University. It was established in 1551 by Saint Ignatius Loyola and my teachers were the cream of the Jesuit crop. The faculty was a showcase of stars with the best Jesuits in the world: Frenchmen, Spaniards, Englishmen, Germans and one American. They were serious scholars. They tested their theses on students who, in turn, challenged them on their positions.

The *aulas* (halls) were filled to capacity at 700 or 800 with young men from all over the world trying to learn more about God. Each morning there were four classes:

Moral Theology 8:30 a.m. to 9:15 a.m.
Christology 9:30 a.m. to 10:15 a.m.
Canon Law 10:30 a.m. to 11:15 a.m.
Church History 11:30 a.m. to 12:15 p.m.

If you were taking the full load, it meant that every day you had four different 45-minute classes. In Latin. Without a southern drawl. Most of us had three out of four classes. I skipped Canon Law. Scholastically speaking, the spirit of competition was incredible. The caliber of men was beyond conception.

After a morning of hard work, 12:20 p.m. and the big green buses couldn't get there fast enough. We usually got back to the college from the university about 12:30 p.m. depending on the downtown traffic. That part of Rome is now closed to vehicles. I can't imagine how long it would take today. We would pour out of the buses and race to our rooms, dump our books, make a potty-stop and head for the dining room.

North American College student

I don't drink coffee. Never did. It's probably because outside my window at the college was a coffee plant where they did something with the beans and on an empty stomach the smell of coffee made me queasy. I couldn't wait to get to the dining room for the midday feed.

Our main meal at the North American College was at 1:00 p.m.. It was always hot and wine was served, but pasta was a far cry from country-fried everything. Would you believe that one of the desserts we had (when in season) was peanuts in the shell? It was a practice to file out of the dining room and proceed to the chapel for a prayer following the meal. Once we were all in our pews and a deafening silence came over us in prayer, there was only one radical disturbance. Imagine over two hundred guys working their gums after the meal trying to clear their teeth of peanut residue. Can you hear it? If I could spell it to make the sound I would.

Since none of us understood Latin yet, one of the priests at the NAC served as the "repetitor" telling us what had been said in our classes that morning. We spent the afternoons studying, but after the eight o'clock evening meal we adjourned outside to the porch for a little social time until they rang the bell for bed. Some guys smoked, some guys bought candy bars before the store closed, but mostly we talked.

Bill Levada was from California and three years ahead of me. He was brilliant but unassuming. Little did any of us know, he would go on to become a teacher at the Gregorian, a cardinal and the highest ranking American at the Vatican. He and I were never close friends, but we always spoke after dinner. I found him interesting even though he was not an athlete or thespian or musician. Bill was a scholar, analytical and a deep thinker in theology, while my theological demeanor often found itself struggling with the *campo sportiva* where I excelled as an athlete. I think Bill Levada found me to be an interesting character, so much so that he invited me to serve at one of his first Masses that December in the catacombs in Rome.

It was a privilege to leave the college early in the morning with a newly ordained priest and feel the Holy Spirit where the first Christians shared bread and wine around a table. That scene is depicted quite vividly at the home of Saint Priscilla in those catacombs dating back to the second century. These are the same actions I perform in the Eucharist or Holy Communion as I have each day for fifty years.

I got to know Bill through my best friend, Miles Riley, who was also from California. Miles was one class ahead of me. We became close friends because of soccer. I was the only guy on the team besides him who had played for several years before coming to Europe. My time in the seminary in St. Louis had been a good training ground for soccer. The North American Martyrs were the worst team in town. They hardly ever won a game. It was no mystery why they were called the Martyrs. My arrival didn't help much, although if we could beat up on the smaller but faster Europeans who grew up with the game, at least there was hope.

Miles was all that I wanted to be. He had a great smile, personality, was great at storytelling, exciting to talk to. I was jealous of him. He was from California, a great tennis player and a great swimmer because his family belonged to country clubs. He got me on the swimming team at college and I did pretty well. My specialty was the breaststroke. (I had a strong frog-leg kick taught to me by a guy from Indiana who represented the NAC in almost every event except the breaststroke.) Miles was interested in music and sports and good at relating to people. I thought those qualities were more important than being a theologian.

I was out of place in Rome. There was very little emphasis on personality. I was an athlete with good communication skills and good looks. If you could quote scripture and knew canon law, that was more important. I would have to be more buttoned-down if I was ever going to live up to the Roman training and be a leader in the American Church.

I was thankful to have the ear of my old friend and mentor Father

Harry in the Italian countryside near Subiaco

John Martin. He too was living in Rome and the superior of the Maryknoll house on Via Sardegna 83. Again, it was a weekly visit for me to go to confession. He was my spiritual advisor but we always shared some social time afterward and, on more than one occasion, a can of Budweiser. He had befriended the Marine Guard up the street at the U.S. Embassy and they would regularly supply him with hops from Germany that were brewed in St. Louis then shipped around the world in cans. A few of my classmates also found Father Martin engaging, both as a confessor and as a guy who might pop a can once absolution was given.

James Foley Kogler, Roy Riedy, Wayne Ressler and Harry Schlitt—aka JFK, Rufus, Wimpy and Fuzzy—became the closest of friends during our first year in Rome. Athos, Aramis, Porthos and d'Artagnan had nothing on us. We all enjoyed each other's company and found some kind of bond that was unique and lasting. It might have been our love for singing and laughing and kidding around.

JFK had a Perry Como type voice that went with his bedroom eyes and his calm approach to almost everything. He was a brilliant man who had deep concerns and feelings for anyone who did not have the blessings or graces that he enjoyed. Rufus was a classic Renaissance Man. He knew art and literature and took it as a personal devotion. He used to get a thrill out of looking at an old painting or an 800-year-old church and would excite anyone around him with a little laugh and a giggle describing art history or a battle somewhere. Wimpy hailed from Cascade, Iowa, a town with one Catholic school and not much more. Fresh from the cornfields to the spaghetti factories, he took it all in. He was the absolute most real person you could ever meet, so honest and truthful without any guile. He said what he thought and was what he was. He was the real deal.

Until you were ordained as a priest, Thursday afternoon was your only free time. We called it "Black Days" because we could go off campus wearing our plain black cassocks. It was the closest we got to casual. The rest of the time, we wore black cassocks trimmed with blue piping and small round blue buttons from

Harry exploring Italy

top to bottom. They were tied with red sashes and accented with white Roman collars. Everywhere we went, tourist and resident alike recognized us as American seminarians thanks to our red, white and blue.

At the same time, America was slipping farther and farther into our past. Letters came from friends and relatives, but the thin airmail sheets only underscored just how far apart we were. They would often comment about a particular event in their part of the country, be it tornado, forest fire, or earthquake. It was only interesting if it was where you once lived. And there was never enough fact in a letter to lead you to seek further information.

As students in a foreign country, it was not part of our training to be up on current affairs. In fact, we knew hardly anything about what was going on in our country or, for that matter, the world. These were the days before e-mail, the Internet and iPhones. There was no texting, TV, radio, CNN, not even local broadcasts that we could watch or listen to in Italian. There was no baseball. The best we had was a sub-sized *TIME* magazine in a twelve-page, no ad format. It was our closest connection to the States.

Bishop Helmsing, who by then was in Kansas City, corresponded with me, offering encouragement as I struggled to adjust to my new reality. The most important words I heard from him were these: "Do your best, angels can't do better!" He wrote this to me after I completed my first year at the Gregorian University. I had to repeat one theology course in the summer as I was unable to understand what the examiner was asking in my final oral exam. We only had exams once a year and they were all done face to face. You had one hour with four professors. Each would ask you different questions in Latin and you were expected to respond in kind. My fluency in Latin had not developed and I was at a loss to know what they wanted me to say. I was embarrassed, but a lot of guys were in the same boat. Anyway, Bishop Helmsing understood and helped me through this disappointing first year abroad.

I was at the noon meal one June day in 1962, when the rector approached the table and asked me to go to Roy's room and check on him. He was not at his place in the refectory. The rector knew why but I didn't. I got up from the table and raced upstairs to the fourth floor (almost 200 steps) and knocked on Roy's door.

He was sitting on the edge of his bed smoking a cigarette and wearing a suit and tie. His bags were packed and standing near the door. His bed was stripped and his closets open and empty. I was shocked.

"I can't believe you're leaving Roy!" I blurted out. There is an empty feeling when a close friend decides the priesthood is not for him and chooses to leave and pursue some other life. "You would make a great priest. You have so many more gifts than I do to offer the people of God. Please, reconsider."

"There isn't anything I can do about it, Harry." Accompanying his gravelly voice that was so masculine were two small tears from each eye rolling down his cheeks. Like any guy he quickly absorbed them on his sleeve not to betray delicate feelings. We both stood, hugged, and it was over.

I carried one of his bags downstairs and waited with him until the taxi came to take him to the airport. I didn't have the courage to return to the dining room and share the news with the guys. Instead, I slipped into the chapel and prayed for Roy and the continued grace that I would need to become a priest.

"Where's Roy?"

That afternoon, I had to explain what I didn't know about him leaving so suddenly. I never saw Roy again until he returned for my ordination in December 1964.

The summer sun was blasting in Rome—so much so that even the cold marble floors and the statues and fountains adorning *la città* seemed to call for an all dog alert for a trip to the beach. You can imagine my surprise when Miles came by my room and invited me to hit the waves at Fregene, a beach town near Rome, with his sister. She was in town on a work-study program out of Loyola and the Olympic Village dormitory where she was housed was sweltering.

I was up in an instant tugging at the first of a hundred buttons.

"When do we leave?"

"Not me, Fuzzy." Miles always used my childhood name. "I have to study. I have an exam tomorrow."

It was late June and oral exams were in the final session at the Gregorian University. Mercifully, I had passed through that vale and summer school had not yet begun.

"She's out front," he said. "She's driving a Triumph."

Say no more. I was out the door.

I spotted her from the waiting room in a red convertible.

Harry on the Italian Riviera

Sleek and curvaceous, that sports car was a dream. I think it was called a TR3. Its driver was cute as a button and just filled with personality like her big brother. He ushered me from the front entrance of the college to the car, kissed his sister and we were off. I was twenty-three and she must have been every bit of nineteen. Needless to say, it was one of the most enjoyable days of my life. I can still see her hair blowing in the breeze as we passed through Cinecittà (Italy's Hollywood) to the black sands of Fregene singing *Come il Carbone*, a popular song referring to the suntan you could get while enjoying the Italian *spiaggia*. That expression "a day at the beach" took on a whole new meaning for me.

Afterward back in my room, I was still humming the suntan song when a classmate (from Philadelphia) knocked on my door and said he needed to speak with me. He then unwrapped a tale of woe that another of our classmates, scrupulous as he was, was about to report me to the seminary authorities for spending the day with a young woman at the beach. All kinds of sick thoughts were racing through his mind about the many pitfalls that I had exposed myself to that afternoon.

Knowing the truth and knowing that I had been doing a favor for a guy gave me the moral high ground. I also knew what a lucky guy I was to have had the opportunity to spend a day at the beach with a young American girl instead of whatever else might have been in store for me—either straightening my sock drawer or making a holy hour in the heat of the day.

There were not many choices that would have trumped what I enjoyed that day with Miles' sister. It was the beginning of a friendship that lasted until her death last year from cancer. Her brother thought it was a great idea even when I was forced to defend myself and my honor to a narrow-minded seminary student. As it turned out, that guy decided the priesthood was not for him and left six months before ordination to become an actor. Somewhere in that Roman Holiday was the work of the Holy Spirit.

In my time, students in Rome were not allowed to come home for the full four years they were in college. Once there, you were there. An exception might be made for the death of a family member. We were usually done with classes and exams by early July. Then we were given a month to travel the Continent. We had to go with at least three other seminarians. Safety in numbers I guess. Every year a different itinerary was planned in advance so you could see and hear the sights and sounds of other cultures. One summer we hitchhiked in Ireland (the Catholic trip), another time we went to The Netherlands (the sex trip). Germany, Austria and Switzerland were mainly about beer and chocolate, France was for wine.

Twice during my Roman years I traveled to the most important Marian shrine in the world, Lourdes. It affected me profoundly, in part because of my parents. I was very impressed by the spiritual environment, all the open prayer and the possibility of divine intervention.

6. People of God

LIVING IN THE VATICAN for four short years, I saw a lot of pomp and circumstance. But I also was privileged to be there during the papacy of John XXIII. He always seemed to be happy even though he was surrounded by old men who were followed by a cloud of darkness and doom. The world and all it stood for was based on what the devil was doing. They heard only wailing and gnashing of teeth. Everything was so negative. John XXIII was about light and hope. He said, "Let's open a window and get some fresh air in here before we all go down the drain into muck and misery." (That last part is mine.)

Looking back, I was lucky enough to have been in the right place at the right time, being a student in Rome when Pope John XXIII convened the Second Vatican Council. Most of my time at the North American College ran parallel with Vatican II. It was probably the highlight of my four years in Rome. An ecumenical council is unique because all the Catholic bishops in the world are invited. Ninety percent of them come. Vatican I in 1869 lasted just a year, but long enough to pronounce papal infallibility. The one before that was in Trent, 300 years earlier. It lasted for three popes, eighteen years and twenty-five sessions.

Vatican II opened on the eleventh of October in 1962. I had been away from Missouri for one year. The Fathers of the Roman Catholic Church all over the world gathered in assembly in St. Peter's Basilica to discuss the pre-prepared papers that were presented to them for vote into Church policy and practice. I didn't know many of the bishops who were there but enough to know how seriously everyone was taking the daily meetings and long sessions of listening to documents called *schemas* that had been written well in advance on such things as the liturgy, the role of media and the role of non-clergy, including women. I was in great admiration of these 2,500 men who all seemed so old that they should not have to sit through classes like I was doing.

74

Anytime that I felt the Gregorian University was boring and overworking me, I thought about all those men who were for the most part kings in their own corners of the world, their dioceses, and here in Rome they were simply schoolboys like me trying to adjust to the times and customs of a changing world and a changing Church. They would stream out of St. Peter's draped in their long red robes and bearing briefcases full of paperwork, knowing they didn't get it all in the classroom (the largest in the world, where you could hear a pen drop—St. Peter's Basilica). And knowing they would have to go home and study more closely what they had not been able to absorb that day.

It was the same for me.

They were meeting at the same time that we were in the Gregorian auditing the greatest minds the Jesuit order of teachers had to offer. I would hear what had been said that day on the floor as it was read to us by the repetitor during our noon meal. But, as I said, it was read. I for one, had to look at the written word and read more closely to understand.

Cardinal Ritter, the archbishop of St. Louis whom I hadn't seen since leaving home, visited me at the NAC while he was in Rome for the Second Council. We had a wonderful exchange. He was very proud of a little guy from Cape Girardeau who was now studying theology in Rome. Bishop Helmsing, his successor Bishop Ignatius Strecker, and my former pastor, now Bishop Marion Forst, were also in town for Vatican II. They came over to the college for dinner often, once bringing news that the Yankees had won the World Series over the Giants. Sometimes they took us out for pizza and beer or to a soccer match. In return, seminarians helped out the visitors from home however they could.

I loaned Bishop Forst my typewriter, which he used to chronicle the Council and the struggle for the soul of the Church. In his daily journal he described fellow Midwesterner Cardinal Ritter as "well offsetting" conservative counterparts from New York and Los Angeles. Cardinal Spellman, a supporter of Senator Joseph McCarthy and war in Vietnam, and Cardinal McIntyre who was pro-John Birch Society, were more closely aligned with the dogmatic Curia than with their countrymen. Ritter (the de-segregationist) spoke on the floor advocating freedom of conscience. Forst himself submitted a paper arguing in favor of dropping Latin at Mass.

Fresh off the press from St. Peter's to our dining room came the documents that were discussed and voted on that morning by the Conciliar Fathers. After the reading of the documents at table, a bell was rung by the college rector who would say:

"Tu autem Domine miserere nobis," to which we all would respond: *"Deo gratias."*

Then the chatter would commence. The guys who understood Latin and the documents better than others would proceed to slice up every word until eyes would brighten and minds would open to the fact that we were a changing church and it was happening right before our eyes.

At the time I took it all for granted.

I'm sure I perked up when I read about the importance of media and communications to the Church. Our rector at the NAC, Archbishop Martin O'Connor, had authored a proposal on the "entertainment media." He was a prophet in his time and a man who understood the seriousness of social communications. It was much more than game shows, soap operas and reality TV. It was a molder of minds and a power to be reckoned with. But little would I have realized then that I would be working virtually all of my fifty years as a priest trying to meld the meaning of Church teaching and modern communications. And that never included the Internet and what could and can be done today.

I recall the rector's advice to one of my fellow students in 1962, "Father, take good care of your teeth, you know television is coming for us all."

Father Edward Egan, the future cardinal and Archbishop of New York, was the repetitor at that time and he was my homiletics professor. He repeated what had been said that day in Latin about the prospect of Mass in the vernacular. He was also teaching me how to preach.

He had a deep voice and said, "Harry, you're going to be a wonderful homilist but sometimes you're walking on eggs."

It was the first time I had heard the expression and my face curled up in the query mode to see if he would go any further with an explanation. After class, my pal Wayne from Iowa reminded me that's what I got for being on the cutting edge with the stories in my preaching. Apparently talking about squirrel hunting did not resonate in Rome.

One Sunday afternoon to celebrate the fourth anniversary of John XXIII's papacy, bishops Strecker, Helmsing and Forst invited the Springfield-Cape Girardeau seminarians out to lunch. Our number had swelled to three with the addition of Justin Monaghan. Bishop Strecker had been looking for priests for his new diocese and the young Irishman was eager to try his luck in America. He had signed up to go to work, as soon as he was ordained, in the missions of southern Missouri. Instead of attending the seminary in Ireland, his U.S. bishop sent him to Rome to the Irish College. I knew Justin because he played soccer for their team. When students at the NAC staged plays, seminarians from other English-speaking colleges were invited, so I had seen him around.

His eyes were larger than pumpkins when I asked him during lunch if he rode horses. His knowledge of America was mostly from western movies where everyone traveled on horseback. He began apologizing fervently to Bishop Strecker for his inability to ride a horse. The bishop looked at him curiously then saw me and knew that I had filled Justin's head with Roy Rogers, Gene Autry, Hopalong Cassidy, the Lone Ranger and all the others he had seen depicting America as a horse and buggy nation where streets were paved with road apples and dust is the order of the day. Over the years Justin and I became very close friends.

Ever since *Sports Illustrated* began publishing, I've wanted to be on the cover. Of course, it's a dream. When people see me in public I often get the curious asking, "Are you so-and-so? You look just like him!"

"No," I say. "Perhaps you have seen me on the cover of *Sports Illustrated*?"

The closest I ever got was when I was the only American in Rome chosen to play on the All American University soccer team. It was a tremendous honor. While my entire NAC team was from the U.S., the All Star team was 90% South American. We were set to meet the mighty All European team in a Roman college-level version of the World Cup.

I was also the only one who took a shower after practice. The Germans, English, Scots and Irish always teased me as we sometimes practiced on the same pitch together as the Europeans. At least I could understand what they were talking about in the dressing room. My teammates from Brazil, Paraguay, Argentina and Mexico were never in the locker room. They used to towel off with their sweaty jerseys and put on their cassocks and head for the bus back to their colleges. By taking a shower and the razzing, I avoided the interior of a motorcoach that might be stopped in traffic and . . . oh my! What an olfactory delight that would have been!

North American College Martyrs soccer team

At the height of my soccer career, I was the center forward for that team and in the All American vs. European final, I scored the goal that made the difference. I recall the little man playing next to me, born and baptized Jesús in Argentina. In Spanish it's the same as Jesus.

"Jesús, Jesús, passa la palla!"

He finally did and I scored. I even made the newspaper back home in Cape. It was a great moment for me but embarrassing to the delegation on the sidelines who heard me yelling, "Jesus, pass the ball!"

My only other college experience in sports that I relish was being on the field in Firenze with *Gli Azzurri*, the Blue. This was the Italian national football team and they were preparing for an international match. My friend John Mahoney and I had known each other since we played soccer together at Cardinal Glennon where he was a freshman when I was a senior. I was thrilled when he accepted the scholarship to come to Rome knowing we would have somebody strong on the North American soccer team who would excel. He was a wonderful soccer player and silver-tongued to boot. He had met the coach of the Blue before one of the team workouts. Professional soccer was just getting popular in the United States and the coach thought it might be good for the sport for a couple of Yanks to see just how far behind we were. He arranged for the two of us to dress and come on the field with the players.

It was exciting to put on the shorts and the shirt and dash out on the field. That was truly the most exciting part. It didn't take long for us to realize that we were light-years behind these young men who were in training and playing professionally. It would be like most of us entering the batting cage of a Major League Baseball team and trying to hit a ball thrown at ninety miles an hour. After about thirty minutes, it was evident to all that just being on the field and taking our kicks was a waste of time both for their training and for the coaches. We were grateful for the opportunity and thanked them profusely as we headed for the locker room. Incidentally, we didn't shower. No need! We hardly broke a sweat!

This reminds me of the words of Dom Hélder Pessoa Câmara from Recife, Brazil:

"When you dream alone, it is only a dream. When we dream together, it's the beginning of a reality."

I can still dream about the cover of *Sports Illustrated* but unless I catch a foul ball at a Giants game—in my mouth—no way, José!

Pope John XXIII died on my 24th birthday, June 3, 1963. He had known about his stomach cancer when he called the Second Council, holding on to life long enough to shepherd the first session and irreversibly alter the course of the Church he loved. I was there in St. Peter's Square and mourned with the many who had gathered to gaze and praise at the little window where he had given so many blessings, where millions had come before to experience the grace that came with his making the sign of the cross over us all. I used to get goosebumps at hearing his voice and words of blessing. The blessings of John XXIII were a passing thing but his definition of the Catholic Church is something that has carried over throughout the entire fifty years of my ministry.

When the pope died, his body lay in state in St. Peter's for three days. Those inside the Vatican wanted to show he was dead. They did not reckon on so many pilgrims, me among them, lining up day after hot summer day to venerate the remains. They didn't cut it off. You could smell the stench of the corpse outside the church and when you filed past you could see it was black.

Once again my time in Rome would be marked by an historic event. The Cardinal Electors were called to a papal conclave to select the successor to John XXIII.

Conclave . . . "with a key."

The cardinals of the Roman Catholic Church gathered at the Vatican, sequestering themselves in what is called a conclave. It literally means that they close the door, lock it and don't come out until there's a new pope. History tells us that a conclave has lasted years in some cases or only a couple of days in others. When travel was more difficult and took more time, it made sense not to rush into things. Here, there was the impetus of the Second Council.

Pope Paul VI opened the second session of Vatican II on September 29, 1963, picking up where his predecessor had left off. Cardinal Ritter, Bishop Forst and the rest of the delegation were back at St. Peter's and the Fathers of the Church resumed deliberations on the *schemas*.

My relationship with Father Martin was growing year after year. He always teased about how important he was to the Church by using the expression *"in petto"* which in English means "inside the breast." The pope would make cardinals from around the world. Naturally he had friends from his own country and culture whom he favored, but he could not appoint them for just that reason. And so it was said that he carried them *"in petto."* So that he, the pope and God would know that if the pope could, he would elevate them to that office. I used to tease Father Martin about being made a cardinal and he would simply look down and with his fist to his chest say, *"In petto, young man. In petto."*

I was asked by Father Martin to assist some Maryknoll bishops who were attending the Second Council with menial tasks, like translation and errands to the drug store or clothing store. Maryknolls were missionaries. They wouldn't have the slightest idea how to translate documents from Latin to English. They had no Latin background, no sophistication of studying in Rome and being around the Vatican. They were not the executive types. They were the hard-core roll up your sleeves types. If you had to build a dam to get fresh water, that's what they did. The things that were important in Rome were not important in mission country at all.

The universality and the unity of the Church were never more apparent to us than the day we heard that President John F. Kennedy had been assassinated.

We were in our rooms when the bells rang and, quite unusually, the alarm went off. We went to the chapel and the rector, Archbishop O'Connor, made the announcement that the first Catholic president of the United States had been shot. We stayed an hour and prayed, then got the message he had died and remained a couple of more hours in quiet prayer. Shocked.

I was in the chapel much longer than I expected, thinking of him and asking God to give him the gift of eternal life. I felt very close to President Kennedy because I believed that he was raised with the same set of values and moral standards that my parents had passed along to me. I felt an affinity because we were both Roman Catholics. Whether it made a difference or not to anyone else, it did to me. I loved the guy and was particularly fond of his speech even with a Bostonian accent. After all (John 3:16) God did send His Son into the world so that all who believe in Him might enjoy that eternal life. We had that in common.

Perhaps in a nod to the new decree on communications, Pope Paul VI allowed television cameras inside the Vatican. He spoke directly to American audiences expressing profound shared grief. On Monday classes were canceled and that evening a solemn requiem Mass was offered for the repose of John Kennedy's soul.

On the same day that the president died, the Vatican had delivered the long-awaited announcement that Latin would be dropped at Mass in favor of the vernacular. For the first time in the history of the Church basic communication, word of mouth, was sanctioned between priest and the people during the holy sacrifice of the Mass.

My first encounter with Warren Holleran was on a Thursday night, as that was when the spiritual directors addressed the student body. Warren gave a talk on "Faith" illustrated with the Old Testament story of Abraham having to sacrifice his only son, Isaac, as requested by God. Warren described the emotional moment so vividly that I can still see the glimmer of the knife Abraham raised to thrust into the young boy's body. That memory is etched in my psyche and will never go away. Tears began to form in Warren's eyes as he spoke of Abraham putting down the knife and beginning his journey of faith, a trip he was taking at his own expense. What profound meaning this story would have for many generations.

Sacred Scripture, the Bible, when fully revealed, can give you the kind of goosebumps that any great writing can. Like the two guys on their way to Emmaus, my own blood began to boil and I became on fire, burning with the rudiments of what would be my life as a Catholic priest. Once ordained, I would have the privilege and the honor of studying and reading and renewing my faith every day with these sacred writings.

I loved to go to Venice. It's really my favorite European city, with the exception of Rome. It's so romantic and full of charm and intrigue. JFK, Wimpy and I always stayed in cheap B&Bs but usually on one of the canals. A favorite pastime was to lean out the window when American tourists were coming from the train stations and sing a line or two of an Italian pop song and then listen to them ooh and aah about *bella Venezia*. It helped that we had our own Perry Como.

It was another day at the beach when I had a major comeuppance. Rarely did we see young American girls . . . unless they were someone's sister in Rome. So coming to the beach in Venice was a real treat. There was a touring group of young Americans giving an acapella concert that night at some theatre in Venice. I played volleyball with them. My Italian was good enough and by this time my tan was *come il carbone* (like coal). I could hear them on the other side as I played with the Italians. "Don't hit it to that guy!" Then I would run over to their side. It wasn't fair, but funny!

I 'fessed up at one point and then began chatting up a young girl who kept asking me what I was doing in Italy. I didn't want to ruin the glow of being around a pretty lass so I didn't want to say I was in Rome studying to be a priest. I kept avoiding all the questions that would lead to that true and honest disclosure. We talked, laughed, swam and tried to get away from the large group. As the sun began to go down and there we were, she asked what I would be doing that evening. I told her I might come to the concert. She was thrilled!

We gathered our towels and shirts and headed for the ferry. She again stopped me before we boarded and said, "Now tell me honestly, what do you do in Rome?"

"I told you. I'm a student in philosophy."

She smiled and with a little grin on her red face said, "You know, my brother is back in the States studying to be a priest. He has calluses on his knees just like you from doing lots of kneeling in church."

Now really, how many of us ever looked at our knees for some sign or relevance as to what we do in life?

"Oh nuts," I exclaimed, "you're right. I do have knobby knees and you're right again, I am studying to be a priest and I shouldn't be flirting with you like I've done all afternoon. I'm sorry!"

I didn't go to the concert. And no, I never saw her again. Nor did I pursue anyone else during my time as a seminarian without telling the truth about what I'm doing, what I'm studying and what I hope to be when I grow up.

The date for my ordination was approaching fast. Even though graduation wasn't until the spring, the NAC ordained its men in December. This gave them a leg up on the American men who were ordained in June at the end of the academic year. Seniority in dioceses was based on your ordination date.

At the same time, the third session of Vatican II was drawing to a close. According to the now familiar routine, after the main meal and chapel, it was out to the rec room for more discussion of what the Conciliar Fathers had said that morning about our Church. Surely, one of these days we would hear that priestly celibacy was out the window with the Latin language and priests celebrating Mass with their backs to the people. Alas, all these years, nothing yet in that vein. But as young men in our twenties, we just knew that it was a matter of time. More on that later.

"OK, OK," I thought, "the leaders of the Church are talking about what the Church might be in the future."

It had never dawned on me that a new definition of the Church itself would be read to us at table on that miraculous day. The Church was now the "People of God."

So what, you say?

This is what. Whereas before the Church was strictly vertical in nature, it now was defined as horizontal. In other words, our Church used to be:

God
Father
Son
Holy Spirit
Pope
Cardinals
Bishops
Monsignors
Fathers
Religious (sisters and brothers)
Laity (everyone else)
and Pets.
Oh, I forgot Angels. They were right before the Pope.

It was an up and down measure of the hierarchy.

The words could not have been clearer. The Church is the PEOPLE OF GOD. That includes all my brothers and sisters of other faiths, religions, beliefs. The window was now open and the fresh air that Pope John XXIII had promised from Vatican II could be inhaled and exhaled without being impaled. One need not be afraid to speak out as a member of the Church, as part of the Church. We were a new and different Church. We were now open to welcoming and greeting and pointing out the good and the positive—without dependence on the grace from God that had to go through all the ecclesiastical channels that we expected before the Council.

No longer would I have to be afraid of playing with Donny Werner (Lutheran) on my block back home. He, like me, was a person of God.

7. Priest Forever

MY PAL JIM PURCELL had a similar personality to Miles. He never met a person he didn't impress. Never could come into a room without being noticed. He played soccer and we enjoyed many of the same things. He was a class behind me. The year I was ordained, he took care of my family, as people usually arrived while we were still on retreat. I had filled the same role for Miles when he was ordained the previous year.

We didn't see our families until the day before ordination and then only for a couple of hours. I was almost nervous waiting in my room. There was a knock. I opened the door and there they stood. Charlie, Johnny and Della. After more than three years apart, you can imagine the thoughts and images that went through my head. I'll only tell you one. They all looked so much older.

The Dirnberger-Schlitt clan didn't really believe in hugging when you could handshake. A big round smile replaced the kiss. They all loved but our cultural background made it difficult to express it the way other families did. I recall the smiles and the pride that we all had because the grace of the priesthood was going to be part of our family. We exchanged a gift or two and my brother John had brought two cans of Stag beer which he knew was a favorite of mine in Missouri. They were warm of course but that didn't seem to hinder their consumption in my little room where we all huddled together and tears began to flow. It was an emotional moment and the Schlitt family was out of sorts as that was not our typical *modus operandi*.

The next morning my buddy ushered them around the city and got them to St. Peter's Basilica for the ceremony. It was a cold damp day in Vatican City with the rain slowly making the cobblestones slick outside as a buoyant group of American families made for the church. It wasn't much warmer inside. Jim made sure my brothers found the bar near the sacristy where you could get a hot coffee and a brandy to ward off the chill that crept through the marble floor into your bones.

Quite a few folks had made the long trip from home. The matriarch, Armella, came with her sister-in-law Audrey. Both aunts were widows. The pastor of St. Mary's in Cape, Monsignor

Prostration during Ordination, St. Peter's Basillica, December 16, 1964

Leo Kampmann, was there along with Father Joe Keusenkothen the pastor in neighboring Kelso. Father Ed Riley, the rector of Glennon who had disapproved of my water skiing and whose hair I used to cut, was all smiles that day (although a little long at the collar).

Flickers and Charles attended my ordination. They had come with Charlie and Mary. She was just as gorgeous as the first time we met and both of them were looking prosperous. I hoped they too saw me like a little brother. Johnny and Betty had brought friends Bill and Cathy Karnauskas with whom they'd invested in land and made a bundle. My Roman friends were also there. I used to go down to work with orphans on Saturday mornings and I had invited two of them. The owner of my favorite restaurant and her stunning look-alike daughter came decked out in style. And of course, there was Father John Martin, the man who had put it all in motion.

The new rector of the North American College, Bishop Francis Reh, ordained me a Roman Catholic priest on 16 December 1964. The ceremony lasted well over four hours. It's a long ceremony just like the time it takes to prepare oneself for the order. With sixty-one other young men at the Altar of the Chair I promised obedience to the Bishop and his successors and received the sacrament of Holy Orders.

I'd made it.

Warm tears streamed down Della's cheeks as I gave her my first blessing as a priest and embraced her. She whispered in my ear that our mother would have been so proud to be there on that day. My brothers pumped my hand until my arm hurt.

Wimpy, JFK and I got an early Christmas present seeing Rufus again. With his giant smile and his humble demeanor he hadn't changed a bit. We were together at every function and it was like old times.

I celebrated the holy sacrifice of the Mass for the first time in the catacombs of Saint Priscilla on the Via Salaria where the oldest known painting of the celebration of the Eucharist adorns the walls. Another of my first Masses was in the chapel at the Maryknoll House where I celebrated with Father Martin by my side. Afterward he made bacon and eggs for breakfast.

I had a joyous Christmas in Germany with my family. Charles and Flickers had taken a side trip to buy a boatload of Carrara marble for his burgeoning chain of hotels, but then joined us in Munich. I've kept up with them ever since.

I thought I would be married within five years of my ordination. I sincerely believed that priests would be allowed to marry and raise families and I think most of my classmates felt the same way. It was at the tail end of the Vatican Council and with all the major changes that had taken place during our four years in Rome, it seemed likely. After all, Vatican II had opened the windows and let in some fresh air. Worship was in the vernacular now and we were putting our eggs in the Scripture basket once again and doing all kinds of new things that would allow the Catholic Church to be more available to the world.

It was also a turbulent time for young priests. Many found themselves unable to cope with the changes that had taken place in the 1960s, the different view of sexual mores and what was right and wrong with the way we (the Church) looked at things. Sex at that time took on a new meaning. The Sixties were termed the "sexual revolution." I missed at least half of it as it had not yet made its way to Vatican City and the Pontifical North American College where I lived.

My experience in Rome could never be duplicated or surpassed. The losses of being there were always overcome by the winning ways of learning something new and different that hopefully would be helpful the rest of my life, even if only spent in southern Missouri with people who might not ever travel outside their zip code.

In late spring, I was awarded a Bachelor of Sacred Theology. It was said that I excelled in Sacred Scripture. I was getting ready to leave Rome and go back to the States when Mrs. Ohrman offered to pay for me to go wherever I wanted before returning to my first priestly assignment in America. I asked for a trip to Africa to see firsthand how missionary work was done.

I landed in Nairobi and experienced being the only white person on a bus. I thought of Rosa Parks and all that had transpired in the South of the USA. However, I was coming from the airport and for all they knew I would be another white man bringing the good news of Jesus Christ to that part of the world.

For a couple of days, I stayed at the Maryknoll house where I met so many good priests who came there for R&R before returning to the missions. I had rides from many of them in the month I was in Africa. Some were on picki-pickis, the local term for motorcycles. That's another machine I had not mastered.

Father Maurice Zerr was a Maryknoll priest from St. Louis who ended up in Kenya among the Luo tribe. He was their first connection to the outside in that third world setting and he was my host.

When it's night in Africa, it's really dark. Father Zerr handed me a torch once the car had stopped on this deserted desert road in the middle of the bush. We stopped in order to relieve ourselves on the side of the road. There were neither filling stations nor rest stops in the Serengeti. As soon as I flipped the flashlight switch, bugs covered my entire hand and wrist right up to my shirtsleeve. It was an unusual feeling and a bit disconcerting as I had not expected it. That's when this missionary priest advised me to turn off the torch before unzipping my fly.

Every new experience in life is food for meditation. It didn't take me long to realize how the visually impaired are really at a disadvantage to live in total darkness.

Roads didn't go all the way to our destination so the next morning we had to abandon the car in favor of a smaller vehicle. Following Mo Zerr through the jungle on a picki-picki was no small feat. Every now and then, he would look back to see how I was doing. I was always 100 yards or more in the rear as I couldn't go fast in the sand without turning the damn thing over.

At one point, I looked up to see a large animal in the path. Mo had told me when this might occur to simply lay on the horn and it would frighten the beast to move along. The second piece of advice was to rev the engine to the point of just noise and most beasts would dash back into cover. In doing so, I killed the engine. My emotional state was wrapped in fear of being gored to death by a rhino. I hit the starter pedal and missed completely thus drawing blood on the inside of my calf and shin. Now I knew I was dead for the animal would smell my blood and would know where his next meal was coming from. With a sigh of relief, I looked up to see that the path was clear. No sign of the animal, no sign of Mo Zerr.

When I finally arrived at the village, he was busy greeting the natives, speaking in Luo. He barely noticed me coming in late with blood on my trousers. It didn't take long for him to feel sorry for me and he asked if I would join him for a small repast of monkey before we had our liturgy.

Mass in the bush was something else. Drums were beating for most of the day, letting the natives know that the priest was there. They began around ten in the morning and at five in the afternoon the little mud church was packed. People were standing outside and peering in the holes in the wall where windows might be, if they had glass. They didn't. I recall the odor and the screaming of babies, but more than anything the expression of faith in the music and the drums. There were no violins, no oboes, no horn section, no director, only the voices and drums of people who came great distances on foot through the bush to pray with Father Zerr.

That night after we had again feasted on monkey, Father asked me to show them the newspaper that I had bought at Heathrow Airport on my way to Kenya. It was the Sunday edition and had the pictures of astronaut Ed White floating outside his Gemini IV spaceship with the brilliant blue earth beyond. I can still see the widening of their eyes as Father explained in Luo how man had flown into space. As he pointed to the sky and continued his explanation, I saw in their faces an absence of belief. They had never seen an aircraft much less a spaceship. No matter how close to God this priest might be, certainly the sky was reachable only by God.

The evening ended. We rested in the mud chapel on sleeping bags that had been rolled up on the picki-pickis. Mine had collected a lot of sand in all the spills I took on the bike. The following morning, we were on our way to the next mission. It didn't take long for me to discern that I did not have a true calling to be a missionary in Africa.

After flying one-third of the way around the world, I arrived where I'd started, back in Cape Girardeau. Three days later on a Sunday afternoon, I celebrated my first solemn Mass in the Cathedral of St. Mary, in my home parish. Bishop Forst was there and gave the homily. There were thirty-five visiting priests in attendance.

So when I returned to Missouri from Europe as a priest, Mrs. Ohrman gave me her no-mileage 1958 Chevy Impala and offered to adopt me as her son. It was a classic car, beige and beautiful. I felt like I had died and gone to heaven when I got behind the wheel of that automobile. My oldest brother Charlie saw the merit in the adoption scheme and told me to accept. She was worth a lot and as her only child I would probably be her heir. I had already had wonderful parents and felt this would be disloyal and an insult to them. Besides, I was twenty-six years old and if there was anything my adult-onset circumcision had taught me it was that there were some things men just shouldn't do.

I did not accept her offer, but I kept seeing her over the years and she helped me with a number of projects the rest of her life. When she finally passed away she was ninety-seven years old and many newspapers carried her obituary with a large headline: "Margaret Ohrman, godmother of Catholic education." She only had one living relative, a first cousin, who was named beneficiary along with religious and educational institutions and many other charities. I was left some money but nothing in the range of the $13 Million that comprised her estate. Good lesson for me: listen to your older brother.

Part II

Evolution

You sift through my travels and my rest;
with all my ways you are familiar.
Even before a word is on my tongue,
Lord, you know it all.

Psalms 139:3-4

Is he lucky, though?

Napoleon

8. Blackrobe

SPRINGFIELD, MISSOURI, is the acknowledged buckle on the Bible Belt. In 1965 it was home to as many bible colleges as Catholic churches, along with the world headquarters of the Assemblies of God. It was a land of speaking in tongues, beehive hairdos and a megawatt radio station broadcasting country music to places as far away as Tulsa and Topeka. Favorite pastimes included bowling, knitting, fishing and Bible reading. The population had doubled in the prior twenty years to over 100,000. Nearly everyone was white and only five percent were Catholic. It was night and day from Rome, or from St. Louis for that matter, and it was the first place I was assigned as a priest.

Bishop Strecker, whom I'd gotten to know during Vatican II in Rome, was my Ordinary (ultimate boss). He appointed me as the Director of Discipline at the Sacred Heart House of Studies. It was the minor seminary for the diocese, which spanned the entire state. I was also assigned to teach at the co-ed high school, Latin to the sophomores and Preparation for Marriage to the senior girls. The irony was lost on me.

I lived next door to the seminary at the Sacred Heart parish rectory with two old priests. They made me think of the men who had surrounded Pope John XXIII, they were always so negative.

I had lost track of my old friend Floyd when I left for Rome. I just had heard he was in a parish seventy miles away in Joplin and at dinner I brought up his name. The chewing stopped and over his glasses one of my gray-haired roommates said for them both, "He's one of those love priests."

He could have meant that Floyd took the scriptures more seriously than the rest of us and practiced what Jesus taught as the first and most important commandment, that is to say, all things are based on love. But I believe that Floyd's naysayers were more concerned about his definition of love and probably felt he spelled it l-u-v.

I was doing my best to adjust to the norms in my new hometown. I was so focused on being a priest and doing a good job. I'd lived in a foreign country but there I was back in the U.S. and I had never taught, had never been around high school kids.

On the first Friday of every month there was a Mass at the Cathedral, next door to St. Agnes High, especially for the students. I was assigned to be the celebrant. I was excited about delivering my first homily to the teens and I had prepared well. I was in the sacristy putting on my vestments when I heard shouting and laughing and scuffling out front. The kids in the pews were horsing around and the sisters who accompanied them weren't batting an eye or lifting a finger to stop them. To my mind, this was all wrong. When it came time for me to preach, the sermon I had planned fell by the wayside.

"The Book of Proverbs tells us that fear of the Lord is the beginning of knowledge," I intoned. "As your teacher it's my job to impart knowledge to you. It's your job as students to respect me. Even if you've lost respect for me, you don't have to be afraid of me." I was getting my footing.

"I'm Father Harry. I am not the Lord and this is not my house." I was on a roll. "This is God's house you're in and you're being disrespectful to Him. God is somebody to be feared."

A hush fell and so did faces. All the joy was displaced by sobriety and the energy fled the room. Order had been restored.

After that first Mass, Father Amel Shibley came over and spoke to me. He was the associate pastor at St. Agnes Cathedral and the kids liked him so much. He had great respect from the student body. He was famous among the high school boys for hearing their confessions on the sidewalk before Mass so they could take communion in good conscience.

"The kids didn't mean any harm, Harry," Amel said. "They're just kids. Go a little easier on them next time."

I headed back over to the high school unconvinced. I had no more than walked in the door when two nuns grabbed me in the faculty room and wailed into me. The Sisters of Loreto were the religious women who taught at the high school. Their mother superior, Sister Jacqueline, had spoken at Vatican II, one of precious few women allowed to address the Fathers. Because she spoke up and was heard, her order was not afraid.

"You were off-course with your homily, Father," the first one said bluntly. "You shouldn't talk to these kids about fear."

The second one added, "Our God is a God of love." She was a pretty young woman who drank too much. Every time we had a faculty party she had three wines and was blotto. After two years she left the order.

It slowly dawned on me that it was a new day in the Catholic Church. I had failed to grasp our role as Catholics in a fundamentalist Pentecostal town. Hellfire and brimstone was not the message of John XXIII. We, the People of God, were about peace and love.

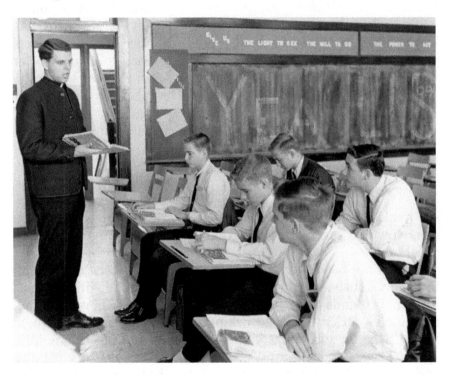

Father Harry teaching at the minor seminary in Springfield, Missouri

I threw myself whole-hog into teaching and gradually I began to connect with the kids. In the classroom I was very strict. I didn't tolerate the kids talking back to me and if I caught them talking to each other I threw erasers at them. At the same time, I could count on them telling me the truth. They were so open. They trusted me with their feelings and knew I respected them. I wasn't going to run to their parents with all kinds of warnings about the future trouble they might get into if they weren't corrected now. I loved the kids and I think it was mutual.

Everything was going along just peachy until I learned that there was more than one girl in Preparation for Marriage who was talking about tying the knot just as soon as she graduated. It bothered me a lot since I still looked upon them as children.

Father Harry and girls from St. Agnes High

About the same time, I met a young lady who had been married and divorced twice and was tending bar at a local pub where the coaches and some male parents would go after games. I often joined them and discovered that whenever I came in she made a point to talk to me. She was not a Catholic but had a deep spiritual sense about her that attracted me and a number of others.

I was not her confessor, but a confidant, and she told me of the many abusive encounters that she experienced with her two former husbands. The first was an entertainer whom she had met in New Orleans while working as a dancer in a club. When he got a better job and a younger woman, she never saw him again. The second husband was a trucker and was very jealous and abusive. He took her clothes and locked her in a house on an isolated farm while he was on the road. She had no family, no friends and no one to confide in, nor go to for help. She was afraid of him and thought the police would only make her life more miserable.

I asked her to come and spend forty-five minutes with my senior girls' class. I wanted her to tell them about her not-so-blissful marital life and assure them that at seventeen or eighteen they wouldn't be left on the shelf, that this was a young age to select a permanent partner in life. The girls loved her and appreciated her candor. Even some parents thanked me for bringing her into the classroom. It didn't go so well with other faculty members who looked down on her as a bartender willing to do almost anything for a tip.

The experiences she shared helped me to see another side of young marriage and how, if you didn't take the time for courtship to find out what you might be getting yourself into, it could be jeopardized. I had spent twelve years preparing to be a priest. To think that at a young age following a brief romance someone could fall in love, get married and expect to live happily ever after seems like a fairytale.

Four years after I first set eyes on Rome, in the waning days of Vatican II, Pope Paul VI sent a letter to the Conciliar Fathers saying he preferred no debate on celibacy. He did not want it aired publicly. Discussions on birth control likewise bore no fruit and the traditional view remained intact. Not quite one year after my ordination, on the Marian feast of the Immaculate Conception, the Second Vatican Council came to an end. Bishop Strecker had attended all four sessions and was on his way home. Along with commemorative rings and medals, he and the other participants received from the Holy Father a copy of Dante's *Divine Comedy*.

I had been left behind by the social changes that occurred in America while I was in Rome. The pre-1960s America that we seminarians had known wasn't waiting for us when we returned. We had that in common with the boys in Vietnam, or would have except there was no awareness of Vietnam, not really. Coming home meant adapting to changing roles for men and women, more open sexuality, rock & roll. And I lived in a town where you couldn't even buy beer on Sunday.

The first and only time I ever had braved the dance floor was when my aunt Armella insisted on a spin the Labor Day before I went to the seminary. I was fourteen and thought, "Why am I even trying? I'm no dancer."

A dozen years later there I was, one of the chaperones at the high school dances. Maybe I identified with the wallflowers. I would go and get the fat ones and the ones with zits and ask them to dance. I was a goofy dancer so it didn't matter if they were. It was an outlet and a workout. It was fun. The parents were happy I got the girls out on the floor and I was never afraid of some little girl running home and saying, "Father Harry touched me." So that's how I learned to dance.

As I got better, I danced with the teachers. One of the sisters was very smooth and surprised me with her moves. There were some college women from Chicago who were volunteers at St. Agnes as part of their work toward master's degrees. Those young teachers knew how to Twist, Swim, Surf, do the Frug, the Monkey and the Watusi. We had a ball.

I was learning how to move, how to live in the outside world, how to balance relationships with my elders and my juniors. There was a thin line I walked between my colleagues and my students, between my students and their parents.

Like the time the coach came to me needing help. He had discovered that some of the boys had rented a house and were using it for a crash pad. A couple of the dads had found out and all hell was about to break loose. We talked them into letting us handle things. We got the principal to come with us and we raided the hideout. The smell of stale beer and cigarettes met us at the door along with some pretty surprised faces. They weren't the only ones who were surprised. We couldn't believe it when we saw the extent of the set-up. There was a bar, a neon OPEN sign and the walls were a web of speaker wires. Crates of record albums lined the room. The floor was littered with comic books, *Playboy* magazines, empty pizza boxes and crushed 9-0-5 beer cans. The party was over. The jig was up.

I wasn't sure what to make of my first wholesale encounter with youth culture. I couldn't tell if they were rebelling against society or trying to lose themselves in it. I did know that the boys were not bad and they were not going to hell; they were not mean and they were not going to be convicts. That's what I told their parents.

Another time I caught one of the seminarians sneaking back in from the park across the street after visiting with his girlfriend in the wee hours. I threatened to tell the rector and have him dismissed from the seminary. It was an awful night. I knew they were in "luv" but had no idea that one day they would be married with a family and become great examples of what a Catholic couple could be. Incidentally, not one of the boys I taught my first year at the House of Studies made it to ordination. That doesn't mean they didn't turn out to be model men who raised families and contributed mightily to their communities.

Bishop Strecker was not only my superior, but also a friend and confessor. I always told him the truth and exactly how I saw things. I believe he recognized the obvious appeal that I had with teens and young people when so many other priests he saw were afraid to get involved. And this was way before all the suspicions and convictions that people have now about priests and youth.

One day he visited the seminary for prayer and a dinner with the students. That evening after the meal, the bishop invited me to take a walk around the park across the street. I could see his little grin as he lit up a cigarette and asked, "What's wrong, Harry? You seem to have lost that happy, loving smile you inherited from your mother that you've had since you were a kid."

It was an easy question for me to answer. I had been living with two priests who saw only the glass half empty. They were the most pessimistic people I had ever been around. Having two meals a day with them was about as much as I could stand. I've already introduced you to my close pal Floyd who was so loving and compassionate toward his parishioners. Whenever I commented about this it was always met with a derogatory statement about how far he had allowed himself to stray from the teachings of the Church. If I brought up young people who were doing so well in school and in their work with the community, or our volunteer teachers from Chicago or the religious women who were so dedicated to the school, all I got was a look that questioned my sanity followed by a sermon on how everything about them was wrong. They didn't want me hanging out with the young volunteers nor the sisters because they would be susceptible to a young guy and vice versa. My job was diocesan babysitter or as one of my buddies called it DBS.

The result of the walk in the park was an order from the bishop to mark on our calendar-of-the-week one day when I would not be available. It was to be a day off or as I called it, a day out. The first week I wrote "out" on a Tuesday, the rector of the seminary called me on the phone. I was next door in an old house, which was used as a rec center for the boys.

"What does 'out' mean?" he asked.

Fearfully I related to him that the bishop had ordered me to do this. He wanted me to have some time away from the boys and my teaching and counseling. This was a new concept for the rector.

I still recall that first Tuesday out. I got behind the wheel of Mrs. Ohrman's Impala but didn't know where to go. So I drove to the highway and headed west for Tulsa on Route 66 knowing that as long as I stayed on the Mother Road I could always find my way home. I went through Joplin but didn't stop to see Floyd. Next time, I told myself. I got to Tulsa around noon and thought I would have a beer or two with lunch. Turns out it was a dry city at the time and you couldn't get a beer. So I had a burger and fries and decided to get a room at the Holiday Inn. I watched TV and went out to a movie. I then tried dinner with a beer and was told I had to join a club to get a drink. I did and the evening ended with a smile.

It was my first day off as a priest. I had been working almost a year and really loved it. I didn't need a day away from the collar, but the bishop could see that I was losing my priestly charism of joy and happiness for my work. So many of my brother priests didn't have the kind of superior with the insight to help them in making better decisions about their lives. My friendship with and admiration for that bishop grew.

It wasn't long after my day off when I got a call from one of the local parishes asking me to join their softball team and their bowling league. The pastor said, "The bishop tells me that you need to spend some time with adults and get away from your closed environment."

How true!

Softball was wonderful and the friends I made were great, but I'll never bowl again. It's like having too much scotch and then getting sick. You simply don't want another drink . . . of scotch. This is how I came to hate bowling, which is right up there with: 1) Going to hell, 2) Waiting in line, 3) Bowling.

Every Friday night, the parish league bowled. And every Friday night I got stuck with someone's wife who was very unhappy that her husband hadn't made it home from the road in time to bowl. Springfield was home to manufacturers of products as diverse as the cheese powder for Doritos and Zenith TVs. Many of the husbands were sales reps who traveled during the week. So whatever anger and animosity the wives felt toward them was directed at me.

Other times, I filled in for a number of women who just didn't feel like bowling that night. After the lane action was over they would show up at the alley lounge, feed the jukebox and ask me to dance. By this time their husbands would be immersed in BS with each other on any and every topic. My sphere of conversation was about school, the seminarians, and rock & roll, which helped me relate to the kids.

Music and athletics had always been important to me. Someone gave me a guitar and I started learning to play it. I missed soccer in Springfield. It wasn't a sport that was played there. I played handball with a Marine recruiting sergeant. We became good friends and he would come to Mass when I celebrated. I really liked the guy. One day after a hard game, which I won, he invited me to join up. It didn't take me long to see how much good I could do serving my country and our troops by signing on as a chaplain and shipping out to Vietnam. I could be such a positive force with our military people. He invited me down to the office and I filled out the papers and signed my name.

Two days later, I made an appointment with Bishop Strecker in order to let him know of my plans. I was excited to tell him that I was going to Vietnam as a Marine chaplain. Of course, as my superior, he was asked to sign off on my choice.

It was a short encounter, as he let me know in no uncertain terms that the people of southern Missouri who paid for my education for the past twelve years were not going to be deprived of my services anytime soon. He had a look of crazed confusion as he smiled at me.

"You will not join the Marines or go to Vietnam or any place else as long as I'm your bishop!" It was the first time he was adamant about anything I'd asked.

I had every good intention, but that time the squeak came from the bishop.

I think I would have made a good Marine chaplain.

One of the state colleges was in Springfield and for three summers I went to graduate school there to get a master's degree in guidance and counseling. It was a lot of fun to return to school as the student. Baby boomers and the first of the Vietnam veterans eligible for the G.I. bill were filling the classrooms. I was enjoying being on a college campus around people nearer my age. For the first time in my twenty years of education, I had professors who were not steeped in Thomistic philosophy and ingrained in Catholicism. It was really different. Most of my classmates were eager to get good grades as they had to get the degree in order to advance in their school districts or careers. The bishop told me that a degree was not essential but learning the particulars of being a good counselor would benefit the students in our schools.

Teaching high school, I saw kids from the country who were never exposed to linguistics. When I was at Southwest Missouri State, I wrote a thesis arguing that studying Latin would increase your score on the Stanford-Binet IQ test. I proved it with my high school Latin students.

Root derivation is so important to figure out what something might mean. On those multiple choice questions there was usually a root word so that when the student would eyeball the choices, one would stand out as having something to do with the question. My students figured out early on that knowing the roots would help them find an answer. For example, the Latin word *spirare* means to breathe. Inspire, expire, inspiration, expiration all refer to the breathing apparatus of the human body. I was taught that all Sacred Scripture is inspired by God. That meant to me that some way (only God knows) God breathed into the authors who wrote what God wanted them to write. The same word is used when God breathed life into the body of Adam to make him come alive. So also God breathed on the first apostles in the upper room so that they would be inspired by the Holy Spirit to go out and renew the face of the earth with this new life given to them by God through Jesus.

Anyway, my students increased their IQs considerably and were never afraid of those choices even though they had no idea what all the words meant. Knowing the derivation of the words, they could make an intelligent guess. And the more success you had in the classroom the better you felt about who you were and what you were accomplishing.

It was a six-hour drive from Springfield to Cape Girardeau and Bishop Strecker asked if I would accompany him during Holy Week to help with the services. I was thrilled and enjoyed the beautiful ride across the 26,000-square-mile diocese through the Ozarks. It was April and the dogwoods and redbuds were showing themselves in the roadside woods.

When we arrived at the rectory in Cape where we were staying, I was met by an elderly housekeeper. She did not care for me because the previous year I had hosted a dinner there for the seminarians and we didn't leave the kitchen very clean. I carried the bishop's bags into the house and as I was walking up the stairs with them, I heard her remark to the bishop that he had brought his "nigger slave" to assist him. Remember, this is 1968 and she was not that well educated. The bishop excoriated her and let her know that her job was in jeopardy and that I should be treated exactly the same as she would treat him. It was good to know when someone like that, who is your boss, also has your back.

Thursday morning, we celebrated the Holy Chrism Mass, blessing the oils that would be used in the coming year for sacraments, like baptism and last rites. Father Keusenkothen from Kelso, who had been at my ordination, was a concelebrant. I took advantage of being back in Cape and went to see Charlie and Mary and Johnny and Betty. Before I was ordained, I used to question who had what for lunch, but when I came back with the bishop, both families made sure I had a big dinner and enjoyed time with them.

The next day was Good Friday and after the services ended at three, the hour of Jesus' death on the cross, it was back across the Ozarks to Springfield and home.

9. Rock & Roll Priest

THE YEAR I TURNED TWENTY-NINE was one of the best of my life. I don't know all the reasons for such celebratory years, but I do know I enjoyed my work in the classroom as a teacher, as a counselor, my private instruction work with kids and being a Catholic priest in a very non-Catholic environment. And 1968 was the year I began working in broadcasting, first on radio and then on TV.

After three years at the House of Studies, Bishop Strecker asked me to take a new post at the Cathedral but to continue my teaching and counseling at the high school. A younger, newly ordained man took my place at the seminary and I was glad to go. I was especially happy to be moving out of the Sacred Heart rectory.

St. Agnes was a lively place by comparison. The pastor, Monsignor Jack Westhues, would dart into the dining room at breakfast saying, "Howdy boys! How's it going?"

Around the table sat three priests. One was an Irish chaplain at a local college, the other an associate pastor at St. Agnes Cathedral and there was me. We were not all awake at the same time. So the monsignor's bouncy energetic greeting was often met with a sarcastic response like, "Oh, I forgot the consecration at Mass this morning."

It wouldn't faze the pastor as he was too busy thinking about the next thing he had to do. He would have given the pink bunny a good run with his endurance. He'd dash out of the room, then all of the sudden the door would swing back open and he would reappear with, "What? You forgot what!"

Then his expression would be met with laughter all around the table.

One time Monsignor Westhues asked me to go to the funeral home and say some words for a neglected derelict whose name was Clyde Crisp. His poor body had been there for almost a week. When I left the back room and entered the chapel space,

I knew immediately that he had been dead for some time. There was no one in the parlor and I approached the podium, turned on the microphone and gave a brief spiritual lecture to myself about loneliness and dying without anyone there to care or grieve.

It was a powerful lesson for me that afternoon. Monsignor Westhues was as close to God as you can get in a lifetime. He was not my style, nor was I like him. But that only proves my weakness and his strength.

Young priests like me who had been ordained five years or less were required to take junior clergy exams. Typically, we traveled to learn from other priests and would meet across the diocese. On one trip, I re-connected with Justin Monaghan.

Justin and I had become very good friends in Rome. In his first parish assignment in the boot-heel of Missouri, the Irishman was a long way from home surrounded by strangers. There was a used car dealer in his parish who had managed to convince Father Justin that an innovative new car with the engine in the rear would suit his needs. It was the infamous Corvair that catapulted Ralph Nader into the national consciousness and was unsafe at any speed. After a couple of months, it broke down.

Did I mention that it was a used Corvair? Justin called me for advice. I told him to return it and demand his money back. He did so thinking this was much better than what he expected, riding horseback.

Justin's pastor would encourage him to come and visit me in Springfield for a weekend now and again when he felt lonely and homesick for his parents in Ireland. He would arrive around 4:00 p.m. and we would commence the cocktail hour way before dinner. Then into the night we would recall our time together in Rome and our answers to all the questions of a Vatican II Church, a Church that was re-tooling itself for the next century. When I'd had more to drink than I should have and could not stay awake, I poured myself into bed while he poured himself another then made his way to the guest room. It was often early in the morn when I would see the light of one of the phone buttons that showed a line was in use. I didn't know until he dried out that Justin would call his mother in Mullingar and his pal in Newfoundland every time he drank too much. You can imagine his phone bills; international calls were at a premium then. When he did sober up, it took him almost a year to pay off the debt.

Father Harry in the office at St. Agnes

Parkview was the public high school not far from where I taught at St. Agnes. I was asked to give a talk there for an art class of forty or fifty kids that met outside of school time. I gave a slide presentation on Rome and talked about what it had been like to live there. One of the girls who heard me that night went home and couldn't stop talking about "Father Harry! Father Harry!" to her father, who happened to be the general manager of the number one rock & roll radio station in town. A few days later I was drinking martinis with him and his sales manager at the Shady Inn, where all the media-types went for lunch, and they gave me my first show.

I was the first priest who was regularly on the air. All the Baptist ministers bought time on radio and TV, but I was being paid.

When I was live on 1340 KICK-AM taking calls on the weekend, I heard from Bible students who wanted to tell me Methuselah did live 900 years. They were burning with love of the Scripture. It was fun talking to these kids who were probably seven or eight years younger and telling me about the Bible. It was wonderful but I tried to explain there was a lot more to it. Like studying scripture in the context of the times. As an example, women were second-class citizens in the days of Jesus.

The station honchos really liked me. I was unusual. They had heard my stories and thought they were good, but theirs was a rock & roll station and people wanted to hear music.

It was Bill Pledger who came up with the idea. He was the station's midday guy, "B. Sharpe." We sat and had a beer at Nadine's Bar next door to the station and he said he thought I ought to mix clips of music into the sixty-second spots I was writing for my show. Nadine's was one of those places that opened early in the morning where old guys would recount the adventures they had while saliva dripped from their lips. It was close by. You just walked out the back door of the station and down three steps and there was Nadine's. So I started experimenting with the hit songs and using those lyrics to wrap around my message.

Bill came to the studio evenings and helped me tear apart songs whose lyrics were apropos for the story I was telling, that would emphatically say in song what I was trying to say in words. It's all done digitally now, but in those days you had to run the tape over the head of the machine and go back and forth until you got just the words you wanted. We worked late into the night and Bill showed me how to take a razor blade and cut the tape and splice it so my message and the music flowed together perfectly. After long hours, we would adjourn to Nadine's and hash out the progress we were making over twenty-five cent beers. If you wanted a clean glass it was five cents more.

I was working Saturdays and Sundays on KICK radio doing three-hour shows and talking to teens and young adults about almost anything. During the show, I also played my one-minute music messages mostly about growth and development from what I had garnered while preparing for my master's degree.

There were ample amounts of drugstore psychology with plenty of examples. The radio gave me a perfect outlet to try out different ways of thinking and approaching young people. It was all done with the idea that it was going to do some good and improve life. I knew from the live calls that there was a deep-seated lack of confidence to say what they meant and mean what they said. So I tried to get to them by saying, "I'll never tell."

Before long I was a well-known on-air commodity and a number of youth groups were inviting me to attend their meetings and speak to them. Most of the time, I was using the Rogerian method of listening and working hard to get them to do the talking and the problem-solving. My education for the master's degree in Guidance and Counseling had exposed me to Carl Rogers. He was an expert in listening to his clients and allowing them to work out their own problems. I loved and imitated his style.

One of my classmates in grad school was a youth minister at the largest Baptist church in Springfield. I met him when I got sucked into a study group to make sure I would be able to get an A or B in the last three classes before graduation. I was intent on getting my master's. The course in statistics with the mean, the median and the mode was very challenging. I would never have passed it without the assistance of my Baptist buddy, the Reverend John Smith.

After we received our degrees, he convinced his pastor to allow me to preach at the First Baptist Church to the 11:00 a.m. congregation. Most of the people knew me from the radio so I wasn't a complete surprise, but a black suit and Roman collar in their pulpit raised some eyebrows. The highlight of my homily was the introduction by Reverend Smith who was so nervous he had trouble keeping his cool . . . which he didn't. After giving my credentials and explaining how our friendship had formed through our studies he announced, "I present to you Father Harry Schitt."

He skipped the "l" in my last name.

After a shocked wave of gasps and giggles swept across the congregation I took the pulpit to thank Reverend Smith and to let them all know why I called myself simply Father Harry.

Dick Jackson was the first one to come up with the name God Squad. DJ was a disc jockey (get it, DJ the DJ). He was on the air at KICK with the likes of "Jungle Jim" Stanley and B. Sharpe and he thought I needed an equally hip persona. He was watching an episode of *The Mod Squad* television series and decided that I must become the God Squad. From that point on, I started every show with a little riff:

Father Harry at KICK

"Hey, hey, hey, It's the old Padre. I'm Father Harry, the mass media minister with much more music in my message. Movin' my mouth to motivate you for more of I'll Never Tell. *That's the name of the show and the word's always 'Go!' on the sporty thirteen-forty in the nitty gritty Springfield city. I'm the pop art Pad' with the mod bod from the God Squad."*

I trademarked the name "Father Harry: God Squad" in 1968 and thought it would serve me well in the future in case I did more work in radio and television. Look on the Internet today and you'll find thousands of groups all over the world who call themselves the God Squad. (I even would meet an Australian motorcycle gang with that name some years down the road.) But

DJ was the first to come up with it as far as I know.

My popularity with young people, who felt comfortable coming to me whether in person or on the telephone on my weekend radio show, was pretty obvious. Naturally, it gave me lots of self-confidence in what I was doing and what I hoped to accomplish. I was reticent by nature unless there was a program. If I could get a kid to know himself or herself better and appreciate who they were and what they had to offer, I would have made a difference.

I was asked to give the annual autumn retreat at the seminary in St. Louis to the students of Cardinal Glennon College. These were all young men studying for the priesthood, about to enter their last four years of theology at Kenrick Seminary. Among them was a serious local boy named Timothy Dolan. He would go on to succeed my old homiletics professor, Ed Egan, as the Archbishop of New York and become a cardinal. It was a five-day silent retreat interspersed with three conferences a day, confessions and private conferences with the students. I still have notes from that retreat. At its conclusion, I asked the young men if they would send me a card when they were ordained priests to let me know whether or not the retreat had meant anything to them on their road to ordination.

I had gained a degree of celebrity from doing radio on KICK. When Springfield finally got an ABC television affiliate, the owner of the new station sought me out as a possible host for a show for youth on Saturdays. Borrowing a page from radio, *I'll Never Tell* was the name of my first television show. It aired on KMTC Channel 27. Its purpose was to assist young people in communication skills. There were a lot of teenagers who never seemed to want to express themselves as much as they could.

It really worked well. It was live with two cameras and a director from Evangel College who thought religion in media was going to be his calling. America was on the threshold of "televangelism" so I'm sure with all the bible colleges in the area, he would have had a good chance of landing a position. In fact, the Assemblies of God turned out some giants of the business including Jim and Tammy Fae Bakker, Jim Robison and the other guy who "sinned" in New Orleans and asked for forgiveness on his show, Jimmy Swaggart.

Little by little, I learned about production, even camera work. When I was not "on" I would take the one stationary camera and operate it myself. Admittedly, I was awful, but everything was new and none of us really knew any better. I can still recall, as a teen band rocked out on the tune *Gloria*, zooming in and out G-L-O—you get the idea. It must have driven the audience crazy but I really thought I was doing something creative. You could never find that kind of action on the six o'clock news with broadcasters and technical people so frozen in their jobs and technique that nothing would ever change. You can go into a TV studio today and discover that all the cameras are robotic, that is they have no human touch and are all controlled by the director in the booth, usually out of eyeshot in another room.

As I said, the show went smoothly as far as we were concerned. The day the station was inaugurated or officially opened, a young reporter from the network in New York flew in to cut the ribbon. His name was Peter Jennings. I remember talking to him about getting my show on the network. He must have thought I was crazy, a young Catholic priest with a national show that had high school bands, scholars, cheerleaders and outstanding athletes, featuring a trio of college students imitating Peter, Paul and Mary.

I guess I shouldn't be too hard on that show. It sold out commercially and after every live performance we (whoever the guests were that week) would make a personal appearance at Shakey's Pizza. The show immediately followed Dick Clark's *American Bandstand* so we had a promising lead-in to capture a large audience. Besides our sponsor the pizza place, I also had a Honda motorbike sponsor who put the two most popular disc jockeys in town on brand new bikes. They left the set during our live show on a beautiful Saturday afternoon with full tanks of gas. The one who went the farthest before running out of gas won the publicity stunt. In every little Ozarks town they went through they were cheered by their radio fans who had seen them leave from the TV studio. It was a great success.

Father Harry on the set of *I'll Never Tell*

It was my close friend from KICK-AM, B. Sharpe, against Les Sweckard from the new station across town, which had just introduced FM to Springfield. We owned the metro radio market but FM was a big hit with the few who could afford the receivers. It never really caught on during my time there. Now you know how long ago it was! We were the transistor radio generation. Les was the winner. By a long shot. He changed his name to Garland, moved to San Francisco and later co-founded MTV. I didn't know it then, but our paths would be crossing again.

B. Sharpe continued to influence my life in a big way. He helped bring the incomparable James Brown live in concert to Springfield, Missouri's Abou Ben Adhem Shrine Mosque. He travelled by jet while his singers and musicians all came on the bus. The radio station sat on historic Route 66 and it was an easy shot to the regional airport. An interview at KICK was set for the day of the show.

As soon as James Brown landed, B. grabbed his keys and me. We went to meet him and talk about the show he was doing that night at the Shrine Auditorium. He invited us aboard his private jet and offered us a beer. When he finished his, he tossed the can out the door of the jet. A booming voice came from the tower informing him that if he didn't pick it up immediately, he could take his airplane and land somewhere else, as Springfield did not need him. He was apologetic even in the wind and with the enclosed tower a half-mile away. He picked up the can.

Father Harry, James Brown and B. Sharpe on the tarmac in Springfield

He made promotional spots for me at the station before the show and could not have been more kind. That night, I introduced James Brown to a sell-out crowd as "The hardest working man in show business."

I have a picture from a rock magazine a friend framed for me. There stands my buddy Bill Pledger, a credit to his air-name in a black turtleneck sweater and shades; James Brown, hip with his soul patch and a big medallion on a long chain around his turtleneck, and me, grinning broadly in my black suit and Roman collar shaking James Brown's hand on the tarmac in front of his red, white and blue jet. I never kept up with him after that concert, but I used his spots.

"Here he is, still snapping the bubble gum, Father Harry of the God Squad."

It wasn't exactly the work one would expect from a priest in the Catholic Church but little by little I wandered from the traditional mold of the parish priest and *Going My Way*, into a media guy who was quite content being able to influence young people by the thousands instead of the few hundred that I taught each year in the classroom. Don't get me wrong. I enjoyed my teaching days, but the media bug had bitten.

Bishop Strecker allowed me to attend a communications seminar at Loyola University in New Orleans that lasted for more than a month. The forum was mostly attended by priests and nuns. It was conducted by a priest who was a close friend of the great director Franco Zeffirelli whose works included the sizzling *Romeo and Juliet*. It was a full time hands-on workshop from 8:00 a.m. until 10:00 at night. It was so thrilling and challenging that the time went by like the strike of a match. We burned to see the light of the next day and what might be in store for us. That fire never died.

Among the many highlights was the presentation of *The Graduate* starring Dustin Hoffman. The producer came in person after we watched the film and we had an open discussion. I found this fascinating. I was also able to have my own radio show from the university campus. I took calls from the students who were up late at night. It was a blast! My desire to use the electronic media (and my ego) was fanned to the point of making sure I did something about it when I returned.

I drove Mrs. Ohrman's car the 1,000-miles to New Orleans and back. On the twelve-hour trip home I hardly stopped. I had been told I had an unusual amount of talent and a gift for the media. That drive was a metamorphosis for me because I thought I could do something besides teach and do something public not just in a private Catholic school.

Back in Springfield, I went to see the bishop. I told him about my experience at Loyola—and how I was invited to go to New York and work for the Catholic Conference in their communications department. Guess what? I got Part Two of the sermon about staying in southern Missouri with the people who sacrificed so that I could become a priest. My duty was to work in the Catholic school system and counsel kids to a better life. It worked. I didn't follow up on any of the contacts I made in New Orleans. I preferred staying at home, watching study hall, doing morning and evening prayers and coaching the basketball team. It was still one of the best years of my life.

10. Man of God

THE OZARK AIR LINES flight was heading to New York from Dallas, via St. Louis. There was a storm and the plane was forced to land in Springfield. Ozark canceled the flight and put up the passengers in a hotel. One of them happened to be an advertising agent for Pepsi-Cola. This guy had nothing to do and so was checking out local radio when he came across Father Harry of the God Squad. He called the station and told me he would like to see me the next morning. I told him I was teaching high school but could get away around noon to talk to him. Within a week I was on a plane to New York to meet with the board of directors and found myself in a large conference room stuffed with suits-and-ties and one lady, dressed to the max. She was Joan Crawford of Hollywood fame. Apparently she had a lot of stock in Pepsi at the time.

I listened intently as they discussed making me the "Pepsi Priest" and sending me out all over the country to promote Pepsi and their slogan for that year: "You've got a lot to live, Pepsi's got a lot to give." I was to go from campus to campus on a million dollar budget and say positive things to young people and encourage them to live a better life.

Sounds good now, but at the time I was intent on teaching Latin and religion and dealing with the audience that I had developed on KICK and KMTC. I was just thirty years old, but I knew myself well enough to know that my spiritual life and my relationship with God were not strong enough for me to maintain who I was as a Catholic priest if they were to "make me a star."

At the conclusion of the meeting, I recall telling them that I didn't work for money but for the Church. And if I did have money, I would be dangerous. It didn't make sense to them but again, it was my choice. I had to return to my teaching duties. I recall telling Bishop Strecker that I was so happy working with high school students. The temptations of looking into the eyes of college girls who always seemed to be so "needy" would not have been good for my prayer life nor my vocation to the priesthood.

The long and short of it was that Pepsi-Cola aired my little messages in Kansas City and St. Louis for about six months and I never heard from them again. I say "them." It was really this one man who had convinced his board that the Pepsi Priest would be a hit. It has occurred to me more than a few times what might have transpired had I followed the bright lights. Several years later, when I thought I had the balance to do that kind of work, there were no more invitations.

Bishop Strecker knew that my work with radio and television and high school students could use some strong prayerful grounding and so it was at this point in my life that he assigned me as chaplain to the eight sisters of the Carmel of St. Anne. I was the only daily contact from the outside world for this cloistered Carmelite convent. The bishop wanted to bring some balance to my secular media work. I often thought he did this so that I would have someone praying for me at all times. It must have worked, as those sisters were indeed a lifeline to my relationship with God.

I said Mass for the sisters every day, but once a month I would visit with them after I had breakfast in the parlor. They were vegetarians so it must have been a huge sacrifice for them to endure the aroma of the bacon and eggs, which they prepared for me. They were separated from me, of course, behind bars of steel but seated in such a way that I could see all of them. It was always a joy for me to minister to them. I loved those women and their deep, honest loyalty to their vows of poverty, chastity and obedience. For me, it was more like pottery, celery and obeisance.

There was a turntable onto which the sister in charge put the chalice, wine and bread for Mass and anything else that I might need. The bacon and eggs arrived that way as well. I was duck hunting very early one morning and had killed a couple of mallards. At daylight I came into the chapel and put the ducks on the turntable with a note saying, "Sisters, if possible, could you clean these ducks for me?" The next morning the dumbwaiter rotated and there were the ducks completely naked of feathers and gutted and cleaned. I thanked the sisters profusely and said I would not ask them to do it again. This was all the talk every visit I made thereafter. It seemed none of the sisters had ever cleaned a duck before and the feathers were everywhere in the cloister. They were pleased to hear me promise "never again."

The sporting life had always been the ballast for my spiritual life. I was in the prime of manhood. Besides hunting in the fall, I loved being on the water in the summer. I used to go floating the rivers with friends in canoes and felt it was the perfect place to talk to God, whom I always referred to as "Ralph." I used the word Ralph so as not to offend any of my non-religious folks in other floating devices. Ralph often answered me with a renewed feeling of love and commitment to the work I was called to do.

I had snow skied as a senior in college and so one winter when Justin Monaghan suggested we head for the hills, I was all in. Another old friend from my Roman days, soccer pal John Mahoney of St. Louis, said he was game too and he would drive. He was the guy who'd gotten me onto the field with the *Gli Azzurri* and was always good for some fun. We piled in a

Father Harry at Winter Park, Colorado

station wagon and drove all night from St. Louis to Winter Park, Colorado. It was the days of wooden boards and leather straps and more broken bones than needed to be. My agility at water skiing was a given but to transfer those skills to the slopes was unforgiving.

The three of us crammed into one small room in a nice lodge. Après-ski around the fireplace in our new Christmas sweaters, we noticed when a group of young women entered the room. They saw us too and came closer to the fire. John had always had an eye for the ladies and he struck up a conversation with them. He found out they were nurses without mentioning we were priests. Between us we were the perfect man: handsome, funny, and sensitive. John was the first one to spy the mistletoe. The spirit of the season came over us all. We had so much fun. We began singing and toasting when the owners and other lodgers raised their voices in complaint that they were unable to sleep. It was a small inn and the rooms were close together. Irish tunes can be fun but not in the middle of the night when people who think they are in training for the winter Olympics need sleep.

I'll never forget the next morning as we all gathered for breakfast in the common room (except the ones nursing hangovers). Justin went to the window to order his eggs from the innkeeper who looked at him with some disdain. My friend said, "I'll have two eggs sunnyside up, two aspirin and a pistol." With that, the entire room broke into laughter and all was forgiven.

On the same trip, Justin disappeared one night after dinner and John and I went looking for him. We found him in a snowdrift down the road mumbling to himself that life was too cold and bitter to cope with and he was just going to let himself freeze. No way he would freeze with the antifreeze he had in his system.

By the time I got back home, I had decided I wanted to buy myself a new Camaro. I'd never had the pleasure of choosing my own car—the make, the model, the color, the accessories—and I was a guy who loved new vehicles. The beige Impala had lost its allure. I wanted something sporty. I sold Mrs. Ohrman's car to a St. Agnes student and his dad who fixed up classic cars. The kid promptly put it up a telephone pole.

As soon as the worst of winter had gone, I went to see another old pal from Rome, my close friend Wimpy. His dad, Art Ressler, owned the Chevy dealership in Cascade, Iowa. I asked my teenage niece Renda to come along for the ride. She was a great athlete and lots of fun and pretty as a picture. We took the train out of Union Station in St. Louis and pressed against the Mississippi River heading north. Wayne hadn't changed a bit. He was teaching high school and serving as an associate pastor at a parish. He remembered Renda's parents from our ordination and her dad bringing me Stag beer. After the reunion, I toured the lot and finally found The Car.

I bought a brand new white Camaro from Mr. Ressler. He sold it to me at cost. I cruised back to St. Louis in my sport coupe with optional four-speed transmission and a pretty girl by my side.

About this time, I also reconnected with Jim Kogler, my old buddy JFK. Unlike me, he had excelled in his theological studies. He left Rome only to be recognized as an outstanding teacher and shortly after his return to his diocese was asked to teach Moral Theology in the seminary there. He didn't last long, as his bishop ordered him to sign a paper declaring that he would not teach anything contrary to the message of *Humanae Vitae*, Pope Paul's newly issued encyclical condemning contraception in almost any form. This document came shortly after a committee of male and female experts including many from the medical profession had recommended that the use of condoms might be OK in certain circumstances.

You might remember this Pope's stance on priestly celibacy and birth control from Vatican II. As disappointing as his view on chastity for the clergy had been for many of us, it only affected priests. Birth control affected everybody. I remember Johnny and Betty asking me whether they should confess using it to their pastor. The rhythm method had been spectacularly defeated by their six offspring, five of whom were given names starting with "R" in tribute. I dispensed them from their "sin" and told them not to worry about it. At any rate, Jim would not sign the paper and was re-assigned to a rural parish where his influence was negligible.

He took it like a man and threw himself into parochial life. But his intellect and thirst for making a contribution to the Church led him back to the parlor of his bishop begging him for a teaching assignment. After being denied, he left his diocese and set out for the Midwest to take an assignment at a small Catholic college in Kansas City, Kansas.

I visited him there and he came to Springfield to spend time with me. We spoke about him continuing as a priest after I went to dinner with him one night. He had brought along a female teacher who sat between us on the ride home from the restaurant. JFK was smoking a cigar and in his haste to tip the ash in the tray he dropped it on the lady's leg where it burned a hole in her pantyhose. She yelled and proceeded to lambaste him for his carelessness. Me, I had never heard of pantyhose. It was the first time the idea had ever occurred to me. Now I was curious. A few years later, when football great Joe Namath was advertising for a company who made and sold the product, those Beautymist pantyhose transported me back to that incident so vividly I could smell the cigar smoke.

It was such a gas to see each other again that Wayne, Jim and I decided to take a vacation together and go to Acapulco. Roy was a teacher and had summers off like we did, but he couldn't come because he was busy getting his doctorate in literature and directing plays.

We had gone to see him another time with my brother Charlie, his wife, Mary, and aunt Armella. Rufus lived with his mother, Mame, at her hotel in Florida where it was 100 degrees at eight in the morning. She was known for her great Manhattans. Charlie wouldn't listen to JFK and Wimpy on the drive home and got lost in the bayous.

The trip to the Mexican Riviera was a much better idea. We scorched our white legs at the beach and drank so many margaritas the lime numbed our tongues. We indulged in the fabled nightlife as much as our promises to God and ourselves would allow.

Wimpy and JFK had to get back sooner than I did, so when they flew east I went north to San Francisco to see another very close pal from Rome, Jim Purcell. I arrived in the City by the Bay on a dreary day. Jim picked me up in his new car and began driving around San Francisco. He stopped at Ocean Beach and I recall how disappointed I was that the sand was so dark and the water so cold and there was not a beach, as I had known it. That was nothing compared to how I felt as the word came from him that he was leaving the priesthood. He had fallen in love with a nun who was working in the parish where he was stationed and they had formed a relationship that was more important to him than what he was as a Catholic priest.

It wasn't twenty minutes later, when I was sitting at the kitchen table in an apartment off the Alameda de las Pulgas (Road of the Fleas) just south of the City being entertained by his newfound love. It was strange at the time, even for me, but very true and honest. It pleased me that they loved me enough to share their story and their new experience together with me. The many years in seminary formation and religious life did not prepare either one of them for a marriage, but Jim and Bernice made it work. They've been married for thirty-seven years now and have two children and three grandchildren.

I marveled at how they and others in that situation are able to adapt. I don't know why I should be surprised at how successful men can be after leaving the priesthood. They have all had training in prayer and the spiritual life. It should only be a matter of focusing on the family from God rather than the family of God.

Jim Kogler did leave the priesthood shortly after I saw him. He pursued the same woman he had dated in high school before he went to the seminary. He and Susan fell in love all over again only this time it was forever. They had two wonderful children, a boy and a girl. I baptized them both and a few years ago Wimpy and I officiated at the daughter's marriage.

One of the priests who taught at St. Agnes had a much different situation, but with the same outcome. Father Tony and the eighteen-year-old president of the Catholic Youth Organization fell madly head over heels in love. She was a student, but not his student, and stood out from the kids in her class because of her maturity. He walked away from the priesthood. It was a huge scandal that rocked the tiny Catholic community even though they married and left town.

I never went to see my old friend Floyd but heard that he eventually fell in love with a teacher and married. He divorced and fell in love with another teacher. She followed a lesbian lifestyle and, single again, he migrated to Buddhism and parts unknown.

In the late 1960s, there were lots of guys who were leaving the active ministry. Most of them were finding individuals whom they loved more than working in the priesthood and, in some cases, were being found by women who were lovely and lonely and hadn't yet met the kind of man who could fulfill their dreams. No one is to blame when two people find each other. I know for a fact that in most cases their lives have been enriched and the parishes where they worship have been better off for their presence.

That was not the case with Justin Monaghan who also had left the priesthood and gotten married. There were so many sorry drinking tales about him that I could relate, but the one that topped them all was when he finally discovered for himself that he was drinking too much. He had a fierce argument with his wife who hit him over the head with a bottle of Cutty Sark. As the blood ran down his face it mingled with the stream of scotch. He told me that his tongue waggled its way to the whiskey without a care for the blood. That was a sign that he should commit himself to professional care and give up the spirits. His drinking and his marriage were both over. Final approval for his return to the priesthood was given by a beloved friend and bishop who made him toe the line for many years before re-instating him as a Catholic priest.

The choice of a priestly vocation inherently means an acceptance of professional loneliness. Sure there is a fraternity among brother priests, but it is not the same as love. For me, the experience of talking to God is the way out of loneliness and a way of escaping or dealing with the inevitable.

Although I was a broadcaster, I was a priest first. My friends in radio and TV could get drunk on a Saturday night and they had to deal with their wives. If I got stupid, I had to get up and say Mass. I had a homily to prepare and I had to be a model. The difference was that I had a prayer life and the discipline that bound me to it.

I got a call to go to the hospital and visit Patty, an Ozark Air Lines flight attendant whom DJ had been dating. She'd had a D&C. I didn't know what it was and had to ask a friend's wife. DJ was wild for women and he had nothing to do with Patty after "her" problem. After he was gone and the KICK people went out, she was my date. She played the guitar and I played the guitar. That was what we had in common.

Some people thought I was responsible for the pregnancy because I had counseled her. There was another woman whom I'd met when she was writing an article about the cloistered nuns. She was in love with me. More like she was a romantic. It didn't bother me. It was fun.

There was one woman in Springfield I had known since my boyhood in Cape. I knew her parents and had visited them at holiday time as a young man. We were old friends. When her husband left her I used to go visit at 9:30 at night after all my duties were completed. It was late, especially for a priest. We sat together on the couch and watched Johnny Carson. All the adulation from the teens I taught seemed insignificant compared to her admiring smile. There was no drinking, nor unusual activity. She never tried to seduce me but she did kiss me on the lips and I kissed her back because I was lonely and she was lonely and talking to an adult woman who liked me was a comfort.

It was my need for affection that made me do it. It wasn't the devil or any negative, dark, doomsday kind of feeling. It was elation, a natural high that made me feel like a man who was attractive, who cared, and yet I knew I was at the limit of what I could do. I always left her house feeling better than when I came. I'm sure it was mutual because it happened more than a few times.

11. Minister to the Masses

BISHOP STRECKER HAD BEEN my spiritual advisor and my confessor, but he had moved on to a bigger diocese in Kansas City. The new bishop of the Springfield-Cape Girardeau diocese was the future Cardinal William Baum. He had been vice chancellor for the man who nominated me for the North American College, Bishop Charles Helmsing, and served at Vatican II as a *peritus*, or expert. He was very kind and gentle and had a keen mind that only showed itself when needed. In other words, he never made anyone feel uncomfortable because he knew more than you did. There was one occasion when I thought I knew more than he did.

I had been on KICK radio for a couple of years and it was *the* rock & roll stone of steadiness for young people in southwestern Missouri. It was an era when weekends were filled with outdoor concerts held in fields just outside metropolitan areas (think Woodstock). There was such a gathering twelve miles east of Springfield along the Finley River on a 550-acre farm owned by a man named (honestly) Dr. Love. The promoters asked me to do a small religious service on the stage that Sunday morning.

I was both thrilled and frightened for the invitation. It was an opportunity to reach a big group of teens and young adults in person in a region that was only five percent Catholic. Whatever faith they might have, I wanted to give them hope for God. But I also knew it would bring out the worst in my fellow Christian ministers and their communities to see a Catholic priest condoning this assembly of rock & roll sinners by blessing it with his presence.

It was raining lightly that morning and when I stepped onto the stage with my guitar, I was astonished to look out upon 3,000 people sitting on tarps, grouped under sheets of plastic and sharing umbrellas. Many of them had camped the night before after seeing the featured act, the Ides of March. "You're all natural people, or trying to be," I told them. "God's a natural person too." I encouraged them to love God and their neighbors. I let them know I cared and hoped that they would all return home safely and without incident.

It was completely harmless as far as what I said or did, but the next day there I was in the newspaper playing my guitar for the damned, surrounded by those instruments of sin: amplifiers and drums.

As fate would have it, this was the same week that the Greene County Baptist Association was holding its 98th annual convention. There were fifty-eight Baptist churches and 27,000 Baptists in the county at that time, about 25% of the population, and to a person they were riled about the concert. The delegates condemned it in a resolution "opposing past and future narcotic conventions and sexual immorality and lawless behaviour in the guise of so-called 'rock music festivals.'"

Bishop Baum came to dinner where I lived and ever so kindly asked me about the event and then even more kindly asked me not to do it again. I'll never forget how he put his hand over his cup of tea (to see if it was too hot to drink) and muttered how much he admired me for trying to assist kids but asked me NOT to do it again. I promised him I would not. It was my last outdoor concert! But in the depth of my heart I felt that I had done a good thing, a good deed, for a number of young people who were seeking consolation in drugs, defiance and distance from their families.

I took some ribbing from my housemates at the rectory. Father Tom Reidy, the associate pastor at the Cathedral, used to say, "Father Harry is very pleased with himself." But he would ask me for help with his homilies so I knew he respected me for who I was. Those guys were not stand-offish. I was part of the gang. They were not jealous of my appeal with teens and my broadcasting work. They were proud that I could do something that they could not. Teenagers and young people almost had to be forced to go to church, yet I could get them back. The secret was—and still is— that if you can relate to young people and they tell their parents, you can fudge a little and get away with a lot.

My own family reacted to me in the same way and had begun to look at me as their priest whom they turned to for help when the kids were in crisis. I was asleep when the phone woke me at 2:00 a.m. It was my seventeen-year-old niece imploring me to come to Cape immediately because she was pregnant and she wanted me to break the news to her father.

I was in Cape by breakfast and met the guilty lovers at a neutral spot, a motel. I talked to them and calmed things down then called my brother and told him come to the Ramada. He had to leave work in the middle of a busy morning. I told my niece and her college boyfriend to stay put until I had a chance to break the news to her father. It was very emotional for him and our talk was intense. He became very angry at the hapless suitor and demanded to see him.

To his credit, the young man told my brother that he was ready to make the move to be a father and husband, that he loved my niece and wanted to marry her and they wanted the baby. The wedding was two weeks later and the mother-to-be finished high school. They are still together and have achieved fabulous financial success. The baby was their only child.

Another time, I drove to Cape in my new convertible (successor to the gas hog Camaro). I had bought it at the dealership where St. Agnes got its Drivers Ed cars. A couple of young guys had started a business installing 8-track players in cars and The House of Sound sponsored *I'll Never Tell*. I'll never forget the installation in the dashboard of that '68 Olds Cutlass. We drove the car into the studio and I sat in the convertible with a bunch of kids and cranked up the tape player so that it could be heard all over Southwest Missouri.

I was rocking when I pulled up to my brother's house. My nephew was drawn like flies to sunshine and talked me into letting him take the car for a spin in nothing flat. He was my favorite. One of the "Rs." I went inside and my brother immediately asked where his son was and I told him I had given him my keys. My brother hit the roof because the boy had just had his license taken away. He had lit a fire with some other boys and had been thrown out of the Catholic high school. His parents wanted me to talk to him and straighten him out. They thought I would be able to relate to him with my experience in guidance and counseling and my Roman collar. I failed miserably. After I got my car back and drove home there was another incident.

My nephew had been drinking heavily and he was caught throwing beer cans out of a car. When the Highway Patrol stopped him and his friends and lined up the boys, my nephew took off running. He was fast and got away but his friends finked on him. At two in the morning (what is it about two in the morning?) the cops knocked on my brother's door and woke him up asking if his son was home.

"Of course he's here, it's two in the morning!" my brother almost shouted. He told one of his other kids to go wake up their brother. Clean from a shower and dressed in PJs, the outlaw looked perfectly fine. But there were eyewitnesses so the cops hauled him down to the station and arrested him. He ended up going to juvey.

Mel Ryan was not his real name, as he was Jewish by birth and culture. Mel was in the entertainment business. I'm not sure how he heard about me but he did and invited me to work in Las Vegas on his monster radio station, KRAM, Mod Country. It was a good deal for me. I invited another priest, my friend John Mahoney, to go along as a tennis partner. The plan was to drive from Missouri and make only one stop in New Mexico where I was given a contact to help me with room and board.

It was a filling station with a restaurant. Sure enough, the guy was there and invited us to make ourselves at home. He comped the room at his motel and made a pitcher of margaritas for us. I still recall how embarrassed I was for the number of Native Americans just floundering around the place who seemed to be intoxicated. After the second pitcher of agave juice, John and I were in the same condition.

We went to take a nap and then looked for a place to eat without margaritas. We found a spot not far from the motel, which was not far from the highway. John was tall and built like an athlete and was wearing the Cardinal football jersey of Larry Wilson, a strong safety for that team. It wasn't long after we were there that people were asking for his autograph. At first he declined but then as it got more interesting, that is more interest from females, he began signing napkins, T-shirts and whatever he could write Larry Wilson on.

John had always had an eye for the ladies. I soon discovered that most of the patrons were from the Navajo reservation and we were certainly out of place and culture. As I watched a couple of guys mumbling about "Larry's" authenticity, I decided it was time to vamoose. My friend was having a great time and wasn't ready to go, but when I pointed out the grumbling mob to him, he too saw a good reason to leave and we fled. That was the highlight of the drive across the country.

Father Harry in the studio at K-RAM, Las Vegas

Our arrival in Vegas at the invitation of Mr. Ryan led immediately to free rooms at a nice hotel. In exchange for my working on air from 10:00 a.m. to 2:00 p.m., we were also given dinner tickets for a show every night of the week. While I was broadcasting I made lots of friends who also invited me to come and taste their food and sample their drinks around town. John and I played tennis early in the morning and then took a swim and I went to work. When I came home that afternoon around 2:30, we sat by the pool and then played tennis before showering and going out on the town. It was a great vacation and what's more, I was paid for my work.

The invitation came to KRAM asking for my participation in a television debate with a former priest named Kavanaugh. He had written a best-seller called *A Modern Priest Looks At His Outdated Church.* We were both comped at the new musical *Jesus Christ Superstar.* The next day, we were on a television show giving our reactions to the rock opera.

I recall being very shy and timid around the ex-priest. He was older and obviously more sophisticated than me. He spoke well and often. Toward the end of the program I countered with criticism that, from my standpoint, the *Superstar* writer failed to finish the story. It ended with Jesus dying on the cross. For me, that was only the beginning. His rising from the dead would have given the show a perfect ending. Instead, it limped out and was incomplete. Of course, this had to do with the script and not the music itself, which was superb and captivating.

My point was made when several years later *Godspell* was on Broadway and indeed did follow the Scriptures and ended like it should. The TV debate ended on a rather sour note as Mr. Kavanaugh and I did not depart as good friends who agreed on the collapsing infrastructure of the Catholic Church. We were cordial but would never be vacationing together.

In the meantime over at the Stardust, a friend of friends was the band director for the nightly review with tall stately chorus girls parading in feathers and high heels and very little else. I had a case of avocados with me for him from our mutual friends. John and I were allowed backstage before the show to wait for the bandleader to come and pick up the box of fruit. When the security guard asked us what we were doing there, John who was usually very smooth stumbled over himself watching the girls come down the stairs in their feathers.

"We have a case of boobs for Mr. Avocado," he said.

"What!"

"Oh, sorry, a case of avocados for Mr. Magliero."

It was another of those moments that could never be repeated and hopefully would not have to be repeated.

Loree Frazier was an African-American singer who invited me to watch her perform because she said she was a fan just from my one week at the radio station. I sat at a small table by myself up front, as she had informed the maître d' that I might be there. I fell for her in all aspects. Her voice, her gestures, her stage presence, her magnetic personality with the audience all led me to wait for her after the show then join her for a drink in another part of the hotel. We became friends in one evening and she took me around to several other shows to introduce me to her friends. When I left town, it was the end. No letters, no calls, no nothing. I felt so guilty for allowing myself to get so close to her only to have to back off, play more tennis, get into my car and make the long drive back to Missouri. I often wonder whatever happened to her.

My broadcasting work in both TV and radio had increased. I was now flying to Chicago about every other month to appear on a morning show, *Kennedy and Company*, which was the forerunner of *Good Morning America*. WLS-TV was owned and operated by ABC and the network was grooming Bob Kennedy to be the host of its upcoming program.

Kennedy and Company afforded me a lot of eye-opening experiences, one of which was to be a guest at the famed Playboy Club in Chicago. I did not get to meet the founder and brains behind the multi-million dollar endeavor, but I did get to go to the dressing room and meet the perfect woman, that is, the physically perfect woman. This was a plastic model with the proportions Playboy deemed perfection. They wanted me to see it before the show the next morning so that I would talk about the experience.

You can imagine dyed-in-the-wool Catholic viewers seeing the last thing they would expect from a Catholic priest and watching my reaction to such a piece of plastic. I must say, it was really non-eventful. The head bunny lady was introduced and after a few minutes of chit-chat, they brought out the lifeless model. It was not much different from a mannequin anyone could see at Macy's when they changed out the displays. I did my best to make it funny. In the meantime, I got to have a great dinner at the original Playboy Club in a booth all by myself and was given much more attention than I've ever gotten in a rectory or a seminary while dining. I'm sure there were those who would have loved to be in my shoes, but believe me, when it comes to a plastic woman in makeup and a costume, the thrill is gone.

Dr. Gene Landy was another guest on *Kennedy and Company* and he was very impressive. He was famous for his book, *Underground Dictionary*, a kind of insider's guide to the language of the counterculture. He was a psychiatrist known for being the Analyst to the Stars. He would go on to gain great notoriety for his work with Alice Cooper and such notable characters as Brian Wilson of the Beach Boys.

I found Dr. Landy to be intelligent and pragmatic and very easy to talk to. His character recently was portrayed in a movie depicting the life of Brian Wilson. It proved that he had a meaningful and major role in helping Mr. Wilson cope with reality. When I encountered Dr. Landy, his professionalism and work with Wilson was his calling card to the public media. I liked him.

He invited me to his home in Beverly Hills and I took him up on it. Much to my surprise, his son was completely out of control, using expletives in every sentence, being extremely competitive at a simple game like pool and openly disrespecting his father. It was a serious disappointment to me that a famed mental giant had such little control of his own kid.

We went to dinner and I was asked to drive his big car because he was apparently afraid of being stopped by local law enforcement. This made me nervous but with a silent prayer and a joke, I took the wheel. Fortunately there were no stops. The dinner was too long, the drinks were too plentiful and the conversation began to be repetitious. I was ready to drive everyone home, say goodnight and be gone. Not so fast. I was a guest so I had to sit up with fame and fortune until all eyes were closed and I could go to my room.

The lesson was again helpful to me. It was another brilliant star that blinded me to the truth. I could not be what he was nor proposed to be, and to me that was a great blessing. I have no idea of his life or whereabouts nor do I want to drive his car, play pool with his son or go to dinner on the beach.

I invited my eldest nephew to Chicago to see one of my appearances on *Kennedy and Company*. That morning the guests included Kenny Rogers & The First Edition. I thought this would be a good introduction to show business for my nephew as he was quite talented, although still a young man. The experience might inspire him to work hard at his craft and become a famous media personality someday. It was fun and we had a good time. We were invited to Mr. Rogers' show that night at some Chicago club. I loved his music and used it quite a bit in my God Squad radio spots.

Years later, I got a cease-and-desist letter from his production company. In nearly three decades of using people's music for public service spots, this was the only time I was ever told to stop. I never understood, as I thought it would be a compliment to him to use his material. I never portrayed the music as mine in any way. Oh well, his loss.

With Cleavon Little and Melba Moore on the set of *Kennedy and Company*

Back to my nephew. He enjoyed the show, the visit, the business, but later told me he was not sure he wanted to work in a field dominated by so many gay people. It shocked me, yet I could understand his point of view. Eventually, he opened a dinner theater in the South.

My only real experience along those lines occurred when

Paul Lynde was a guest on the Kennedy show. He was terrific and a favorite of mine on the hit game show *Hollywood Squares,* which aired for many years. The man was so creative and funny and his approach to life was genuine. We were on camera together as he was the featured guest and I had already done my bit. The show had hired a chimpanzee to recreate a shtick Paul had done at the recent Emmy Awards with his fellow presenter, a chimp. Paul was a great sport and took it all in and, because of his talent, made the most of it.

After the show, the producer pulled me aside and warned me to be careful, that Paul would probably invite me to dinner and then inquire about my personal life. He knew that as a priest I was single and might think I was interested in the same sex. Right on cue, Paul Lynde ambled over and asked me to dinner. I said no but thank you.

"Well let's have a little breakfast then," he said with a smile. "I know we were both here early and you must not have had time for more than toast and coffee."

I agreed and we went to the commissary in the building and talked for about an hour. He kept being interrupted by autograph seekers and I'm sure they wondered about me. He was kind, courteous, considerate and very much a gentleman. When he was convinced that I was not gay, he apologized and said how much he enjoyed our conversation and wished me well. I wished that my nephew, who was basically afraid of gay people, would have had the chance to make his acquaintance. After that, Paul Lynde's appearances on TV were a must-see for me and I always will have a warm spot in my heart for this great comedian and person.

I had met Bill and Cathy Karnauskas when they came to Rome for Miles O'Brien Riley's ordination and I was his wingman. They bonded with me because I was not from wealth and seemed more like their kind of people, unlike the Riley family. Miles' mother, for example, had ordered the pool at the Cavalieri Hilton to be filled on December 22 because their pool in Menlo Park was full. That seemed a bit excessive. Anyway, we became good friends. Bill and Cathy came to my ordination the next year because his California real estate investment had paid off. They always invited me to visit out there so finally I did.

I drove around in their big yellow Malibu convertible. I drove on the 405. I had no idea of all the pollution. By the time I got back my eyes were burning so badly I had to do cold packs.

I was visiting them in Fallbrook when they decided to fly their little plane to Las Vegas. It was fun until we arrived at the big airport and tried to land behind a 747. We bounced around in the jetwash for a minute or two but finally landed.

At lunch that day, Merv Griffin was sitting with Arthur Treacher and Don Rickles at a table across from us. My friend asked me to introduce myself and let him know that I had just been invited by Pepsi-Cola to become the Pepsi Priest. I was bashful so Bill went over. Merv got up from the table and came over to me and was as warm and friendly as ever a man could be. We talked for a long time and he asked if he could go to confession sometime during our visit. That night we were comped to his show and invited backstage. He introduced me to his wife and son, as well as Arthur and Virginia Treacher who turned out to be such lovely people.

I recall sitting there with Arthur and he predicted that the next voice down the hall would make an appearance and say exactly what he said, "Oh, Arthur, you were simply divine." In walked Carol Channing with her huge red lips that no one could miss saying in her deep lusty voice, "Oh, Arthur, you were simply divine."

It was quite a week for me as I was invited to escort Merv's wife to a different show each night while he was working at The Riviera. It was funny when the maître d' would see Mr. and Mrs. Merv Griffin on the reservation sheet and there I was and what a disappointment it was for them. I never did tip like Merv or even like I was supposed to since I didn't know what I was doing except enjoying the Las Vegas nightlife.

Miles Riley had arranged to meet with me while I was in Las Vegas. I saw his million-watt smile across the room and soon we were bear-hugging and he was calling me Fuzzy and telling me I hadn't changed. He had been my best friend in Rome.

Miles had sent me a handwritten invitation to come to San Francisco and assist him in setting up a communications ministry. He wanted to talk about it face to face. He knew I was doing radio and TV in Springfield, Vegas and Chicago. Miles said there would be an immediate need for my services in San Francisco. I could begin with at least two radio shows and one television program. He had paved the way.

I was on fire with excitement, burning to follow my dream of doing more in the world of media for the Church. Since the short summer stint in New Orleans that sparked my desire for the ministry, it had been building. I would have to say good-by to my classroom teaching and my teen counseling in Springfield, but I could hope for a similar set-up in San Fran.

Miles' proposal, much like Bishop Helmsing's inquiry about Rome, was a surprise and a challenge. I had no idea how I would be allowed to go to the West Coast, to a different and unique diocese, to do radio and TV work. I was excited but I held back because I didn't know if it could actually be done. The Gemini broadcaster and the Gemini priest were twin sons of different mothers but the Father was the same. I asked Miles when he wanted me to start.

The connection with radio and television that followed in the next forty-plus years made it clear and evident to me that the Holy Spirit was truly guiding my star wherever it would shine most brightly.

I came home to Springfield for the last time and found a postcard waiting for me in the mail. It was from seminarian Tim Dolan and simply read, "Thank you. I'm going to be ordained a Catholic priest." Now, looking back on what he has accomplished as a "churchman," it does not surprise me that he would remember to say thank you after the experience we had in St. Louis. He was the only one from any of my retreats who ever did.

The future Cardinal Dolan had found that his vocation was true. I heard mine calling me. Bishop Strecker had said "no" to New York and "no" to the Marine Corps. Bishop Baum was much more pliable when it came to utilizing my talents in communications after he exchanged letters with Archbishop Joseph McGucken of San Francisco. It's a big deal for a bishop to release a priest to another diocese. It's like losing someone you counted on to work for you the rest of their lives, someone you had trained and educated. Then all of a sudden they're in a different state under a different bishop.

Baum was generous and recognized what I might be able to do. Or he was afraid I'd pick up the guitar on a Sunday morning and head for a rock concert. Or maybe it was the squeak of an archbishop requesting my presence.

"Two years, Harry," Bishop Baum said. "Two years."

High school ended in May and I packed up my life in Springfield. Monsignor Westhues and the housekeeper walked me to the curb. As I was leaving the Cathedral to move to San Francisco the last thing he said to me was, "God bless you. I know you'll never come back to Missouri."

Little did I know, he was right.

"No," I said, "I'll be back in two years. Not to worry!"

I headed east on the familiar road back toward my birthplace. Pastoral assignments always take effect July 1 and I wasn't due in San Francisco until then. My last month in my home state was spent south of Cape Girardeau in a little town called Benton. I was asked to go there to fill in for the St. Denis parish priest who was sick. This gave me a chance to visit with my family before I left for California.

Benton was a town of mostly Catholics, many of them my relatives. I had an uncle who lived four doors down from the church on the highway. Two doors from him lived cousins on my dad's side, uncle Leo's daughter Mildred and her husband, Sam. Theirs was an unusual family with more than a dozen children. Seventeen to be precise, although three had died just days after being born including premature twins. Sam and Mildred had babies like there was no tomorrow.

I recall that my sister-in-law Mary had been in the hospital with her twins (numbers six and seven) when Mildred was there with her tenth. Mildred went home the same day she gave birth. My brother Charlie had thought that his wife could do likewise.

It took a special woman to be the mother of so many kids and have them turn out the way they did. Sam had the disease of alcoholism and was up and down as a useful person to the family. Mildred managed to make ends meet and that family was always an inspiration to me.

One of the younger daughters had just made her profession

as a religious woman. Her name was Mary (same as one of the dead twins) and she was a Franciscan nun. There was a large wheat field between the rectory of the parish where I was staying and Mary's home. I recall how my heart leapt when I saw her walking through the grasses on her way to visit me. That June was a lonely month for me and I was just about to begin one of the most exciting journeys of my life.

It was a blessing for me to get to know Mary. She and I spent many hours together listening to music and enjoying the back and forth conversation of Scripture and liturgy. Neither one of us were saints and I knew that my weaknesses and sinful aspirations were a surprise to her. I shared from the heart and she knew it.

Leaving that agrarian Midwestern society for the big city of San Francisco would mean a whole new life for me. I don't know what happened to Mary. I never saw her again.

I got in my convertible and started driving west.

Part III

Maturation

*Behind and before you encircle me
and rest your hand upon me.
Such knowledge is too wonderful for me,
 far too lofty for me to reach.*

Psalms 139:5-6

*You should never hesitate to trade your cow for
a handful of magic beans.*

Tom Robbins

12. Golden State

WITH THE MISSISSIPPI RIVER at my back and my future straight ahead, I retraced the route of my early priestly life across my home diocese to the Queen City and onto the familiar contours of the Mother Road. I left behind the rice fields and the wetlands of my birthplace and the neighboring wild and scenic waterways, dropping down from the Ozark Highlands into the plains. It was days away from summer and I had just turned thirty-three, the age the Bible says Jesus was when he died, crucified by a mob. I don't know why most Catholics think of this when they reach that age, but in my experience this has been the case.

To get from the Bible Belt to Babylon by the Bay you have to go through Las Vegas. I stopped there on my way west and worked for Mel Ryan for one week. It was to be my last stint on KRAM but Mel said he came to San Francisco often so we would stay in touch.

From Vegas I drove to Los Angeles and spent a couple of nights. I had stayed in touch with Merv Griffin and he invited me to appear on his television show with CBS. The night arrived and they had overbooked so I got scratched and was subsequently introduced to the audience as his almost Pepsi-Priest friend.

I watched and listened to a number of comedians and pitch people warming up Merv's audience before he came on stage and thought I would be able to do the job. I wanted to open for him when he was doing the daily talk show for CBS in Hollywood. Merv and his producer, a very kind Catholic man named Murphy, were setting up a gaggle of game shows that are still running today and would eventually make them both millionaires. I sat in his dressing room that day and told him how earnestly I had prepared and how eager I was to show my stuff (that's show off, now that I know better).

All I had to do was go out in front of the live audience and warm them up. Tell a story or two and then give them a serious lesson in life, all in a humorous vein. I had rehearsed some shtick and thought I was ready for the big time. I made my pitch to the two of them about the possibility of trying me out when I got maybe the best advice of my life from Merv Griffin.

Merv listened attentively as was his custom since he was one of the premier interviewers of his day. After recognizing that I was serious, he said to me, "Harry, you know how many comedians are out of work? Do you know that I get a dozen calls a week to do the job you're asking to do? I have to say no to all of them. You are a priest. None of those guys, nor any of us in this business, can do what you can. You can forgive sins, change bread and wine into the body and blood of Christ. Why in the world would you want to entertain these folks in the audience who come here to see a free show? Thank God for the gift you have as a priest and keep being a priest."

He was absolutely right. There was no need for me to even think about it. I walked out of that private office and into the green room outside the studio with the comedian who was going to warm up the audience. I wished him well and gave him a blessing. When he left, I knelt down and thanked God for the advice and the gift I had been given.

I drove up Highway 101 to San Francisco and did a lot of soul searching, realizing once again that my talent was not on stage or in entertainment, but ecclesial, and I should make the best of it. I spoke to Merv a couple of times on the phone after that but we never got together again.

I arrived in the City by the Bay July 1, 1972, on a Saturday early afternoon. I remember because the good friend and close buddy who invited me out West had to dash off to Mission Dolores to hear confessions right after I got to town. Miles had just enough time to take me to my new quarters in a big house on Diamond Street in the Castro district, near Most Holy Redeemer. There were three other guys living there, all conscientious objectors who were working for my friend, and one lady. She was the main squeeze of the guy in the room across the hall from the only bathroom, which got constant use during my short tenure there.

I recall not knowing what to do with myself when I discovered a small black and white TV in the kitchen. The St. Louis Cardinals, my team, were playing baseball against the hometown Giants.

"Perfect!" I thought. "I'll go up the street and get a beer and watch the game in color."

The first beer sign I saw, I went in. I thought a watering hole named the Missouri Mule might have Stag on draft. I noticed that the ball game wasn't on and that several, if not all, of the male customers were conversing intimately and as if they loved one another. I didn't know I was in the first gay bar in what was probably the first gay neighborhood in the country. A guy from Cape Girardeau had not had experience with a gay bar and its patrons. This was a far cry from Paul Lynde at a commissary. I quickly resorted to a six-pack from the local liquor store and settled for the black and white at my new digs.

Miles soon returned and we talked far into the night. He said that my accommodations would only be for a couple of days and that a permanent place would be forthcoming. It wasn't and that was OK as I ended up in a bishop's suite while he was away on his annual one-month vacation. I had a garage for my convertible and food every day. I didn't have to queue up for the john and my mattress was not on the floor. I could take a walk and feel safe and was in the same rectory as my friend.

The Archdiocesan Communications Center was on the fourth floor in the old Young Men's Institute building on Oak Street and there were handball courts, a gym and a pool in the building. What a place to work! I couldn't believe my luck.

With its Ionic columns four abreast, Fifty Oak was a grand old building. The communications work we did from there was hand-to-mouth. We had no subsidy, no regular income, no traditional means of support. We did all our shows as public service, so there was no advertising, no solicitation for donations, no real revenue. Miles and I both believed that the Apostles would have given anything for the tools we were using to spread the Gospel. The Archdiocesan Communications Center, or ACC, was our primary ministry.

At first it was only the two of us and the COs working there. Like other associate priests, our salaries came from the

Archdiocese. We were given room and board in parishes where we helped out with weekend sacraments. I had received a kind letter of invitation from the pastor of Sacred Heart and was living there.

Miles already had a Sunday morning show called *For Heaven's Sake* that aired on the ABC station, KGO-TV, and another one called *Mosaic* that aired on KPIX-TV, the CBS owned and operated station. I filled in for him as host on occasion. ACC produced both shows. Our goal was to bombard the local airwaves with quality programming and break into the national market. Our dream was to broadcast ACC productions internationally.

In a period of just a few months, I had landed my first major market radio show. *Faith Forum* aired every other Sunday morning at nine on KNBR-AM, NBC's flagship on the West Coast. I delivered thirty minutes of music and meditation, recorded in the KNBR studios, produced by ACC and heard as far away as Hawaii. We grew to a paid staff of three plus a secretary/bookkeeper. When we sold a video or film we put the money in a pot and those guys split it up.

The activism of the Sixties and the anger about the Vietnam War converged outside St. Mary's Cathedral. Demonstrators protested the money spent on the edifice instead of helping the poor. We decided to start doing a youth liturgy at the Cathedral on Sunday evenings that would bring in kids. It would be their Mass.

At about the same time, the "Father Harry" spots were being picked up by an alphabet soup of radio stations. I happened across my old pal from Springfield Les Sweckard. He'd landed as program director at KFRC, San Francisco's Top 40 powerhouse. I didn't know he had changed his name and my appointment was with a Les Garland. We were both a long way from Springfield. *Father Harry* hit the Big 610 airwaves and the kids couldn't get enough. KYA, simulcasting on AM and FM, began airing the one-minute God Squad spots. A mild equivalent to Beatle mania swept through the Catholic high schools. From Archbishop Riordan to Presentation and Mercy, teenagers clamored for more of Father Harry.

I started doing a program on Sunday nights that drew a

different radio audience than either the morning religion show listeners or the rock & roll teens. The gig on KCBS-FM was one of my favorite recording opportunities. I would enter the Transamerica Pyramid building around 9:00 p.m. and go way up into the City's tallest skyscraper. I can't remember which floor, but while I was playing music and offering *Lovenotes for Listeners* I could feel the building sway in the wind. My producer would always smile when I pushed the talk-back button and asked if there was anything unusual going on.

"No," was his response, "only your show."

Our Sunday evening liturgies at St. Mary's Cathedral were a great hit. We began with a team of young people and worked with them on all the aspects of the weekly celebration. The group would meet for hours and go over everything from the greeting to meeting afterward. We designed a printed bulletin with hymns and readings that were new and modern. We had a rock band with a wide repertoire so that almost every ear could find something that was pleasing. My friend and co-worker Miles had a wonderful talent for re-writing the lyrics to popular songs so that the worshipers could immediately recognize the tune from the radio or their record collections and simply use the words that Miles had crafted. We had young artists who would design the bulletins with cartoons and pictures depicting what the Scriptures were saying to us in the liturgy. All those things were indicative of liberation from rules and regulations that was the blessing of Vatican II. It was a win-win situation.

We had various priests as celebrants and they were asked to come to a Tuesday night meeting and present their homilies to our Liturgy Board of youngsters. The board would critique the sermons and offer suggestions to help the priests speak to the kids and not above them. It was humiliating for some and a growing experience for others. I recall one priest, who is now a bishop, telling them how much it meant to have feedback that was honest and direct. It would only make his Mass more meaningful. And it did.

It was post-Vatican II and there were not yet stringent rules as to what you could or could not do at Mass. So one priest delivered his homily from inside a "tiger cage," simulating the ones used in Vietnam to hold POWs, prisoners of war. He made the point about how horrible the war was and how imprisoned we are when we don't free ourselves to speak out against it.

We had commuters from as far as a hundred miles away coming to share this new form of liturgy. There was also a whole gang of those kids from fourteen to twenty-five who knew me from the radio and came to see Father Harry in person.

I had met the director of *Godspell* during my *Kennedy and Company* days. We became friendly enough that when the touring company came to San Francisco, I invited him and his cast to attend the Sunday evening liturgy at St. Mary's. We had more than 8,000 young people at that Mass and the performers arrived from the matinee downtown just in time to do the music and the homily. That was another highlight of my experiences with the wonderful Chicago TV show that carried over when the road cast came west.

We also had a writer from Los Angeles who would fly up almost every Sunday just to attend the Mass. He was famous for creating the "Flying Fickle Finger of Fate" award that was given on the popular TV show *Laugh-In*. The first award in 1968 was to the U.S. Congress for ignoring the will of the people in refusing to pass gun control.

Sometimes in later years, the writer would come up the center aisle and begin to give his life story. We would have to ask him politely to cut it short and then cue the band for the next hymn before he would surrender the microphone. He too was a well meaning individual who experienced God in the service.

Miles used to make a big thing of hugging everyone after Mass. The girls lined up. They were all sizes, shapes and colors. His mother would often say to me, "What's the big attraction that my son holds for fat girls?"

"They need love too," I replied.

I did not have the same gifts as Miles. I would seek out one or two small groups or families each week and get to know them. Over the years I was able to maintain closer friendships with them because I knew them better. It was a good combination. Miles was for the many, I was for the few. Whatever we did together, it was successful.

Late on Friday night after a full week, Miles would telephone his mother and ask if there was anyone staying at their beach home at Pajaro Dunes. It was a beautiful place on a big beach with tennis courts and bike paths and, of course, the surf. We would jump in his car and not stop until we hit the market near the house where we would over-buy everything. "Never shop with an empty stomach" is so true. When we got the groceries up the stairs and into the kitchen, it looked like we'd be there a month and a dozen others were going to join us. Mrs. Riley always wondered how many people we were feeding.

"It's only me and Father Harry," Miles would assure her.

"Will you be eating two pounds of bacon apiece and washing it down with four quarts of orange juice each?" She made her point but we kept repeating ourselves.

It was in these remote and quiet environs that many ideas were spawned and plans were hatched to grow the work that Miles had begun in 1971. I was determined to get rid of talking heads on TV and bring something to the screen that was more exciting. People talking about their religion was a lot different than people talking about their faith. The latter packed more emotion and made the characters more alive and appealing.

Inside Out was a show that I began on KRON-TV. The idea came from giving youth retreats and seeing how interested the kids were in meditation, quiet and the chance for some introspection. We were trying to elicit the deeper feelings that they carried through the teen years when they had no avenue for expression without looking silly to their peers.

I had made close friendships from the Sunday youth Mass with two adult women who were deeply spiritual. Joan was married with three beautiful daughters who were all involved in show business. She was a counselor to lots of priests who were leaving the Church and marrying. She was hired to give priests' retreats. She had such a calm way about her and a terrific way of dealing with men. She was a tremendous listener and very sympathetic. She used to shed tears at the slightest emotion when she felt someone was hurting. She was genuinely concerned about priests. Her focus was human liberation. Our friendship led to a number of media projects that were viewed by thousands.

Elsa was a psychiatrist and teacher. I had great admiration for her and looked up to her as a feminist figure in my life. Elsa was my personal advisor for a number of years. She was my senior by ten or fifteen years but it really didn't matter. She had a remarkable ability to transform quiet into a cacophony of spiritual growth for those who took her counsel. Elsa was my guest on *Inside Out*. It didn't take long for her to be the star of the show. Her female intuition and insight into the smallest things brought light to both my panel and the audience. It aired at midnight yet we had a wonderful audience for the show. It aired again early on Sunday mornings.

As a result of our relationship, I was invited to be the co-teacher in Elsa's psychology class at a neighboring community college. Every Tuesday night, I would get in my car and drive the freeway for an hour to share three hours of instruction with this talented and lovely lady. The class did not know I was a priest until about the third session. By that time they had revealed more and more about themselves. I became a whipping boy for all the disappointments that many of them had had in their attempts at a happy marriage, and a martyr for my Catholic beliefs.

It was astonishing. People weren't interested in learning psychology or the mechanics of thinking. They were looking for someone to solve their problems. It was like there had been an ad in the newspaper, "All of you who have troubles in your life, come to class and we will listen to you and help you overcome your woes." These were not people who had any respect. These were people who thought they'd been led astray.

There was one woman in class who'd had an abortion and who had all these feelings that had lasted a long time. She couldn't bear the guilt she had taken upon herself and blamed the Church. Another man was a pilot with a terrible drinking problem. I was stunned by the ugliness of the names he called me. Maybe I over-analyzed the situation, but it felt like they were taking things out on me because they were unhappy people and because I was a priest and a Catholic and had a major commitment in my life to the faith and to the Church.

I recall standing in the parking lot more than once after class with the good doctor and having her heal my wounds. It was a long sad ride back to the City for me on most of those Tuesday nights. Driving home by myself, I didn't turn on the radio; I didn't listen to the ballgame. I reviewed everything. Why was I doing this? Was it doing anything for my growth? Was I really helping people as a priest? Was I making any progress passing along any spiritual lessons to anybody? Or was I just a dartboard for people to zero in on and do away with their self-inflictions. You can imagine my meditation. It was such a joy the next day to be at the office on Oak Street.

My commitment to the Church was deeper than psychology. I only lasted two semesters as a college professor. My energy level and my ability to take it went way down. It was a difficult time for me and even today, when I drive by and look over at that college, I get shivers.

ACC continued to flourish. We landed a second show on KRON-TV. We came in with creative that they loved and got the green light for thirteen weeks of *Hot Fudge Sunday*. The new program featured sketch comedy and was in the vein of successful burlesque shows like Carol Burnett and *Laugh-In* and the local live theater sensation *Beach Blanket Babylon*.

We called it "religious variety." In an especially hard-to-forget episode, I was decked out in a red cape, with one hand clutching the hood around my face and the other swinging a picnic basket as I pranced through the woods to Grandma's house. "I'm not afraid of the big, bad wolf," I squeaked in falsetto. "I have faith! And, I know how this story ends."

"This is Brian Roberts, your blue-eyed brother, from atop Nob Hill with much more music . . ."

Brian was a great disc jockey and my show followed his for a long time on KYA radio in San Francisco. I would come on at 6:00 a.m. and he would be going home after a midnight to six shift. He was always very pleasant to me and very friendly. We shared the same engineer, Superharlo, who was famous from the jocks constantly ribbing him on air about everything. I got to know him as a Vietnam vet, a handball player and a very private person.

Roberts was so good that when the Armed Forces Radio and Television Service was looking for a jock to do a daily radio show overseas, two AFRTS guys came to interview him. They would later hire me at the suggestion of my blue-eyed bro. Apparently, they couldn't pay him enough money to do the extra work. In the meantime, they listened to my programs, asked for a demo

Father Harry's *Love on the Rock* was #1 on AFRTS

and within two weeks I was flying to Hollywood to the old AFRTS studios on Pico Boulevard. I was assigned to work with a man named Frank Cangialosi. He was a wonderful producer and became a great friend. I officiated at the marriages of two of his daughters and just recently married the daughter of a daughter. I also baptized a whole mess of kids from all their unions. What a thrill for a priest to have that kind of connection after so many years. I can't tell you what it does for a spiritual ego.

Some of my most memorable moments came from my affiliation with Armed Forces Radio. At one time it was changed to American Forces Radio and then it went back to "Armed." I think it's back to "American" today. I'll pay attention when I hear them at holiday times and the announcers talk about the overseas distribution. I used to be able to brag that I had an audience larger than the Pope's. I had 600 different outlets around the world as well as 250 ships at sea and it was estimated that I reached 60 million people. I still get e-mails from those who listened to me every week on AFRTS.

It didn't take Armed Forces long to get my name and my show known around the world. It also didn't hurt that I was producing radio spots for KFRC, KYA, KCBS and KNBR and getting help from a number of radio personalities like Dr. Don Rose, who in his day was the best in the country. We became close personal friends. Again, I had the privilege of giving the sacraments of marriage and baptism to his family. Don and his wife, Kae, were great supporters of mine for many years.

I have been the culprit behind more than one blunder when trying to pass along the life and teachings of Jesus Christ. The infamous Zebra killer struck only a block away from where I lived at Fillmore and Fell. The City was terrorized over a six-month period by sixteen random killings with no apparent connection. Half of the attacks occurred within a few blocks of Sacred Heart or Fifty Oak. On any given Sunday I would peruse the Sacred Heart congregation for suspicious characters. There was one such individual whom I profiled for my own satisfaction. He often came to church with a brown paper bag. Now and again he would put it to his lips and take deep breaths. I was unaware of glue sniffing and the apparent high that it can affect.

On a particular Sunday when I was feeling brave, I asked him why the paper bag? He had not yet put it up to his face. It looked like it contained something heavy as I tried to sneak a peek. He quickly grabbed the bag from the pew and scurried out the other end of the bench and through the swinging doors into the street. It wasn't until about six months later that I was told the bag held a gun he had used in a crime and he kept it with him until he had a chance to dispose of it off the Bay Bridge. I never followed up and never saw the man again.

Reading the papers and knowing that the Zebra killer might be nearby kept one wondering about where you lived and how long you might live. It turned out the murders were racially motivated black-on-white crime. Two of the killers lived three blocks from Sacred Heart. Four members of an offshoot of the Nation of Islam were finally convicted of first degree murder and sentenced to life in prison. There was no death penalty in

California at that time.

Marcellus spent most of his life in jail. He too had a problem with guns and absolutely no problem running the neighborhood where I lived. He liked me, I think, because I was never really assaulted, except for the one time late at night crossing the street when a dark sleek car swerved on purpose to hit me. I jumped on the hood of a parked car and avoided what could have been my demise. It was awhile before I came out of the rectory into the streets at night. Marcellus used to tell me not to worry. He had the backs of all the priests he knew. Comforting.

Sacred Heart parish was an active place and there was always something being carted off, unless it was tied down or locked up. I was in the front parlor of the rectory talking to the parish secretary and as we glanced out the window we saw a man carrying the Sacred Heart of Jesus down the street. The statue was large and cumbersome and I knew he would not be able to run with it so I burst out the door and yelled. He dropped it and ran. The plaster Jesus suffered a severed hand and chipped lower extremity, but it went right back on the pedestal that afternoon. The sextant put some glue on the base so our namesake could no longer be taken unless by crane or gorilla.

One Saturday afternoon during football season, I made my way to the church to hear confessions. There wasn't much business as the parish was not well attended and even fewer were coming for the sacrament of reconciliation. As I opened the door and switched on the light I was met with the horrible smell of human feces. Someone had mistaken the penitent's side of the confessional for a restroom and had used the church bulletins for wipes. I spent the entire time for confessions using disinfectant and trying to rid the box of that stench.

This particular parish was a con stop. It was inner city and there was more than one talented person who could con the priest out of something. My favorite was a guy who took me for $45 one afternoon. He drove up in a big Cadillac and said he had been at the Crosby Invitational in Carmel. He was a professional golfer who had been robbed. He took me out to the car, opened the trunk and sure enough he had an impressive array of clubs with a huge bag and shoes to match. All he wanted was a few bucks to get a meal and a room and some gas. I only had $45 and he took it all.

Fifteen minutes later the pastor came to my room.

"Did you give some money to one of our alcoholic friends?" asked Father O'Connell.

"No," I said, "I gave some to a pro golfer who had been robbed."

He laughed. "You've met Dave. Go down the block to the liquor store with a big Cadillac parked in front. You'll find him inside buying a pint or two for the road home. He lives in Oakland. He plays golf and cons coins from young priests like you. How much did he get?"

"Forty-five dollars," I confessed.

"Oh well, too late now," said the pastor. "He's already spent that and will be on the move to the next rectory where he might find another young priest who believes his con."

I was still kicking myself early the next morning as I made my way to KYA radio to do my regular 6:00-9:00 a.m. shift. The public service director set up my guest schedule so I knew little about whoever I was to host that morning. Much to my surprise the guest was Ginger by name, a transsexual who'd undergone physical reconstruction. She was representing COYOTE which stood for "Call Off Your Old Tired Ethics." Ginger was interesting to speak with and a delightful interview. But I knew that as soon as we opened the telephone lines the first callers were going to ask about sex and how she was able to do it or not do it. I was right. She handled it with great aplomb letting the listener know that she was a person like any other but with an unusual physical challenge that she couldn't help. She was born male but had always felt she was female.

What a lesson for a young priest with all kinds of preconceived notions about transsexuals. One lasting memory was the smell in that little air tight studio from both of us. It could have been a gym with fifty young men practicing basketball. It was definitely male hormones that told the truth about both of us.

We must admire people who are born different than we are and who have to go day after day explaining both to others and themselves what a challenge it is to try and fit in no matter what we do or where we are. Go Ginger! She did give me the opportunity to call off my old tired ethics.

The Diocese of Springfield-Cape Girardeau had a new bishop. To no one's surprise, Bishop Baum had been made Archbishop of Washington. He had risen to the episcopacy only three years earlier, but his time at the Second Vatican Council as a *peritus*, and his work in D.C. at the National Conference of Catholic Bishops, had earned him acclaim and respect. He would go on to become cardinal and serve at the Curia in Rome. As of this writing he is the longest serving American cardinal in history.

My new boss was one Bernard Law. He had been ordained for a Mississippi diocese and his civil rights work there aligned him with Protestant ministers. That led to ecumenical work on a national level, fostering dialogue with other Christians. Next stop Springfield-Cape, where 95% of the people were non-Catholic.

I flew back from San Francisco in December to attend his installation in Springfield. Bishop Law shook my hand in the reception line and said he would like to see me early the next morning at his home. That was it! With fear and a bit of trepidation, I arrived to a warm and friendly greeting from a man I barely knew. He was direct and decisive.

"Harry, I want you to return to work here as soon as you can. I'm calling back all the priests of this diocese who have been serving the Church in other ministries."

My smile faded to disappointment and I was very concerned about having to leave California. I told him that I had begun working for the Armed Forces Radio network and had one of the most popular shows in their history. I was always tops in the category of religious network shows. My television shows commanded a large audience and my two other live radio programs were making me a "mass media minister" beyond my wildest dreams.

"No matter," he said. "I want you back."

I went to my best friend from St. Agnes and to my first cousin, both priests, and pleaded my case. Tom Reidy and Phil Bucher worked in the chancery office with Bishop Law and I thought they could help me. They did.

Within two months, the bishop came to San Francisco. He

followed me around the entire weekend. He came to the studio at KRON and watched me tape my weekly TV show *Inside Out*. Then Sunday morning he got up early to accompany me to the KYA studios for my radio program *Weekends with Father Harry*. That afternoon he went with me to a fund-raising luncheon in Menlo Park. That evening he stayed in and listened to the live broadcast from KCBS. I took him to the airport the next day.

I'll never forget his smile of support and his encouraging words as he told me that I could never do what I do for the Church from southern Missouri. I now had his full blessing to continue my media work and to permanently change my diocesan status from Springfield-Cape Girardeau to San Francisco, if I wanted.

The Catholic Church has a system whereby a priest is slated to minister in the part of the country where he is ordained and serve as a priest in that diocese until he dies. (A diocese is set up similar to a county in a state and is determined by population and distance.) However, there is a process called incardination and excardination through which a priest, with an invitation from one bishop and the permission of another bishop, can transfer. In Latin, *cardo* means hinge—you literally hang by the hinge of your bishop to serve where you do. Bishops are very intense when it comes to a priest leaving the service of the diocese where they are the chief shepherd (remember Bishop Strecker?) plus I had been one of the first two priests ordained for the new Diocese of Springfield-Cape Girardeau. Even so, I went through this process and thanks to Bishop Law I was able to make my permanent home in Northern California. I was incardinated in the Archdiocese of San Francisco in 1974.

That was a decision that the future Cardinal Bernard Law made for which I will be eternally grateful. He had the foresight and the humility to see that my ministry was good and fruitful and meaningful, even if it wasn't happening in his own backyard.

13. Hot Fudge Sunday

THE MCGILVERY SISTERS were twins from Santa Barbara. They weren't identical, but they were both a lot of fun and appealed to the Gemini in me. Libby and Lizzie became regulars at our Sunday night Mass at the Cathedral. They came from a very talented family of artists. Their mother's work was displayed in a Beverly Hills gallery. Their father was a lighting director in Hollywood. One of the twins was a sculptor and the other was a budding filmmaker. Libby worked at the modern art museum and Lizzie worked for me.

Pretty and outgoing, Liz knew television production. She was looking for full time work and thought ACC was a good place to start. She came to see my partner, Miles, about a job.

Miles was interested in every cute girl who came along who had unusual talents. Lizzie was bubbly and smart and bursting with energy, eager to contribute in any way she could to our multimedia operation. Miles interviewed her but he didn't hire her because we couldn't afford anybody. She came on as a volunteer TV producer for my show *Hot Fudge Sunday* and we started working together every day.

We mostly did radio and TV production at ACC but we also dabbled in slide shows, posters, logo designs and presentations for groups trying to establish their brand. We had some conscientious objectors who were allowed to do service with us in lieu of going to Canada until the heat from the draft board had ended. They were all excited about any new venture we might find ourselves encountering at the Archdiocesan Communications Center.

Miles and I had begun fund-raising for a film to foster vocations to the Catholic priesthood. Raising money was not that difficult as we got a number of older pastors excited and interested in the project. Our idea was not to film the priest in his daily work but to get reactions from lay people of how one priest or another had influenced their lives. It worked out well.

The Priest sold many copies and we used it on our various television programs. Every place we had a show, it aired. On all three networks and the independent station, we introduced *The Priest* as a show within a show.

Our success with ACC's first attempt at a documentary was cause for a celebration. Mel Ryan from Las Vegas was the one who had put me onto the Down Under on Taylor Street at Post, a block from the Academy of Art. It was not an Australian restaurant, but located down under an apartment building. It had been a basement storage area and the odd crannies made for intimate dining. I had befriended the owner and he gave us a deal on the upper room and we treated our staff to dinner.

Father Harry on the set of
Hot Fudge Sunday

Miles invited Lizzie. He was interested in her but she wasn't interested in him. She liked Miles and used to laugh at his stories. She just didn't take him very seriously. He could captivate a room when he walked in, but his experience at romanticism was very limited.

Lizzie and I had gotten to be good friends working together on *Hot Fudge Sunday*. I was five years older so she had a great respect for me. I'd been around longer and was semi-famous from my spots on KFRC. I admired her artistic talent. She created an animated open for our program. On the stage came a glass, then two plops of ice cream, hot fudge pouring over the top and a cherry on top of that. HOT FUDGE was stacked above SUNDAY and under that were the cherries and the cream. She did that and I thought it was a terrific opening.

We talked and laughed the whole night at the Down Under. At the end of the evening, she didn't want to stop talking. We were both having a good time. She had no car, she took the bus everywhere, so I drove her to Chestnut Street to a favorite saloon of mine. Long after dinner was over, I sat there gazing into her eyes wondering why I had never met anyone like this during my twenty years in the seminary and as a priest. It was one of those instant, magnetic, immediate attractions, and everything was interesting, funny, intelligent, endearing, and in depth. There were lighthearted expressions of deep feelings. We closed the place still talking.

She lived three blocks away but it was two in the morning. I ended up driving her home and much to my surprise, kissed her on the lips. It seemed innocent enough, but for the first time in my life it enlightened me with an inner glow almost like a luminescent halo bursting out from the inside of me. I didn't quite know how to react, but as I drove back to Sacred Heart I recall that I felt God had sent me a special gift and I better both enjoy and explore this relationship.

The next morning, I was busting out all over with smiles of joy and frowns of guilt. I guess it was written all over my face because several people I dealt with that day remarked that they had never seen me so up and down.

I really don't want to write another story about a priest falling in love and then trying to make that great decision whether or not to leave the active ministry and renounce the vocation. Let it be said that I did fall in love. I did consider a change but it lasted only a matter of hours and I was back on the track to ministry. It was more than a challenge, one that was only overcome, I'm sure, by prayers and her good sense—the sense to realize that our relationship was not going beyond what we had enjoyed.

Still, it was easier said than done. We continued to work together producing a weekly show and we started spending more time with each other outside of work. Liz played softball and I went to her games. She was really good at tennis. On Sundays she and I would hit the courts, then have pizza and go for hot fudge sundaes at Ghirardelli and walk along the wharf. We had lots of laughs as well as soul searching talks about the future and what we might be able to do as a team, a couple. As much as I would like to relate all those beautiful moments we shared over such a brief time, I really didn't have it in me to cast a shadow over all the work I've been able to do as a priest.

When you make a promise that you're going to live a celibate life and all of a sudden there's someone in your life that you think about, and your mind is captivated by that person, you invariably end up thinking about that promise. My thoughts became more and more intense so certainly my relationship with God became more and more intense—because I was being led down a road that would lead to a fork. So I prayed about it a lot. I thought about it every day. I prayed at Mass. It only went away when you were doing something else, reaching out to other people.

I thought about my mother. If she were here today, what would I say? I'm in love enough to be able to share my failings and my successes with her. I would want her to support me in my life whatever my choices. I was in love, but more in love with priesthood than a person.

Pride in priesthood is not sustaining.

It wouldn't last if I . . .

My brothers. . . What would my brothers think? Do they love me or what I am as a priest? Pause for thought.

You fill a role for the people in the parish. They expect something from you as their priest, not as a human being. The relationship is spiritual and distant and also dependable. Charlie and Johnny and their families looked to me as Father more than brother or uncle.

Eventually, Lizzie decided to move back to Santa Barbara. Her father had retired and her parents lived there, and the rest of her family were all close by. Letters flew back and forth between Liz and my confidante, Joan Ohanneson. They had gotten to know each other and became friends at ACC.

"You and Lizzie were made for each other for life," Joan used to say, which didn't help me particularly.

I lost another significant person in my life not long afterward. My Chicago colleague Bob Kennedy died that November from cancer. He was forty-one years old. It had been more than two years since I had last seen him but his death came as a big shock. He had been a mentor to me and had he lived and gone on to *Good Morning America* in New York I am sure he would have furthered my media career.

If you didn't like the sound of my voice, you would not want to turn on any radio or television in San Francisco on a Sunday morning. Up at five, I would go to KYUU-FM and broadcast live from 6:00-9:00 a.m.. Then I would listen to my pre-recorded self on KNBR while driving to Sacred Heart for the ten o'clock Mass. Following the Mass, I could catch any number of my one-minute spots that aired on KFRC. I would be home in time to catch my show on KRON-TV at one in the afternoon. Then it would be a long dry spell before Sunday night at nine when once again I could be heard on KCBS-FM. The market was still covered during those days by virtue of all free airtime and I had the privilege of doing whatever I could and, by the grace of God, a lot of good for lonely people who listened to the radio.

Sunday mornings on KYUU

We did hundreds if not thousands of radio and television programs at ACC. We saturated the market. If you were in San Francisco during those years and didn't know Father Miles and Father Harry, it was your fault. We had lots of publicity and lots of friends in the media world. We did weddings, funerals, baptisms and graduations for so many people who simply knew us from the airwaves. At one point, I referred to myself as "marrying Harry" because of the calls I got when people would say to themselves, "Oh, I know a priest—let's get that guy from KFRC."

As Archbishop McGucken used to tell Miles, "I'm not sure

what you're doing there, but keep it up. People are talking and affected."

I met these two cops one night after recording in the Transamerica building. There was a restaurant and bar near the mezzanine of the Pyramid called Ripples. It was unusual because in the men's room above the urinals there were TV monitors and they were not advertising anything. They all had funny sayings and you stood there being entertained while relieving yourself. It is my recollection that they also had TV cameras in the waiting room outside the women's bathroom and those monitors were at the bar, but there were too many embarrassing moments for this to catch on.

My two cop buddies were so familiar with the neighborhood and Chinatown that they invited me to backrooms and bars where tourists would never go. They were good guys. Both had gone to Catholic schools and were great emissaries for San Francisco law enforcement. One of them was a motorcycle cop and I would see him now and again watching the streets and patrolling for the filming of the famous Quinn Martin production *The Streets of San Francisco*. I got the opportunity to play the part of a priest on a couple of episodes and enjoyed the experience. I was able to meet Karl Malden and the young Michael Douglas in his prime.

Whenever I went to AFRTS in Hollywood, I would try to catch up with Lizzie. I never really seriously went back to try and refuel the fire of our love, but I did see her a couple of times a year. Each time we both felt something that moved us, but it wasn't enough to return to where we were in our relationship in San Francisco.

In all my years as a priest, I've never enjoyed living with an individual more than I did with Father Dan Sullivan. He was a recovering alcoholic, chaplain for the fire department, a native son of San Francisco and a genuine good guy. I looked forward to getting up in the morning just to watch him do the crosswords and have him ask me what I was doing that day. He never failed to show a greater interest in me than he did in himself. He had so many stories about his disease and what it had done to him. But that's his life and those stories are not mine to tell.

His best advice to me was when the telephone would ring in the middle of the night and I would answer and listen to some poor soul who, while the cubes were tinkling in the glass, would review their entire life. I would be up for an hour or two thinking I was doing God's work.

Next morning Dan would say, "Who was on the phone so long?"

"I don't know, someone who needed a kind word and a large ear."

He would laugh at me and remind me in a gentle manner that when the person hung up they would go to sleep and never remember a word they said or heard from me. I, on the other hand, would now have to drag my body, with the toothpicks still propping up my eyelids, and go to work for ten hours and then come home exhausted. Chances are the phone would ring again the next night. Dan assured me, and I believed him, that I was wasting my time counseling late at night with anyone who was already in their cups.

Other rings during the night were from the firehouse dispatcher alerting Dan that a fire was at such and such address. It was usually in our neighborhood and often because people still smoked in bed and fell asleep with lighted cigarettes. I'll never forget the one building, just kitty-corner to the church, which served as a cheap motel (flophouse) for any number of derelicts. The firemen all knew the building by heart and it was just routine when they were called there. It gave me a chance to put on the white chaplain's hat and stand near the trucks and watch the action. Coming from a small town and never having witnessed such activity, it was quite a thrill.

I can still see one man clinging to his little black and white TV, hanging from the window exhorting the firemen to get his big ass outta there. They put up the giant ladder and rescued him but would not let him bring along his TV. He was crushed. It might have been all he really had.

I got to know a few firemen in those years and knew the ones who had the disease even better, as they would come by the rectory before going back to work or their families.

Dan asked me one day if I owned a gun.

"Sure. I have a .22 caliber that was given to me in Missouri."

"Well, you don't have it any more. I gave it to the police to melt down."

It happened that one of our guests was thinking about suicide. He went into my room, found the gun but couldn't find any bullets. He put the gun under his pillow and went shopping for some ammo. The housekeeper discovered the pistol before he returned and a disaster in the rectory was averted. I really didn't miss the firearm. It was part of my past. I haven't touched a gun since, nor do I intend to.

Gun control is so much in the news these days. I have nephews who all have more than one gun but they hunt and use the guns for sport. To listen to them talk, you would think they were ready to go to war.

I remember Governor Jerry Brown of California talking about the rampant gun violence across the Bay in Oakland. He said when we send guys to jail for using guns they usually spend the time planning how to get even when they got out. They return to the same location, the same house, the same family even, to get their revenge. That leads to more shooting and more killing and, what's worse, more danger for the people who live in those areas.

The land of the free has the highest incarceration rate in the world. The walls and barriers keep getting higher and shinier with the barbs that glisten in the sunlight. We need to spend more time getting to know each other outside those walls rather than simply looking over them and preparing ourselves to explode with vengeance.

The Golden Rule about doing unto others what they've done for you gets all mixed up. That expression is about love and was never meant to be twisted into an endorsement of revenge.

Business was booming at ACC. I was hosting a new TV show Sunday mornings on KRON called *Tell-A-Vision*. It was a half-hour program where I tried to point out positive things and good news stories that viewers were only getting a tiny slice of from the typical news shows. "If it bleeds, it leads." I don't know where I heard that but it has been proven true for so many news shows that dominate the airwaves.

Father Harry with his Gabriel Award

Tell-A-Vision was unique for its time and, I might add, quite popular. It was done on a shoestring with mostly volunteers who were trying to make their way onto the communications scene. After Lizzie left ACC, Kathleen Emrey took her place as my producer. Mike O'Leary and Jim Swanson were under Kathleen. We're all still friends to this day.

One day I hosted Don Novello, whose portrayal of Father Guido Sarducci, a Catholic priest from the Vatican, was all the rage. He was very clever and very funny. One of his bits he did on my show was an observation of the different methods of capital punishment used at different times in history. Because of how Jesus died, Catholics make the sign of the cross. If Jesus had come later, the Padre wondered, would we be making the sign of the noose? Or the sign of the guillotine? The sign of the electric chair? I think you get what I mean.

There was a great deal of negative press and Archbishop McGucken got more than one letter about my show. I went to see Bishop Francis Quinn who at that time was still Father Quinn and pastor of the parish I would lead years later. His views were closely aligned with those of the present day pope, Francis. He was an activist who protested the death penalty, supported nuclear disarmament, immigrants, minorities and women in the Church. We walked around the block and within twenty minutes he had me feeling good about myself and about the decision I had made to have Padre Guido on the show.

Years later as a gag, I was asked to drive Don to a Robin Williams opening and people were questioned about who was the real priest (another occasion when I was glad the good sisters back in the monastery were praying for my vocation). I did a similar advertising promotion for J.C. Penney when they had William Christopher dressed as a chaplain like his Father Mulcahy character from the very popular TV show *M*A*S*H* about medics in the Korean War.

I always closed *Tell-A-Vision* with the Storytellers Prayer that I copied from a book. It was anonymous then, but today the Internet credits it to Mrs. Bruce Cramni, one-time president of the National Story League:

> *Show us, O Lord, how each life may be a story told in the beauty of truth, open through the wages of friendship, revealed by the spirit of love, yielded to the joy of service.*

That prayer has provided me with many a homily during my priestly life. The words are ripe with spirituality. Since we all have a beginning, a middle and an end, we all have a story.

I'm not sure I could even spell it, but it happened to me and taught me a few good lessons. It's not a broken neck but it was close enough to scare the devil out of me. I know, I know, I could use a few more frightening moments from Beelzebub.

It was a hard overhand serve that did it. I was in the park near the hospital playing tennis with Lizzie. I usually tried harder than I should to win but this was ridiculous. I served so hard that I twisted my neck. The next day I went to Detroit to accept some broadcasting awards. Carrying a heavy bag full of trophies made it very easy to injure the rest of my neck in such a way that it could only be repaired by a laminectomy.

I took all the drugs I could but to no avail. I still remember the Sunday afternoon when I told the pastor that I was in such pain that I couldn't watch the NBA finals on TV.

He knew me well enough to say, "Let me take you to the hospital."

Once in the hospital, the doctor immediately put me in

traction. I told him I had Mass at the Cathedral in a few hours.

He said, "No, you don't. You have an appointment with some pain pills, some nursing care and a thorough examination by a specialist."

I told him not to worry, I would be right back after Mass. It would only take a couple of hours. It was my turn to preach and we were drawing about 1,000 young people at our Sunday evening liturgy. It was fun, faith filled and fulfilling for all, but especially for the celebrant who could feel the spirit in the music and the participation of the kids. It was a great spiritual high of the goosebump kind and not repeated that often so if you had the chance you couldn't miss it.

Needless to say, I was not able to escape the hospital. In fact, they gave me some kind of drug that would not allow me to count to ten using all my toes. However, the pain subsided and I was resting comfortably. It didn't take the neurologist, Dr. Kenefick, long to tell me that he would have to do surgery and the sooner the better. By then I was fully aware that I would not be able to play or work with that kind of injury.

So, a laminectomy!

It was the first major surgery since what Dr. Ritter had done for me when I was twenty-two. (I had to tell that story. I just couldn't pass up one of the funniest happenings in my life.) The whole thing laid me up about six months.

Here's the lesson. Remember when Karl Marx said that religion was the opiate of the masses? He didn't use the word crutch, but that's what he meant. In that long period of recuperation, I wondered how people deal with such pain and helplessness without faith in God and the hope that is needed to look forward to healing. This doesn't even take into consideration the gift of charity or love that comes with a healthy mind and a healthy body. To feel miserable usually breeds more misery around you because of the lack of spirit. I can't imagine going through an ordeal like that again and not having the crutch of Catholicism to give me faith, hope and love.

During the recovery period after my neck surgery, I received a blue stationery envelope with a "Dear Harry" letter. Lizzie let me know that she understood (better than me) that what we had was so good, so special and so dynamite that the explosion which might come after would destroy us both. The little blue letter that said my relationship with her was over came down on me like a ton of bricks. I was taking pain pills and hurting but the emotions that I felt from the letter that I read over and over again were so debilitating that I just didn't feel like life was worth the struggle. I'm sure it was prayer and the sacrifices that so many had made on my behalf that helped me through those beautiful but challenging times.

I remember my brother's visit to San Francisco. Johnny and Betty made the trip out west to see me while I was recuperating from the spine surgery. We went to dinner at Scoma's and the hostess, Mary Ann, seated us at the best table in the house overlooking the Bay. I wanted to be very honest and up front with my brother. John loved me so much and was so proud I had become a priest that it really broke his heart to listen to me tell him I had fallen in love with a beautiful woman and had been so tempted to leave the priesthood.

I felt it was advantageous to my vocation and my life as a man that I had had this experience. I told him I was pretty solid there was no chance I was going to leave the priesthood because of her. I can still see the look on his face. I never talked to him about it after that, but always knew in my heart how disappointing it was for him. I felt at the time that it was very selfish on his part, but I don't think I ever appreciated how much he cared for me.

The little blue letter from Liz that said we were through had put me in touch with my feelings. As soon as I could manage travelling on my own, I headed south to see her. She was more beautiful than ever. I took her face between my hands and said what I hadn't put into words before. "I love you, Lizzie."

I drank a bottle of wine with her and again she told me she wanted me to leave the priesthood. Again, I said I couldn't. I had said no several other times but I had finally recognized what this limbo love would mean for her and her future. "It's time, Liz." I said quietly. "It's time for you to have a career, get married, have children."

I knew it was time for me to move on as well. My brush with mortality had re-connected me with the purpose for my existence. To have meaning, my life must revolve around God. If I forgot or abandoned that simple truth, or cast it aside, or became wrapped up in my own little world, then I would cease to exist.

Love for another . . . with Liz . . . with Dan Sullivan . . . brother John. God had opened my heart through love and I learned a secret about myself, one I'll never tell. *Love me as a brother.*

Eventually, I was able to keep up our friendship but put down our love. I met Lizzie's fiancé and there was never any jealousy of him. Our deal was over. He wasn't concerned about me. He didn't have an inkling about what had happened and I wasn't part of their life. I was glad she was marrying somebody because I wanted her to be happy and not mooning over what we had. We rarely spoke until she asked me to perform their marriage. I ended up officiating at Lizzie's wedding. It was a most difficult moment when I had to say the words of the vows and know they were meant for another man and not me.

Yes, I'm still good friends with both her and her husband and visit with them from time to time. I baptized their twins and years later was the celebrant for the son's wedding. I know that there will always be a place for her deep in my heart, but different. Joy for her happy marriage and her children is all I can muster for someone who meant so much at an especially vulnerable time of my life.

14. No Matter Where You Go

IT WAS AN OLD MAN in Arkansas who once said to me, "No matter where you go, there you are." I held his wisdom as gospel.

The Sunday night youth Mass at St. Mary's Cathedral had morphed its way into a family Mass, as more and more moms and dads wanted to come and bring the rest of their children. Soon, we were trying to please older people and we lost our true identity. It didn't help that the pastor of the Cathedral at that time was eager for us to find another church to hold our services. The associate pastor used to tell on the kids with Coke in the Cathedral, or the young adults smoking in the back, and the pastor would get all upset. We went to Mission Dolores with a new musical group of young black singers and lost our rock & roll identity. It was now more gospel-oriented and the crowds dwindled. We had to make a decision whether to continue with this Mass or go to mass media and give the bulk of our attention to radio and TV. We decided to move on. It was much less satisfying but we were able to reach so many more people. The TV Mass I still do today dates back to the late '70s when Miles offered it Sunday after Sunday.

My personal life was interrupted about this time by a religious woman who worked for us at the Archdiocesan Communications Center. She was a good lady who came from a wonderful family and just got mired in feelings for me that were not mutual. It was one of those love/hate relationships where one moment I would be her knight in shining armor and then I'd turn out to be the back of the horse he rode in on.

She showed up everywhere I did, including Mass away from the convent where she resided. I finally went to her superior and asked for advice. It was evident to me and to my close friends that this would be a major hit to Sister's ego and possibly a stumbling block for her dedication to the religious life. It was. When she was asked to leave her job at ACC, it was too much to

173

bear. She was assigned to different work in a different part of the state. I never heard from her nor saw her again.

I know these kinds of relationships happen every day but until you are personally involved, they don't seem to register. This could be a real weakness of the Catholic priesthood. There are so many of us being so busy coaching people that we forget about the game itself. We could set up a game plan and write it on the board but have not experienced it ourselves.

Padre Guido Sarducci used to chastise the pope in a mock Italian accent, "You no play-a the game, you no make-a the rules." Remember the priest who could prove on the blackboard that kissing was a serious sin? Finally a young lady challenged him and proved it wasn't.

I recall one day when I was playing the part of the priest in an episode of *The Streets of San Francisco*. We were shooting a scene at San Francisco State University about a young woman who was getting off the bus and then was raped and murdered on campus. My part in the scene was to go down on one knee and bless the body of the deceased then greet the detectives as I departed. I had a total of about five seconds on camera.

If you know film production, you know that it takes hours to prepare and get the scene just like the director wants it. During that time I became very friendly with the young lady who played the part of the corpse. She was excited to be in the show and have a CU, a close-up, of her face on national television. As the day went on I offered to drive her to the airport and keep in touch as I felt she would one day soar to stardom. Not so.

During the first take the director yelled, "Cut! Father Harry, you're staring at the victim."

She was cute. I was distracted. The director instructed one of the producers to take the sheet and completely cover the corpse. So much for the young starlet's desired close-up. No, I did not take her to the airport. She would not talk to me after the incident and so the "cover up" ended our relationship.

It did not curb my interest in film.

Working fourteen-hour days and nights had its advantages. It was hard to be left behind and there were plenty of creative minds around to keep us all challenged. There were always five to ten conscientious objectors who were doing their service time with us at the ACC. Most of them had artistic talents and all of us were pretty much against the war in Vietnam. Even though I had once volunteered to go there with the Marines, now I saw things differently. I was never again going to own a gun. I still have a bad feeling around them and even though I come from a gun-toting family of hunters, I shall not return to that sport. Killing fish is enough for me. After all, it is said by some of my friends, because of their cold blood, they feel no pain. I wonder why, then, when you land them they flop around so much and you have to club them so you can remove the bloody hooks that protrude from their gums. I'll never really know.

Sometimes I broke up those long days by getting on the old elevator and going down to the street to get on the even older streetcars and head toward the waterfront where there were many movie theaters. There were very few good movies. In fact, it was my first lesson in really bad grade B movies. They mostly depicted ignorant blacks, crooked cops, rich white slavers and scantily clad women. They had no redeeming value that I could see although I confess it took me awhile to stop going. If I learned anything from them, it was that I could make a movie. I saw many films during that period of my life and most of them were late at night when there were very few patrons.

Miles and I were still trying to crack the stained-glass ceiling with a mainstream hit. We tried to replicate the success we'd had with *The Priest*. It took a few years for us to garner enough money to produce *Sister*.

We didn't want to tell the story of how Sister gets up at 5:30 every morning, brushes her teeth, goes to Mass, grabs her books and teaches class all day. We wanted to tell the story from the point of view, POV, of people whose lives were affected by sisters. Something like, "Sister Rosemary is such a wonderful person. She teaches my kids and helps them learn. She deals with sick people and never gets sick." We were thinking students, patients, kids in orphanages and pregnant girls.

There were two problem we hadn't anticipated. One was that religious life was waning at the time we were making this picture. Sisters weren't fostering young girls' vocations any more. There were more co-ed schools because of fewer religious teachers and the expenses tied to lay teachers. The other issue was that different orders of sisters had different charisms. If you wanted to be a religious woman, but didn't want to teach, you wouldn't be interested in the Sisters of the Presentation of Mary. You would choose the order that, say, had a charism for working with the poor. Or if you wanted to be a nurse, that would be the Daughters of Charity, like those who taught my sister, Della.

It did not go so well as by this time the interest in female religious life had waned. All the older women were now retired in homes and the younger ones were not particularly interested in teaching for peanuts in the Catholic school system. It was a whole new era for Catholic schools with the religious orders leaving and salaried lay teachers taking their place.

It cost $10,000 to make *The Priest*. *Sister* cost $12,000 and was far less interesting. It was used as a tool for vocation directors, and we used it as an insert inside our show *Mosaic* and talked about vocations in Des Moines.

Our big joke after the dull thud of *Sister* was that we would make a sequel and call it *Son of Priest and Sister*. Lo, these many years later, it is not so far-fetched. In fact my friends whom I wrote about earlier fit the bill.

The famous basketball player Rick Barry was a guest on my show *Tell-A-Vision*. He was quite a star in his time and not very likeable to the general public. His talent however could not be denied. I went to the Oakland Coliseum when the Golden State Warriors were practicing and played one-on-one with Rick. We shot B-roll, the images shown while the talking head gives information, for the upcoming show. We edited the film so that when Rick shot and missed (rarely) I would rebound and make my shot. It was easy to do in post-production so I really did learn a little bit about film-making.

I had a chance to visit with Rick many years later, sitting in Franklin Milieu's box seats at a 49ers game. I told him about the video wizardry and it was like he never heard me. He knew he was a great athlete and he also knew that I was not. It was silly to imagine that anyone would be fooled by a little editing.

The following week on the show, I entertained the great rock impresario Bill Graham. I had an early morning appointment at his office ahead of time and the first thing that struck me was the overwhelming display of awards. He must have gotten one for everything he ever did. The walls were plastered with gold records and autographed pictures and what seemed like an endless display of proclamations. Every table and available flat space was covered with trophies and more pictures signed by important artists.

Bill himself could not have been more affable. We had a few laughs about his Jewish background and my Roman Catholic presence in the middle of rock & roll and then went on to our business. I was there to give him a heads-up on the questions I might be asking during the program.

That man had answers for questions I never asked. He was an absolute genius about the work he did. There was no star big enough and no act beyond his reach. He could put together shows and make something out of nothing. That is the true definition of creation (to make something from nothing). His interview consisted mostly of me nodding my head in dumbfounded agreement and complete admiration for what he had to say.

I also was working on a TV piece featuring the homegrown band Journey and wanted to see if the interviews could be done from their trailer. No problem. Bill said he would arrange for backstage passes. There I was at the Oakland Coliseum the night of the concert watching Steve Perry and the others go through an old trunk of throw-away clothing to see what they were going to wear on stage. I got to spend time with all of them and then watched the performance from backstage. It was deafening and a sellout. They were climbing the charts on the way to the top. I always felt that Bill Graham made all that happen. He was a powerful man in a powerful business at the time.

While I'm at it, how about Gideon & Power? You probably don't remember them, but Gideon Daniels was a first class guy who didn't make a lot of money at his craft but who had feelings to the depths of his toes and could make music for the masses. He put together a show for *Tell-A-Vision* that included a piece about flowers. He called it "flowers while you live." The whole idea was to have a party for close friends while they were still alive when they could actually smell the flowers and admire their beauty.

How many bodies have you seen in funeral parlors and churches covered with flowers and the person they are for is incapable of appreciating their beauty and fragrance? Gideon put this to music. On one occasion, we staged a party like that for Miles' mother who very much appreciated what had been done. She did indeed enjoy the scent and the beauty that surrounded her. When she really did pass I recall seeing flowers again but they didn't seem to make as much sense around the coffin as they did the way Gideon presented them.

NBA All-Star Jerry Lucas was brilliant. I have no idea what his I.Q. was but I do know from experience that he could remember almost everything. He walked in the studio and shook hands and greeted my entire audience by name, first and last. We did the show and then he stood there in front of the set and said good-by to each and every one of them by first and last name. My mouth was agape as I stood in amazement and heard him say without a stammer or a stumble the names of more than forty people.

He told me that there was a lot of downtime in professional basketball when you really didn't know what to do with yourself. He would take city telephone books and memorize them. You might have seen him do the same on Johnny Carson or another talk show. But when you saw it live and in person, it took on a whole new meaning. He also memorized the entire Bible. I had only to give the name and the number and he would launch into chapter and verse with a wry smile knowing how much I was impressed.

These are a few names of the many people who made an impression on my life while I was growing up and still have their effect. I was not much at memorizing and I know how important it is to recall people's names after you have met them. Ask any successful politician or bishop and they'll usually be blessed with that kind of a talent. My skill for recalling names is very limited. That would surely have been an episcopal disqualifier in my early days. Today, it doesn't really matter as I see some of the hierarchy who dodge the chance to meet their flock. Sad.

I jumped at the chance to meet some far-flung members of my radio flock.

I love Australia. I love everything about it—the people, the customs, the accent, the land, the water and all that it entails. Maybe this comes from my childhood mental and spiritual fascination with incarceration (that still continues). After all, the whole blooming country was pretty much put together by ex-cons who were banished there because they were corrupting civilization with their wicked presence.

My first trip came as a result of the popularity of my radio work as Father Harry of the God Squad. The show had been picked up by several stations down under and one in particular, 3DB. They brought me over first class on Air New Zealand with room to sleep and sheep's wool blankies to keep me warm and cozy. It was my first experience with such a long ride and the conveniences and having so much TLC made it an outstanding trip.

In exchange for the gratuity, I assisted the radio station with their annual fund-raising effort for the Royal Children's Hospital Appeal on Good Friday of Holy Week. The entire country, literally everyone, stops to remember not only the death of Jesus Christ on the cross, but also all the sick little children suffering and dying in hospital and the poor families who cannot afford the critical care their children need. The media makes an all out full-court press recruiting as many celebrities and top personalities to visit the medical facilities, as well as urging each and every citizen to dig a little deeper to support the effort. 3DB was no exception.

The morning DJ, Ric Melbourne, was an absolute wacko on the radio. He left very little to the imagination when it came to entertaining an audience and holding them for the better part of the morning as they weaved in and out of traffic and loaded themselves onto all sorts of transport to get to work. A morning with Melbourne in Melbourne would bring a smile to your face or a tear to your eye if he were advocating a cause.

I was asked to sit in with him for a few days to get to know the audience, take some phone calls and be the set-up man for Ric. He used phrases on me, which I never fully grasped, like "shaking hands with the unemployed" nor did I have an inkling as to how deep into the mud I was going. The station manager did and on several occasions asked him to tone it down. Ric and

I became close friends and remain so today. I've baptized two of his sons and spent time with his family both over there and in the United States.

On one occasion, I was asked to interview a famous television personality. It was early morning and Ric and I had been laughing and cutting up for more than an hour. Into the studio steps this elegant looking gentleman with an entourage of assistants. He made his way to the guest microphone, put on the headset and smiled at me with a warm greeting, "So you're the famous disc jockey priest?"

"Yes, thank you," I responded, then naïvely asked, "Now what is it you do?"

Little did I know that he was an entertainment legend. He was on the air over the entire country five nights a week. Not only was he the Johnny Carson of late night Australian TV, he hosted the first national show and had had a number one music program on television for nearly a decade. It wasn't until a day or two later and a number of sly references to my ignorance of the "man" that I started noticing his face on billboards and in magazines and his name in general conversation. He was such a kind and professional man, that he took my oversight with good grace and actually had some fun with it. I will never forget Graham Kennedy's genuine acceptance of my faux pas. Just like many classy entertainers, he recognized that, being from another country, I wouldn't be familiar with Australian celebrities. I appeared on several national TV shows that year but, alas, not his.

The ultimate judgment of my success or failure was that my popularity in Australia spread. The number of radio stations airing my work soared along with the invitations to return the following year. This left a very good taste in my mouth for the country that is so supportive of Americans and most of our politics and people.

On the way back, I went to Japan. I spent about two weeks "in country"—that's what they call it when you are overseas and doing time in the service—and finally ended up in Tokyo for one last appearance before my flight home. The programming guys were always telling me about how popular I was with the Japanese teens in country. After a long morning prepping work for a TV show that I was going to appear on that afternoon, I took a walk along the streets of Tokyo. It was just before noon and as I approached a stoplight, I paused and I could hear my voice on a car radio, blasting away about some new group that I really loved. Then I passed some kids on the sidewalk with a boombox and they too were listening to Father Harry.

My chaperone later told me that I was taped and translated into Japanese. I still have the little booklet with English on one side and Japanese on the other and an audio cassette of *Love on the Rock*. My spots were used as a learning guide for youngsters wanting to improve their English skills. If Father Moon Mullen, my English professor in the seminary, knew I would be an influence in that regard, he would have canceled his subscription to the English language and put in for a transfer to the real moon. My chest was bursting with pride as I made my way along the streets of Tokyo, thrilled that the young boy with terrible English skills was now being imitated by kids in Japan. But the real story follows.

I was picked up by a producer and a Catholic chaplain and driven to a TV studio somewhere downtown. It was a Saturday afternoon music talk show aimed at teenagers. I had my little pitter-patter all set to wow them. There was a live audience with a lot of kids screaming and yelling the star's name. Sorry, I never got it. They played an excerpt from one of my spots and then there was applause.

What happened afterward was all in Japanese and translated by some young guy who spoke so fast I hardly knew what was coming next. But here's the gist of it.

"Father Harry, why you call yourself father?"

Fair enough question. I explain and it's translated. "Father" is a traditional Roman Catholic title for a priest.

"Ahh! Father Harry, if you call yourself father, why you have no children?"

So I start over. It's then I realize that I might as well just smile and give the impression that I'm having a really good time. I was at the mercy of the translator and the host.

It was a good lesson for me. I thought I was in control. I didn't even speak their language. The laughs and misunderstanding were on me. After that experience, I returned to the hotel and waited for my ride to the airport, but not without lots of smiles of realization that I was in another country.

It was the same year *Billboard* magazine gave me the honor of "Radio Personality of the Year." I went to a dinner and got a plaque. I have no idea where it might be today. I know that my producer Frank Cangialosi was very pleased.

Dr. Don Rose was scolding me. "You're a priest! What do you mean about this not being a miracle?"

He was the KFRC morning man and a nationally known personality. At one time he was the highest paid radio jock in the country. He had suffered a heart attack in 1972 and some unfortunate surgery cost him the use of his leg. Even after eleven operations, the limb was frozen as his knee would not bend. It was difficult but not impossible for him to maneuver. He was also an easy mark for a slippery piece of fruit on the sidewalk.

I had become very close with Don, his wife, Kae, and their children. The closer I got to them, the more we talked about miracles and what might happen to restore his leg to full capacity. I was working at KRON-TV at the time and together we came up with the idea of making a pilgrimage to Lourdes. I had been there during my Roman days and experienced the profound power of the Marian shrine.

At first, there was great hesitation at the station because it seemed more for Catholics and not very exciting. However, when I introduced the possibility of a miraculous component, the program director began to salivate. He knew of Dr. Don, as did anyone who lived in Northern California at the time.

We put together a crew and off we went to France. Our time there was joyous and exciting. Don took the famous plunge into the waters of the River Gave de Pau and immediately felt warmth and change in his body. I was with him and saw a difference. But miracle, I thought, no way. He was eager to share the news with his family and with great joy we departed from the holy grounds of Lourdes. Up to that point, Don had relied heavily on his cane and a brace for walking. Following his holy dip he said he would no longer need it.

We returned to California and he went to see his doctors for X-rays and got the good news. They could not explain it, but the bone in his leg was healing in a way that they thought was never possible. We shot the end of the video on a golf course where he sank a long putt.

First Class Miracle aired that Christmas, won several awards including an Emmy and generated a new interest in that little village in southern France. KRON even submitted the documentary for the Peabodys. For my part, I didn't really need a miraculous occasion or magic to deepen my faith. Frankly, I was still incredulous, but deeply pleased that my friend Dr. Don had what we prayed for and asked God to do for him through the intercession of Mary the Mother of God.

I suppose there are few events in American history like the mass suicide that took place in Jonestown, Guyana, in 1978.

I was living at Sacred Heart parish on the corner of Fell and Fillmore, about six or seven blocks from the Peoples Temple where the magnetic preacher Jim Jones carried on every week. In fact, he was so good that the nuns who taught in our grade school at Sacred Heart would ask me to go lightly on the Sunday homily so that they could make the twelve o'clock service at the Jones temple down the street.

I never attended in person, but from time to time was keen to give it a shot. I used to drive by and in the back lot I could see that the congregation had begun collecting things to ship or take with them to the South American nation, which was to be their new home as a Christian community. Pastor Jim must have been some kind of preacher to pull off what he did. It's unimaginable. I can't for the life of me figure it out.

There was a popular magazine at the time called *New West*. In August of 1977, a feature article about Jones called "Inside Peoples Temple" was published. When Jones got wind of the impending exposé he fled to his Guyana outpost and began evacuating his followers from the City by the Bay to Jonestown. By the time the story broke, more than 700 believers had left their lives behind for the Promised Land setting the stage for the horrors to come.

The co-author called me shortly after his article appeared

and began to nose about my business. He interviewed my friends and co-workers in search of dirt so that he could smear me before I ran off with my little media audience and committed some terrible crime.

I'll never forget my first visit to the Press Club of San Francisco and having lunch with this guy. He then coaxed me up to a private room for a game of pool. I was neither fond of pool nor a player of any great shakes. After a few balls fell into the pockets, he began to inquire about my pockets and how full they were from the three radio shows and the two TV shows that I was doing. I think he thought it was a slam-dunk that he had another celebrity preacher in his sites and was ready to pull the trigger.

Little did he know that all of my work was public service and I was lucky if production costs were paid. Getting rich as a priest takes an unusual talent. "After all," I told him, "If I were rich, I'd be dangerous." Only one more interview followed and that was the end of that. *New West* magazine soon faded and I never heard from that reporter again.

I had a similar experience with *People* magazine. They shadowed me for two days taking pictures and the person doing the interview was supposed to follow up. The telephone never rang. I was left with some lovely black and white glossies. Special to me was one of me sitting at my desk with the dog, Cesar, who lived in our rectory. I was wearing my black robe, petting the black dog and over my desk was a radiant picture of an angel.

It happened to be one of Charlie's three angels, Farrah Fawcett. She was a hot item at the time and her poster with the long, flowing blond hair reminded me of one of my nieces. Anyway, it made the shot and I thought, "Oh no! What if it appears in the magazine?" It wasn't exactly like having a picture of Mary or a crucifix above my desk.

By the way, the dog was named after Cesar Chavez, the great Catholic immigrant worker who changed the lives of farm laborers in California.

Father Harry in his office at Sacred Heart

When I first moved out West, I couldn't get enough of the delicious, inexpensive grapes the likes of which were seldom seen in Missouri. Miles took me to task.

"Harry! You can't eat the grapes!"

I was mystified. They'd been washed. They tasted great. I couldn't imagine what the problem was. That's when I learned about the plight of the farmworkers and Cesar Chavez.

I never met the man, but I admired him from afar as his courage and foresight were out there for all to see. In the early '70s, there was doubt as to whether he would succeed in his mission or fade away like many other protagonists of worthy causes. This man not only followed his political and social ideals, but dressed them in a firm and fervent spiritual life that has led some to believe that he is one of our modern saints. I wouldn't go that far.

Oh, the dog! Yes, he was a huge Great Dane with a wonderful personality. He was coal black and his ears had been fixed so they pointed to the sky. It was the first time I had ever lived with a dog and the first time I learned to love one. On Sunday afternoons, I would take him to South Beach for a run and he obeyed me like I had trained him all my life. He did trash the backseat of my car as sand and saltwater were too difficult to clean off him once he had his exercise.

There was a sign on the front door of the rectory. It said, "Beware of the Dog!" It was a rough neighborhood and the owner of the dog bought him so that there would be some visible protection around the residence. I always thought the sign should read "Be Aware of the Dog" because he was such a fine animal.

Cesar grew older during my time there and at the end, an elderly priest moved in to live with us and used to feed him cookies late at night while he was watching Creature Features. That meant that poor Cesar couldn't hold himself during the night and always left a warm greeting at the front door for whoever had the early service. Remember, this was a large dog. It was no small matter to clean up that pile before Mass. Disinfectant and a shovel were in order.

I once sat at the kitchen table helping the sextant of the parish with funeral arrangements. His twin brother had passed the day before and we were talking about the service. He was so upset and his emotions were running wild, when all of a sudden he turned white and to stone and keeled over at the table. He knocked over his coffee and flipped the spoon high in the air.

I was trying to revive him when the elderly Irish priest (the one who loved late night snacking) said to him, "George, would you be having some chest pains? I would go up the three flights of stairs for me own heart pills, but I would be afraid I could not make it down in time."

He was right. George was dead. We had a double funeral service that week for twins. It was a first for me.

That year saw a double funeral for popes as well. When *humane vitae* arbiter Pope Paul VI died it was not completely unexpected. The death of successor John Paul I two months later was a shock. With the election in October of the future saint John Paul II (dashing my hopes for a Pope George Ringo), 1978 became the first year since 1605 with three popes. Conspiracy theories abounded. The phenomena entered pop culture and urban legend. People dressed as popes for Halloween.

When Harvey Milk and George Moscone were shot at City Hall in San Francisco, I was in my office only three blocks away working on some radio scripts. The sirens and commotion outside the Fifty Oak building were too numerous and blaring to set aside or not notice. On went the radio and the TV and, sure enough, our worst thoughts for something crazy at City Hall had happened.

A group of us ran down the four flights of stairs and into the street only to join people gathering peacefully from all over the City. Candles burned in memory and sympathy outside the magnificent building whose dome was like St. Peter's in the Vatican. I didn't feel I had any anything to offer the group, so I went back to the office and prayed for the two murdered men and the perpetrator.

I didn't really know the Moscone family. My good friend and radio producer, Louise Molinari, knew them well and we talked about them. It was a great blow for her to know the widow closely and appreciate her loss. Years later I attended the Super Bowl at Stanford between the Niners and the Dolphins. I recall going by to pick up people at the Moscone home but never really got to know them.

I never had occasion to meet Harvey Milk. I'm sorry we never crossed paths. He moved to San Francisco the same year I did and we were almost certainly in the same neighborhood near Most Holy Redeemer when I first arrived.

George Moscone, Harvey Milk and Dan White were strangers to me, but White's wife was a longtime acquaintance of mine. I had met Mary Ann Burns in Rome when she was a student and came to visit at the North American College with her best friend, Helen. My good friend Jim Purcell was Helen's brother. I saw Mary Ann again when I was a priest in Springfield. She and Helen drove from California to Missouri in a convertible and let me know they were coming. I met them in St. Louis and we spent some time together touring the sites. I prayed for Mary Ann and her infant son, prayed that the bullets had not ripped her family apart.

The tragedy at Jonestown ten days earlier was even more horrendous as it involved religion, worship, belief in God, and a fellow minister. I don't think I'll ever be able to see beyond those dark glasses of Reverend Jim and wonder how he became so attractive, even to my little congregation of Dominican Sisters who loved his messages. They liked his preaching (apparently better than mine), they thought he was charismatic and dynamic, and that he was filling the joint down there and I wasn't. They never really confided in me about their experience at the noon extravaganza. I think they probably felt I didn't want to hear or know that they were hoping our service would end so they could go down the hill on Fillmore Street to Geary. The Kool-Aid had not yet been introduced. Even today, when I feel someone is just "going along" and waiting to fail with an idea or an ideologue, I think to myself, "They're about to drink the Kool-Aid."

While I've not exactly laid down my life for my friends, I've certainly done my best to assist when and where I can.

Michael O'Leary, native son of San Francisco, was a butcher by trade and when lupus invaded his body, his body went south. After he was diagnosed, Mike had to give up his livelihood. He took several communications courses at San Francisco State and was looking for some kind of internship in television and radio production. It was a perfect fit as I needed help and he could only be paid a paltry sum or lose his disability benefits from the union. Both of us learned by trial and error.

We became good friends. He was the producer for my weekend shows at KYUU. I was on the air live from 6:00-9:00 a.m. Saturdays and until ten on Sundays. I got paid for that work and the money went into the ministry, so to speak.

A radio studio has two sides: one with all the equipment and the engineer where there is often panic and lots of running around to make sure the right stuff goes on the air; then a soundproof studio separated by thick glass where only the talent and guests are present with the microphone. There's a "cough switch" in case bad words are uttered or to address the guest without the audience listening in.

One time my friend Warren Mullen had offered me a free trip to Hawaii. He worked with us at ACC. I had an eleven o'clock flight on a Sunday morning, so I wasn't going to be able to stay for the whole program. I had to leave the radio station by eight-thirty. Mike had to come from the other side of the glass and he was so nervous he almost wet his pants. The next thing you know, I'm aboard Pleasant Holidays in first class with my earpiece listening to my good friend subbing for his friend who had suddenly taken ill.

Father Harry on the air at KYUU

Mike went on the road with me to Idaho as my producer. I had been invited to speak at Boise State University. My God Squad spots aired on KBBK-FM there and I drew big crowds for two appearances at the Student Events Center. Later that same summer, Mike was my producer when I returned to Australia.

My second sojourn to the environs Down Under included several side trips to different cities and introductions to a great many new faces and eventual friends who were very supportive of my radio work. The God Squad had landed safely and the followers were numerous. 3DB radio in association with

Channel 7 arranged a stage appearance for me at one of the local theaters. I had Mike O'Leary and his wife, Barbara, along to assist me. It was a sold out event and I believe well received. I signed many autographs and sold a fair number of audio cassettes. But the highlight of my visit was a press conference held that noon at a quite popular restaurant and wine bar called Churchers.

My driver was a very attractive producer and employee of the station and as we drove up I noticed a shiny Harley-Davidson at the entrance. Apparently in Australia there was another God Squad, a large group of motorcyclists who biked around the country doing good works. We took pictures and shared stories and the Melbourne papers had a field day covering a Catholic priest with a bunch of bikers. I loved it. When I read the story I felt good all over like Jesus mingling with people who were not accepted by the mainstream and frowned upon because they were bikers. This group was not exactly Hells Angels of California fame, but their Christian ministry was centered on the "outlaw biker fraternity."

It was also at this time that I was feeling pretty good again about my tennis game. A visit to the Sydney home of John Newcombe gave me the opportunity to see the "outback"—his backyard with a beautiful tennis court sheltered by trees and lush greenery so that his fame and fortune could not be observed by just anyone. "Newk" was a national hero and an international tennis star, winning sixty-eight career titles. He won nine of ten times at Wimbledon and was among the Top Ten players in the world for ten straight years. He achieved my still-unfilled dream of appearing on the cover of *Sports Illustrated*. I was invited to hit the ball around with his wife. It reminded me of my professional *calcio* debut in Florence when my buddy John Mahoney and I got to don the uniforms and join the *Gli Azzurri* on the field.

Mrs. Newcombe hit the ball and I chased it. She might as well have been playing with a golden retriever and after a stroke or two asking him to fetch. In this case there was nothing golden, but I was the one lurching and lunging for power balls that went left and right and never to me so that I could return. Needless to say, the invitation to continue play did not.

That experience was similar to one I'd had in Ireland when my buddy and I played golf with his cousin who was known to be the best left-hander in the county. After watching us play eight holes, he developed a toothache and left the course to us to pursue relief from another kind of pain. We never saw him again, but we inquired about his fame in the local pub that evening and sure enough, he played almost every day and was indeed the best left-hander. But as far as anyone knew, his teeth were perfect.

It is with fondness that I leave you with this tale, which happened on my way home. I had a layover in Tahiti. It was arranged by the radio station so that I could have a bit of R&R following the hectic schedule of the week before. My first mistake was buying a bathing suit in a sporting goods store where the clerk was insisting that I was shopping from the rack of women's running shorts. My French and his were so far apart. He was kind and tactful and I was, again, ignorant and set in my ways wanting that particular article.

I woke up early the next morning and walked to the beach hoping to do some snorkeling in the crystal water filled with exotic sea life. I got the snorkel gear and sallied forth in a dinghy to an island about 100 yards from the beach. It was filled with friendly people all of whom were sans swimsuits. I looked funny and felt funny and they were babbling in French. I'm sure the comments were not all complimentary. I did enjoy observing the wildlife both in the water and on the island. As they say, when in Rome...

On the second day in order to fit in, I skipped my suit and began swimming with the fish. After I was exhausted, I crawled up on the sand and proceeded to get my bottom burned. The flight home, even though first class, was a very uncomfortable one, which consisted of me scooting back and forth and standing in order to relieve the burn to my gluteus maximus that had fired up my entire *derrière*. Never again!

Bill Stewart was a giant in early radio and made an international name for himself in the world of jazz. My association with him became closer and closer, as he was an on-air personality for Armed Forces Radio. Bill was older now and producing his own shows. He programmed music for several airlines when they began offering that service for long flights across the country or the oceans.

With all that air time it's a wonder people were able to breathe. Those were the words of one of my producers. I never had writers. All I had to do was pay attention to life and what was around me.

Bill invited me to send him a tape of what I thought I might be able to offer. I did. I was able to parlay the work I'd done late at night in the Pyramid on KCBS into a format that fit Bill Stewart's company, Music in the Air. I used the "easy listening" format way ahead of its time, putting in lots of FM music that was relaxing and moody. Like the radio version, I called it *Lovenotes for Listeners*. It got me on every TWA flight around the world.

The whole idea was to assist travelers with the love that they might have left or the one they were going to meet. It was a format with little talk and a soothing voice that made people's face muscles relax. A slow smile might appear and you knew they were feeling something. People who travel frequently or rarely often have a serious purpose for boarding an airplane. Several hours with an open mind, a *tabula rasa*, make for fertile ground to sow with ideas of how much people mean to each other and how seldom they express it.

I was so excited when *Billboard* magazine came to me in the person of Bill Stewart asking if I was interested in doing the show for TWA. He was working in collaboration with the publication. The representative for the airline was to meet me at a luncheon on Sunset Boulevard in a place called Scandia. I didn't know it, but it was a hotspot for big names. The setting was perfect and I was "on." I wanted to impress. I probably had a martini and that helped. And I was celebrating my fortieth birthday.

The producer was a beautiful lady with auburn hair named Ona. She managed TWA's Cabin Entertainment program and specialized in captive audiences. I finally understood what people meant by bedroom eyes. It was an all-afternoon affair. TWA listened for three hours in the studio. I was driven to my hotel and still on fire with the excitement of having a show on all of the TWA flights around the world.

She's in the next room. What wall do I have to go through to be there? I couldn't help myself and telephoned the producer and we talked for another few hours, about me mostly. I was energized. As I said, women have a way of making others feel good about themselves. She and I became very good friends. We grew closer and I found myself opening up to her in a way that I had never before experienced. We had what seemed like a psychic connection. This kind of communion with a woman introduced me to yet another aspect of God's love.

Years later, when Bill Levada became the Archbishop of San Francisco, he remarked time and again how much he enjoyed listening to his longtime friend from the North American College as he made his way back and forth to Rome on Trans World Airlines (now American Airlines, and who knows what they'll be when this is printed). People like Levada were usually eager to come or go and it was a good format for experiencing re-entry.

I didn't have the show long, as one of the most frequent routes of TWA at the time was New York City to Miami. You probably guessed. Lots of Jewish people on those planes. Letters arrived at TWA and Ona Burns, the executive producer for the show, had to tell me that in order to continue with the program by a priest, they would have to offer the same opportunity to both a rabbi and a Protestant minister. There was simply no budget available on the network for that kind of expansion. A good thing ended for me. I'm sure there were some wonderful seeds of love. I lost track of her over the years. She'll never know how much our friendship meant to me.

> *But grace was given to each of us according to the measure of Christ's gift.*
>
> Ephesians 4:7

15. Ebb Tide

IN 1979, THE CBS TELEVISION station moved into new studios on Battery at Broadway to be closer to downtown. Their old building on Van Ness Avenue had been the first in San Francisco built to be a TV station and the Westinghouse Corporation gave it to the Archdiocese as a tax write-off. We said good-by to Fifty Oak and ACC and we opened Bridge Productions in our very own television studios.

Miles was ready to move on, just not to Bridge. He felt he could better serve the Church by working in the chancery office instead of devoting his time and talent to public service projects. After working together for seven years, Miles and I went different ways. He became the head of the communications office and the spokesman for the Archdiocese. He was the go-to guy for interviews and I would see him regularly on the news.

Father Harry and the crew at ACC

We flourished in the old KPIX building. Bridge had a $500,000 budget and close to a dozen paid staff. Kathleen Emrey, Mike O'Leary, Jim Swanson and Warren Mullen, who was a talented artist and a Christian minister, were all being paid at Bridge. Father Ed Kaminsky was drawing a priest's salary. I was the Executive Director and I was drawing the same. We functioned like a mini ad agency but at rates well below the market because we were a non-profit. We were doing lots of public service work. We produced and I hosted a documentary called *Kids from Company "C"* about young cancer patients and it went on to win an Emmy.

That fall, my brother Charlie and his wife, Mary, came out to visit me and see San Francisco. It was his fiftieth birthday. The next day, I had an attack of kidney stones and went down like a rock. I fell to the floor and the doctor who lived three blocks away came to take care of me. I had to be force-fed liquid until it passed. It was the same day Charlie's first grandson was born to daughter Sheila and he was proud he had just become grandfather to a little boy.

Mike O'Leary was on his deathbed for the umpteenth time. Tubes were coming out everywhere and liquids and drugs were being pumped in. It looked like the final time that I would administer the sacrament of the sick to this poor guy who had lupus and was affected by just about everything he did or touched in life.

The lowest blow was when his wife, Barbara, told his mom and dad that she wanted a divorce so that she could get on with her own life. It seemed natural and normal, but under the circumstances, an incredible thought to have.

Mike's brother was holding his hand and verbally giving him every kind of encouragement to rally and come back to us. When I left the hospital that evening, I felt it would be the last time I would see him alive.

He finally got a new kidney from a guy who died on a motorcycle. Mike was rushed to the hospital and we followed him with cameras and documented it on *Tell-A-Vision*. Mike celebrates his birthday but the real celebration of life for him is the second day of June, when he went in for a kidney transplant and came out a new man. His hair returned along with the full use of his muscles and his bodily movement was restored.

After he got his new kidney it just changed his whole life. He got rid of most of the drugs and once again could have children, but by this time it was too late for Barbara who had left him while he was on his deathbed. She ended up marrying three more times and took up with his younger brother twenty years later. That didn't last either.

My friendship with Mike has grown in the nearly forty years I've known him and now we are the best of buddies. For the last ten years he's directed my TV Mass. He's a good director.

That same summer I said good-by to Sacred Heart. I loved Father Dan, but it had never been my parish. I'd been there seven years and I didn't know the names of the people in the pews. I'd greeted them and shaken their hands, but I never had been a part of their lives. I wanted to make more than friendships, I wanted lasting friendships.

I began living in the Marina district at St. Vincent de Paul. It was an unusual living situation as there were four priests in the rectory. The pastor was a retired colonel in the Air Force. He was in the position of authority and it was his home not mine. He was a frightening figure for the kids in his parish. I didn't want to become him. He always liked me because I worked for Armed Forces Radio. He predicted (incorrectly, thank God) that I would one day be a bishop. His premise was based on the fact that I still had hair. I had to remind him that bishops cover their heads with zuchetti, or little purple beanies, so the amount of hair does not really count.

The Colonel, as I called him, gave great sermons (not homilies). He always preached in a bellowing voice. He was an orator from the old school and not accustomed to using artificial means (like sound systems) for projection. He was the sound system. Poets and prophets were no match for this man who could recall almost word for word suitable phrases, which fit his Gospel preparation. He often dragged out old yellow paper, not yellow paper from legal pads that we're used to seeing, but white paper that had been stored away for so many years it was yellow and papyrus-like, as it had hardened over time. He taught me to save my notes so that I would never be short of a good sermon. He was giving me sound advice. Most people came up to me and said, "Thank you. You were a wonderful homilist."

"Going to the well" made it simple to extract from yesteryear what he thought was still a winner and an inspiration for the faithful. Most of the older people were accustomed to his style and mode of oratory. However, many of the young people moving into the Marina at the time, as it was a hotspot for young singles, didn't quite have the same reaction. I think they thought he was colorful and interesting but really didn't have his finger on the pulse of the times or the young boomers, who were mostly from the East Coast and still looking for a place to pray. One that they could call home and let the folks know they had landed in a safe haven on their way to heaven.

I could tell numerous stories of my stay in that residence, but will conclude with this one. Toward the end of his life, the Colonel got a bit sloppy with his wine at noon and his cocktail at whatever time seemed cocktail time and the archbishop had to give him a warning.

"Monsignor, if you don't ease up on your drinking I'm going to have to make a change at your parish."

That was all he needed. He didn't have to go away to dry out or take a course or see a psychiatrist. He only had to be told that his priestly ministry was in danger of slipping away. From that time on I never saw him take another drink. He often treated me to big dinners on Sunday night at the Presidio and would have the chef heap huge amounts of meat on my plate and then tell the steward to pour more wine, never for him, only for me. I learned a lot from that man.

Now when I feel unprepared for a talk or homily that I'm asked to give, I go to the well. My paper isn't yellow but the theology is old and true for me but perhaps not what the youth of today would consider stylish.

I spoke to my friend Burt yesterday about his interview with John Lennon. Burt's retired in Greenbrae now. Back then, he worked for a record company and was the last one to interview John before he was shot and killed. He had several albums with him as they were waiting for the limo to pick them up in front of the Dakota in Manhattan and take them to the recording studio. There had been a persistent individual who pestered him for an autograph and Burt convinced John to sign one of the albums he had and then give it to him. This man turned out to be the killer. He was waiting later that evening when John and Yoko returned home from a recording session.

I was on the air the night John Lennon was murdered. It was December 8, 1980. The phone lines at the station lit up like crazy. I was working as a radio personality at KYUU-FM on weekends and I had played a lot of John's music on my show. I had several callers asking me to participate in the candlelight vigil service at the Marina Green.

I was pleased and surprised when I arrived to discover that there were so many Lennon fans in the Bay Area. Thousands came and they sang and they cried.

I offered a prayer near a statue on the Marina Green and watched the flashlights and cigarette lighters break the darkness with their warm glow. We stood together singing *Give Peace a Chance*. The whole demonstration was not very long and I never saw a report on it from any media source.

I was invited to speak at the National Association of Broadcasters. It was at the Hilton in Las Vegas and the hall was filled with 8,000 broadcasters from all over the world. I spoke about what a privilege it was for us to have such a powerful medium to bring all we do to people around the globe. I talked about "light" and what we could do to brighten a world full of gloom and doom. I got a rousing response and was feeling like I should be a major star in show biz, just like I told Merv Griffin years before when he gave me the best advice I ever had. Then I blessed the food we were about to eat and waited for my chance to meet the headliner.

After I sat down, he came driving in on a golf cart, took his seven iron and got up on the stage. The featured entertainer at the NAB was Bob Hope. For the next ten minutes, he told some of the oldest, not funny, jokes I have ever witnessed. I said to my pal Warren who was traveling with me how sorry I felt for Bob Hope. He must be getting old.

Then he signaled to the band leader to strike up a tune. The full orchestra went into a medley of songs that included every state in the Union. He had a line or a reference for each one of them. As their part of the country was recognized, the delegation from that state stood and cheered. Bob Hope ended with a wonderful tribute to the military people who serve our country mentioning of course Armed Forces Radio. I was in front at the head table and felt once again like I was in a special place at a special time.

When he finished, I was eager to shake his hand, have my picture made with him, and say thank you. But the standing ovation continued as he mounted his trusty golf cart and drove out the back door into the sunset.

I asked his producer if there was a chance for a photo op and he told me that Bob didn't do that. He was on his way to play eighteen holes and this was his time for recreation.

And to think I felt sorry for Bob Hope!

By this time, I was a fixture at the NAB conferences and had since moved over to the annual meeting of the Radio Advertising Bureau. Through the tutelage and good fellowship of Bill Stakelin I was invited year after year to participate with them, either as a motivational speaker or to lead a prayer breakfast.

In the evenings, there was always great entertainment. The general in charge of AFRTS invited me to attend a cocktail party for 5,000—mostly men in broadcasting. I wore my black suit and my collar and didn't stand out as the military brass were also in uniform.

I was introduced to an admiral and his two aides, a man and woman both in their early thirties. We were about ten feet from the dance floor and a well-known musical group was playing many of my favorites. My toes were dancing out the fronts of my shoes. I just couldn't help myself and said to the female lieutenant, "Would you like to dance?"

"Oh no, Father Harry, I don't dance. But thank you."

The music wouldn't let me rest.

"Well, I don't either but I did learn a few moves while chaperoning teenagers in high school," I said. "Come on, you can do it."

I reached out for her hand and she drew back.

"You don't want me to dance with the admiral, do you?" I said. "Come on!"

So we hit the hardwood. I took both her hands and began a spin when I realized that she really didn't know much about dancing.

The music slowed just a bit and she whispered in my ear, "Father, I had a riding accident when I was a young girl and I have a prosthesis, so I really can't twirl like you're suggesting."

Oh my! A wooden leg and both feet in my mouth. And again I learned a valuable lesson.

Every year a different branch of the military would send me out into the field to get to know my audience, to give retreats and to speak at prayer breakfasts. I spent time in Asia, Europe and at sea with the Navy. I would always ask the top brass what it was that I could do on the radio for the troops that was most important. I pretty much got the same answer from both the officers and the chaplains who hosted me and arranged my visits: "Tell the men and women to be honest and respect other people's property!!!"

Honesty and truth. That was easy. They didn't need any theology or church rules. Many of them had joined the military to get away from the ghetto or the small town or families that were dysfunctional. They didn't always get to know that it was wrong to lie, cheat and steal. I talked to a number of guys who said, "If you don't get caught, what's the big deal?"

Living in close quarters, away from home, you don't possess much. So when someone messed with your things, it was very hurtful and caused many fights and sometimes worse. That was the thing—in the old days guys could settle differences by throwing a few punches and rolling around on the ground. Nobody got knifed or shot or blown up. What a difference with "tough guys" today.

Anyway *Love on the Rock*, that was the name of my show, became the most listened to religious program on the network and held that number one position for the entire time that I worked for AFRTS. I chose *Love on the Rock* because I was talking a lot about love and not luv.

I recall one officer cornered me at a convention and told me

I should change the title because where they were in Iceland was known as the Rock and many of the troops felt I was advocating making love on the Rock. I actually was called into session by the general of AFRTS and the program director, Mr. Brown, to discuss this matter. It was funny to me, but I offered to change. My producer said, "No way," so we kept it as *Love on the Rock*.

Every show was pressed onto long playing vinyl discs. I had a collection of every show, more than 500, and I ended up using them later as place mats at fund-raising dinners. They were always of great interest to people who had collections of LPs. There are still a few in the basement, but I have no way of playing them as that type of technology is disappearing.

When I finally retired from AFRTS in 1994, they were just beginning to send out the shows by satellite. The military had reception dishes at most of their installations and all the ships at sea had adapted as well. That wouldn't affect the talent or production but it sure made it possible for the network to get things out a lot faster.

Twenty years working on Armed Forces Radio put me in contact with many wonderful chaplains in all the branches of service. Whether Catholic, Protestant, Jewish or other, I found them to be a great bunch who were devoted to their men and women and their families. Most of the troops thought I was a chaplain when I traveled overseas to visit them. I was given a high rank and treated like a guest celebrity.

I once had the privilege of giving a retreat to all the Catholic priests in Korea. After traveling for twenty-three hours, I arrived in Seoul completely exhausted. My host was a Protestant chaplain and he said I was due to meet all the Catholic padres at the base church. When I arrived they were all expecting me to give three conferences, hear confessions and lead them in prayer. It was a complete surprise. Once again, the early training in communications surfaced in that I was able to have a spiritually nourishing day for all of us. Boy, did I sleep that night! I must have slept for two days because the round-robin of appearances and visits to different sites was amazing.

Of course, the highlight was to go to the 38th parallel and put on a flak jacket and helmet and be escorted by six fully armed Marines. I had Thanksgiving dinner with these troops in the bunker. Out the observation holes you could see North Korea and the fake town they built on their side. Now that all this is in the news, it brings back fond memories of how brave and dedicated our troops were to have drawn that assignment and survived.

There have been very few incidents over the years on the 38th parallel. Some of our finest men and women who served time in Korea are now raising families and enjoying the freedom that they made possible for us all. A little squeak or two in life is only to let us know how fortunate we are to live in the greatest country in the world. Yes, I am a "homey" and proud of it.

At one point in my life as my radio career began to be more stable and my audience the same, my producer's husband, a friend who was almost the mayor of San Francisco, suggested that I be more controversial. "Take on some of your guests, fight with them," he said. "It goes a long way in gaining popularity."

My fellow Cape Girardean Rush Limbaugh had proven that. Sorry, I just couldn't do it. I was not clever enough or smart enough to know all the alternatives. You need all kinds of excuses and sidetracks if you're going to go down that road. I am also not a person who likes to confront. I will avoid a confrontation on almost any subject if I can. It just isn't my mug of beer or, if I drank it, cup of tea.

Legendary DJ and ad man Chuck Blore's philosophy of "soft sell" seemed to best suit my personality. It was easy to present the Gospels because they really sold themselves. In fact, it was harder to stay out of the way of the Word so that it might manifest in the people you were trying to get to.

Dr. Don won his lawsuit for the botched heart surgery that crippled his leg. With some of the settlement money he invested in a long-held dream to own a sailboat. He dubbed it *First Claz Miracle*.

There was great hoopla at Pier 39 as Captain Dr. Don and his crew of five were readying to set sail from San Francisco for Honolulu. There were hundreds of radio fans, the fireboats of the San Francisco Fire Department, a band and a tiger from Marine World/Africa USA. It was a spectacle. They escorted us through the Golden Gate and we were off for a seventeen-day, five-hour and three-minute sail to Hawaii.

Setting sail for Hawaii on the *First Claz Miracle*

Shortly after passing under the iconic Golden Gate Bridge, I began to feel the notorious *mal de mer*. For the next five days, I paid homage to the white porcelain god begging for mercy. I lost several pounds. A "silver bullet" known in the medical field as quinine finally broke my fever and allowed me to feel human again.

I began reading every printed word on the boat. It was a 38-foot Dufour and there was not a lot of room for anything. You could never be alone except in the head and it held too many unpleasant memories for me. By the way, I read the entire Bible in five days, cover to cover.

We had shifts of two hours at the helm as we sailed day and night with the course set by Don's son who was an excellent reader of the stars. At one point the electronic device that drew up our course failed and, like the earliest sailors, he shot the stars. It was amazing.

At about three in the morning, the alarm sounded and all hands were called on deck. We bounced out of our bunks in the pitch-black night and were told by the person on duty that he could hear a motor. Immediately, we went into emergency mode. An automatic rifle was produced and placed in my hands. I stood in the light with the gun, sure I'd be the first one fired upon by pirates.

I remember being invited to go on the trip as spiritual insurance in case there was anything nefarious that might take place. We were all frightened as our searchlights went around in

Father Harry and Dr. Don

an attempt to identify any unusual craft. We never saw one, just heard the sound of an engine. It was unnerving, in the middle of the ocean, when the waves and the wind in the sails were usually the only sounds.

After that, sleep was not easy. I grabbed as much as I could in daylight as I was too scared to sleep at night. After a few days, we were closer to the Islands and the danger seemed to subside. I don't want to experience that again, even sailing on a *First Claz Miracle*.

Women in the Church. It's not a very popular topic with the Roman Catholic hierarchy. The two previous popes were particularly expressive on the subject, raising warnings and caution flags with every bishop and archbishop working to shepherd their diocese or archdiocese into the 21st century.

Joan Ohanneson was renowned around the country and gave any number of lectures, taught classes, conducted retreats for priests and was much in demand for personal counseling. She was also a very precise person when it came to what people said and how they said it. I was her editor for the soundtracks on a number of her projects and used the technique B. Sharpe had taught me at KICK. We would run the tape over the sound-head and use a razor blade with a motion that could cut to the syllable. Like most creative producers, Joan would change her mind more than once and I would be on the studio floor searching for the last snippet of tape with a sigh or a gasp after a word. But when it was finished, it was magnificent.

I did four half-hour documentaries on the subject "In Celebration of Women's Gifts," with close help from Joan. We interviewed a number of women with all kinds of qualifications and credentials. Some wanted to embrace the priesthood, others were quite satisfied with their present role, whether teachers or administrators of large institutions. We titled the segments *Agents of Change, Mothers and Daughters, Peacemakers* and *Dreamspeakers*.

I predicted at the time that one day we would be ordaining women as Roman Catholic priests. That was back in the late '70s and early '80s. More and more well-educated women religious were turning to more defined work in parishes where there were no priests. Many of these women went to school summer after summer and had obtained masters degrees and doctorates in theology, liturgy, parish administration and a number of other church related subjects. It only seemed natural, to me, that with the lack of men being ordained, they would be accepted. Plus, many priests were leaving and getting married and following other careers. There would be more and more parishes without priests (of the male gender). What to do? I thought we were well on the way. Boy, was I mistaken.

I don't even know where the tapes are today, but I do know

that I was absolutely and unequivocally convinced that one day a woman would take my place on the altar and celebrate the Eucharist with the people of God. I'm in my mid-70s and all talk of such a happening has ceased.

Recently, one of my clerical brothers was remarking how I had been passed over as a candidate for the episcopacy. He was sure I wasn't a bishop because I had supported women priests in the late '70s. I reminded him that the Holy Spirit is still in charge of the Church and that's why I was not introduced as a potential candidate. It had nothing to do with my priestly work or practice in those early days.

Joan would have supported whatever would allow me to reach more people.

> *If you don't know where you're going, you'll probably end up somewhere else.*

That works for me!

So when I was in Minnesota doing a documentary for television about Mothers Against Drunk Driving, I caught his countenance out of the corner of my eye while trying to read the cue cards. He was bopping down a staircase. I stopped and asked, "Floyd, is that you?"

Sure enough, he turned and responded, "Harry?"

We had dinner that evening and were able to go through almost thirty years of knowing each other. Floyd was now a Buddhist. Since we shared eight years of Roman Catholic formation in the same seminary together, I asked him what the great appeal was for him to make the switch in midlife. I was eager to learn how Buddhism had affected him. His main reflection was that they didn't "collect" things. It seems his life in the Roman Catholic Church left him with the notion that we were ALWAYS doing some kind of collection, whether it be in church, or drives for clothing or food or old blankets to send to the missions. His new life seemed unencumbered with such trivial stuff as he was now able to pray, meditate and consider the bigger picture.

As a Catholic priest, I was just the opposite. I had clothes, a car, a home and all I needed. All the collectibles made me comfortable. I was able to collect more memories of my old friend who helped me understand the difference between us.

Floyd also related that he had been married twice since he left the priesthood. He had a bad experience with a woman who turned out to love other women more than men and she left him wondering who he was. The other marriage also failed, but I can't remember why. He seemed to be wrapped up in his new life as a Buddhist. I believe his heart and soul were in it to the best of his ability and he continued to reach out to others whenever and wherever he could. Happy trails to a guy who grew up with me and who took the other fork in the road.

> *Look at the birds of the air. They neither sow nor reap nor gather into barns and yet your heavenly Father feeds them. Are you not of more value than they?*
>
> Matthew 6:26

Life as I knew it in San Francisco was about to come to a close. Things changed when the Federal Communications Commission no longer required those who shared their air with the public to disclose how they were really sharing the air. With the arrival of televangelists and preachers who could buy time and use it to ask for donations, the whole realm of offering religious messages and being on the air for free went by the wayside. Now if you wanted to get to people with your message, it had to be paid for, in advance.

Being a priest and being involved in the communications business was a spiritual enterprise for me, not a monetary one.

After several very successful years, the Church got worried about taxes and making money and closed us down. The Archdiocese informed me that they had a buyer for the building, the old CBS TV station that had been given to the Church as a tax write-off. The figure of $4 Million was out there and they were going to sell it and use the money for Church communications projects. I had no choice. We had to disband Bridge.

My belief today is that the Church was afraid of doing work that could be taxed and perhaps jeopardize its status with the IRS. I wouldn't blame them a bit. But as the director of Bridge Productions, I was never told this nor consulted about it.

The production family at Bridge took another hit with the death of our unofficial spiritual director. Father Dan Sullivan died of a heart attack sitting in his truck up in Glen Ellen. He loved the countryside and found it a peaceful respite from Sacred Heart. Kathleen Emrey and I mourned him together. After we left the funeral home we headed for Union Street and we drank margaritas and cried.

Mike O'Leary was hired to work in the Communications Department with Miles, who thought the Archdiocese needed a magazine. Miles was convinced the Catholic newspaper was too expensive and Archbishop John Quinn shut it down. The *Los Angeles Times* reported the story saying my "turtleneck sweater approach to Christianity" had fallen victim to the changes and I would be leaving San Francisco.

16. Big Apple

JUST TWO DAYS AFTER the Archbishop announced his decision to close Bridge Productions, I received a call from the Catholic Telecommunications Network of America. They asked me to come to New York and work for them as their national sales manager. You've heard how a priest needs permission from his archbishop to change dioceses. They had already inquired whether or not I could serve the Church in that national capacity and Archbishop Quinn had given his blessing. For the first time in fifteen years, I would be without a television show.

ABC Radio signed me to a contract and began distributing *Father Harry: God Squad* in October 1983. Twice weekly, my sixty-second spots were available for the ABC Contemporary stations to download from the network. After ACC and Bridge producing my radio spots for ten years, I was working with ABC in New York.

I was hired over Thanksgiving as development director for Catholic Telecommunications Network of America, or CTNA. I had gone with just a suitcase and a few essentials as they had posted me in a small hotel just around the corner from their offices. The hotel is now demolished. I had a room with a view of the building next door. It was football season and I took a shower, put on my shorts and lay on the bed to watch the game. The telephone rang and it was a strange man in the next building who invited himself over to get to know me. No thanks. I pulled the curtains and deprived myself of fresh air and wondered about my reputation coming from San Francisco. I must say he was a gentleman and never called back.

My friend CW stopped by to take me to dinner the next evening and while we were visiting in the lobby, a small varmint made its way across the tattered rug onto the marble floor and skidded into a gaping hole in the wall.

The next day, I told the boss these two tales and he

immediately booked me into a Sheraton that was farther from the office but in a better area where I felt much safer. It was near the Church of Our Savior and I quickly introduced myself to the pastor and asked if he could use me for weekend assignments in his busy parish. I told him that I would be getting an apartment somewhere in the neighborhood off Lexington and would be close enough to help out.

I'll never forget when he invited me to say three Masses on Ash Wednesday. They each had to be no longer than twenty minutes so that he could get the people in and out as fast as possible. The parish was near Grand Central Station and they came in droves to get the ashes and take communion and then flee to the giant skyscrapers like ants to hills to fulfill their workday.

Eventually that winter, I moved all my stuff from California. I sold my car as it was too expensive to have in Manhattan, and now I was at the mercy of public transportation for the first time since I had left Italy. Giving up your wheels is a big thing as I've discovered with several close friends who are senior to me and are no longer able to drive. It's a personal loss of freedom and should not be taken lightly.

I had taken to wearing a coat and tie instead of the black clergy suit and collar at the suggestion of a bishop in Brooklyn who often came to Manhattan for business. He told me that the panhandlers would take up most of my time and waylay me at every stop whether it was bus, train, or subway if I stuck to the suit. It didn't take long to experience exactly what he meant, so I dressed pretty much like everyone else.

My new home was a seventh-floor apartment where there were only two doors, one to enter and exit and one to the bathroom. The kitchen was on a wall and my bed was a fold-out couch. I had a small table, which served as a desk and for eating. The real plus was four large windows which gave me a view of the Chrysler Building only a couple of blocks away. It was small but convenient and only $800 per month. The size of the place eliminated the possibility of overnight guests, but one nephew who worked for *Esquire* used to leave a change of clothes there because his place was in Brooklyn.

At forty-four years old, I was living alone for the first time in my life and it brought many new challenges. When I left home at the age of fourteen and entered the seminary, there was food, laundry and many little services that you take for granted. Now I had to shop, cook, pay rent, carry things in and out, and up and down seven flights of stairs when the elevator was not working.

The "blue" chicken was my first really bad experience from not knowing what I was doing when it came to the preparation of food. I had cooked a chicken on Saturday night and left it out on the counter. Sunday morning before I went to Mass I put it in the fridge. Monday I went to work then stopped at Lex and 46th at a favorite spot to say hello and howdy-do to some friends before I sauntered home to catch the Monday night football game on the telly. I was famished and looking back at me from inside the otherwise empty fridge was that leftover bird from Saturday night. I put it in the oven to heat it up thinking that whatever germs there might have been would be killed by the second roasting. It didn't taste that bad with a generous sprinkling of salt and pepper. But it left me with the worst and only case of salmonella that I've ever had. It took me more than a week to return to health. My sister, the nurse, called me and a week later I got a package—*The Joy of Cooking*. I still have it and the bookmarked page that warns about leaving fowl out overnight.

When I moved to New York in 1983, I once again came across my old friend Les Garland, who by this time had come up with a little idea called Music Television. I was his guest at the MTV New Year's Eve party. It was the hottest ticket in town. He insisted since we both were from California that we stay up to see in the New Year on the West Coast. A little after three in the morning, I put my sport coat on over my sweaty white shirt and stepped out in the cold. I thought I would get a taxi and get home quickly to shower and go to bed. You know I had not been living in New York long to have such an ignorant notion. Plus, I had no idea where I was. I was counting on the taxi driver to find my address.

So God chose to send a major snowstorm into Manhattan that night. It was beautiful walking in the snow and thinking how important I was to have experienced in person the likes of Elton John, Cyndi Lauper and others who were thrilled to have been on the MTV New Year's Eve show from New York. The good feeling soon turned to agony as the leather in my shoes was now completely soaked from the fresh mush on the sidewalks. My body sweat had turned to ice inside my jacket and the fingers of both hands were beginning to tingle from the drop in temperature.

Once I found Grand Central Station, I knew I would be able to find my way home. I don't know what time I rolled in but I was unable to roll out for about three days as I caught the cold of the century. Again, I was new in the apartment so had not had a chance to stock up on common cold medicine. But "common" cold medicine would not have worked on the super sickness that I acquired that beautiful Manhattan night of my party with the stars.

I met Eddie O'Brien when I first moved to New York City. The CTNA offices were in the same building as the chancery for the Archdiocese of New York and he was the secretary to the Cardinal. He had had a storied career at West Point and in the military. We were the same age and one Saturday morning he invited me to play handball at the New York Athletic Club. Neither of us knew how the other played. After a couple of games it was clear that I spent more time playing handball and less time pursuing theology than he did. He was very kind to me and even though I was more capable on the courts, I would never be able to match the future Cardinal's dedication and commitment to the Church.

I had an unsettling call from Kae Rose, Dr. Don's wife. She wanted to let me know that my friend and mentor was undergoing surgery to have his leg amputated. After all his pain and all his struggles, a log on the path proved his undoing. He tripped and the leg snapped during a recent camping trip and this time there was no more they could do for him or the limb. All I could do was pray for him and his family.

As the sales director for CTNA I visited almost every diocese in the country and traveled 75,000 miles a year. I spent about twenty days of the month visiting bishops and their communications personnel across the States. It was a wonderful learning experience and a good opportunity to see Roman

Catholicism at work both in the cities and the rural areas.

One hot summer day in Iowa, I was waiting in the parlor to see the bishop wearing a light seersucker suit that I had bought the day before. My black suit was drenched with sweat and I could not get it cleaned. It smelled to high heaven. So the door opens and the bishop comes out and his first question after the introduction is why I'm not wearing a black suit like a priest should. I explained about the hot weather and my suit hanging in the hotel getting some air. Needless to say, he didn't go much for the seersucker and I didn't get the sale.

Otherwise sales were easy, as a Catholic foundation had given me a back-pocket promise of taking care of the start-up costs of a satellite dish and all the trimmings for every diocese that wanted one. The local church would have to come up with people to run the operation, tape the programming and pass it along to schools and parishes in their area. It was a lot to ask of a small place in the Midwest that could barely afford one communications person for the entire diocese. But every time a bishop would say to me that he wanted this service but could not afford it, I would offer to write a check to cover the installation. It helped, but it didn't put the service over the top. There were all kinds of opinions and conflicts about the kinds of media that would be delivered.

Every bishop is a king in his own diocese. He says what comes in and what goes out. If he didn't approve of something because it was too conservative or too radical, he could simply say "not in my diocese." All those years when we had at least four or five national newspapers, there was never one that captured the Roman Catholic teachings to the satisfaction of all the bishops and dioceses. I often thought to myself while traveling the country that if they cannot get together on the printed word, there will never be agreement when people start talking about what someone said or what they heard on television.

It didn't take much longer for me to see the handwriting on the wall. I had covered the country and there was not going to be any more great progress with Catholic Telecommunications Network of America. It had to be fully backed by the bishops. It was not. CTNA failed for lack of product and foresight from our leadership. However, the satellite dishes were now in place for delivery and it was going to be up to the programmers to come up with the product that would affect the people in the pews. It was time for me to move on.

The Catholic Communications Campaign was looking for a national director. I interviewed with three bishops and the Director of Communications for the United States Catholic Conference and was offered the job. I raised money and put deals together for national religious radio, TV and print projects.

I still had to do a bit of traveling working for the USCC, but much less. I was responsible for collecting about $7 Million a year and setting up the mechanism for the funds to be distributed around the country and in the missionary world. The bulk of the money came from an annual collection taken in parish churches for the CCC. Every year there were requests for funding from locals and missionaries for their programming. We were able to do an adequate job for most of those who sought grants for their work. Our most important grant was made to the Philippines. The Archbishop of Manila, Cardinal Sin, was an outstanding leader in the Catholic church. He used to greet visitors to the Archbishop's Residence by saying, "Welcome to the house of Sin!" Fillipinos loved him and the humor in the double entendre of his name. He was able to orchestrate a peaceful overthrow of the government there by having Catholic Radio announce to the people to be calm and act in a dignified manner and the present regime would lose the vote. They did.

Once during a report that I gave in a meeting room at LaGuardia Airport, the prelate from Detroit insisted that all the CCC grant money should go to CTNA of which he was now the bishop representative. I opposed him and his response was: "Schlitt, you too can be torpedoed."

It was a shock to me that someone of his stature would not appreciate all the Catholic producers and talent around the country who had done so much for religious education and Catholic media in general. That prelate soon was transferred to Rome and did an outstanding job at the Vatican updating their financial disclosure practices.

It was about this same time that I first heard of the possibility of widespread pedophilia in the Catholic Church. A priest psychiatrist presented his findings to the Bishops Conference in Washington, D.C.. I had read of a few problems in Louisiana, but never imagined that it was across our country and the world. Back then, I felt it was a few men who had lost their way and their minds, and didn't know what to do. I remember one cleric telling me that the word pedophilia was not even in the dictionary before the 1980s (although I've since learned the word was used as early as the 1940s). No one really knew the severity of the condition nor the numbers who were sick with it.

Working for the Bishops Conference, I had regular meetings with bishops and notable Catholic communicators across the country and there didn't seem to be an avalanche of mental gymnastics to figure out what needed to be done. Even the hierarchy in general felt that pedophilia was narrow in scope and only the problem of a few sick individuals. Thus they tried to protect those priests and put them in places where they would not be noticed, nor be the cause of more problems. Many of the bishops first directed that the men be evaluated by people trained in psychiatry and addictions like alcohol and drugs. The go-to group was the Servants of the Paraclete, begun in 1947 to treat substance abuse and located near Santa Fe. "Paraclete" comes from the Gospel of John and is a dimension of the Holy Spirit that is considered a helper, or advocate. Troubled priests routinely were "sent to New Mexico" in the belief that they could be rehabilitated.

It was not my problem and was so hard to wrap my head around that I didn't give it much thought.

"Dear Fuzz." That's the way Jim Kogler used to address his letters to me even when we were approaching our fiftieth year on earth. I had told him the story of being called "Peach Fuzz" by my older brothers years ago in Rome and thus the rest of humanity followed suit, even though most of them were still wet behind the ears at that time.

Wimpy, Rufus and I had gotten together with JFK for one or more occasions in Buffalo while I was living on the East Coast. Wife Susan always prepared a great meal and then would leave us to our old stories of days in Rome. We would retreat to the basement cellar and pick out wines that Jim imported over the

The four Roman friends (from left) Wimpy, JFK, Fuzzy and Rufus

years from some of our favorite places in Italy. We loved Orvieto wines and the Bigi bianco was our favorite. We always cracked a bottle or two and continued the bull sessions into the wee hours of the morning.

Jim had become a partner in a law firm and was very successful. He was an outstanding court attorney with a remarkable knowledge of history. His success didn't last long as he had contracted a strange disease, probably from one of his trips to Africa to visit his sister who was a missionary nun in the Congo. I remember my last visit with him before he died. He gave me his pocketbook annotated copy of *A Man For All Seasons*. Saint Thomas More was his patron saint and he modeled his own legal career after him.

At Jim's funeral, the church was packed with priests and nuns and people he had affected during his lifetime both as a priest and a lawyer. The Bishop of the Diocese of Buffalo gave a wonderful tribute to him and his work. I was sitting there with Wayne and Roy wondering why things had to be that way.

It was after the burial that Roy and I ended up in the wine cellar of Jim's home looking at all the empty bottles we had drunk together over the years. They were clearly marked by a date and the event—his parents' 50th wedding anniversary, his children's baptisms, Jim's own wedding. It was a glance back at the many joyful moments we four friends had experienced. The trip down Memory Lane must have triggered something in Rufus. Until that night in Kogler's wine cellar, I had never known why Roy had left the seminary.

It had been almost a quarter of a century and he had never told me why he thought he didn't have a vocation to the priesthood. That night after Jim's funeral, Rufus revealed for the first time that he had been asked by his spiritual director to leave if he thought he might be a homosexual. Roy was gay and had kept it to himself since childhood. He broke down in tears both of sorrow and joy because now he had a trusted friend and confidant with whom he could share his life. Shortly after that he told Wayne, and the three of us grew even closer. There were many more years of visiting each other, celebrations, and the unbreakable bond of friendship forged in our Roman days.

I crossed paths with another old friend, my producer for the TWA program *Lovenotes for Listeners*. I saw an obituary in the newspaper and Ona Burns' name caught my eye. I attended her father's funeral in New York when I was living there. Despite our immediate attraction in the past, she never even noticed me, although I don't know how she missed the only white guy in the place. That was the last time I ever saw her. She had married and I trust is living a good and prosperous life.

Tim Dolan was someone else who resurfaced at that point in my life. I hadn't heard from him for fifteen years, since I'd left Missouri, until 1987 when I was working in New York. One day I got a call from Washington, D.C. and it was the future cardinal. He had been assigned to work there as a secretary to the

Apostolic Delegate. There was some small business matter he was calling about and we renewed our acquaintance.

Speaking of cardinals, I used to invite my old homiletics professor from the North American College in Rome, Edward Michael Egan, to have a beer with me on Friday afternoons when the offices on First Street would close. We often walked together on our way home. He was a new auxiliary bishop and was Vicar for Education for the Archdiocese of New York. His hometown was Chicago and I'm sure if he had his druthers, he would have rather been in the Windy City instead of the Big Apple. But again. like most devoted churchmen of his stature, he went where he was asked to go.

I don't suppose "Easy Ed" ever had the idea that someday he would be the Cardinal Archbishop of New York. On second thought, maybe he did! Anyway, he never had a beer with me as he always dressed in his black suit and collar and I had on the tie and coat. He was a good teacher and I learned as much from him about the workings of the Church as I did in all my classroom work in Vatican City.

The New York Athletic Club became my second home and my oasis from all the traveling and meetings. It was still men-only in the mid-1980s. A law requiring the admission of women was being appealed. The case ended up going all the way to the Supreme Court. Handball was my sport and it gave me a good outlet to alleviate stress, wear out the body and provide a social group that really didn't give a damn about church politics or church prelates. They knew I could be counted on to be on time for a game and maybe a win if I played someone older or infirm.

When I was interviewed to join the NYAC I had been recommended by Monsignor Edwin O'Brien, who would also go on to become cardinal, and also interviewed by retired fire chief and fire commissioner of New York, John O'Hagan. When I sat down at the first table, the interviewer looked at my résumé and asked me how much I made a year. He gulped when I answered and then asked how I expected to pay my dues there. I thought it was the end and I would leave embarrassed, only to see Chief O'Hagan wink in the background assuring me that I would be a welcome member. That club allowed me more than my share of physical recreation and lasting friendships. One of my best pals is still there and has been a great supporter of my work from the beginning.

My new CCC position required me to collect money, to give away money and to pair money with funds from other grantors so that programming would continue to grow and progress. We were able to put together a wonderful board of directors and the work prospered.

At the same time, I continued making my radio spots at a studio on 57th Avenue owned and operated by a good friend who allowed me to have the studio space for free. I used the same studios as the Beatles and a number of top drawer celebs who recorded there. It was an old church that had been converted to recording studios. The sound was outstanding. He was a godsend for me and responsible for the production of the first priest rap that I recorded in his studios.

Information, Wind, and Water was the title and it contained several tracks that I thought could be successfully marketed in light of my radio following across the country. Not so. Never worked. I used the tracks in some personal appearances, but it never caught on. Rap wasn't far off, but it was part of the city scene springing up from the African-American neighborhoods.

I named the work *IWW* after words my dad used to say about some of his customers in the garage business. All they wanted was free information about their cars, then they'd blow wind about how great they were, go to the water cooler for a refresher and leave. Dad had some good ones. I only wish I had paid closer attention when I was younger.

There was a high-rise going up next door to the old church-turned-studios and the pounding of pilings going into the ground ruined my friend's business. He sued, but a man fell at the construction site and was killed. The legal system then turned to that death and my pal only got his settlement a few years ago, long after he had gone belly up and moved to the Midwest.

It would not be fair to leave out the Eternal Word Television Network and Mother Angelica as she used my name in her autobiography. She referred to me as that smart-aleck young priest from the CCC who was sent down to Alabama to spy on her.

Truly that was not the case. When I was on the road I took notes because I went to so many places and when I arrived back in my office in New York to write up my reports, I simply could not have done it without the legal yellow pages that I had collected.

I stayed in Irondale two days and watched a telethon where they asked for money. I didn't really care if they were supposed to do that or not, but they saw me taking notes and figured I was the bishops' watchdog and would pass along a bad report about their work. During my travels, I met people who prayed the rosary every night with Mother Angelica before they went to bed. I met others who thought it was a joke to have this religious woman representing Catholicism on TV as she was obviously not a theologian and was very strongly bent to the right when it came to her opinion about challenging thought and dogma in the Church.

It didn't seem to bother her, as she became a great success. Her right-hand lady, whom I called the steel magnolia, was a sweet attractive person. She took me to the airport from the Mass at their convent and assured me that I would not be invited back because of my yellow pad of notes taken during their telethon. And to think when I ran Bridge Productions in San Francisco, I was willing to partner with her to have a coast-to-coast broadcasting facility to serve the entire Church. The Holy Spirit was not behind that alliance.

I was living in Manhattan and it was a couple of hours on the train to the Maryknoll house for retired and aging priests. I had gone up before on a Saturday and had a wonderful visit with my friend and mentor Father John Martin. He was the same guy who introduced me to the priesthood and I would say fostered my vocation. No, we didn't do confession and we didn't drink a beer. I just wanted to share my priesthood with him and he was always excited to hear about whatever I had done or planned to do. I hadn't returned for almost a year, as I had to do so much traveling and time seemed to whiz by.

I met Flickers and Charles in New York and we went to

dinner. They had been very successful in the business world and very generous to me when I had asked them for assistance along my priestly pilgrimage. We had one friend in common, the Maryknoll priest Father John Martin. Charles' family had supported the Maryknoll missionaries. When Charles was in high school, he had thought about becoming a priest. He met Father Martin about the same way I did. One day he met "Flickers" and then began to doubt his calling. He went to see Father Martin and told him his dilemma. Father Martin suggested that he would be better off going home and marrying that "little girl." So he did.

Flickers and Charles kept up their friendship with the priest and Father Martin used to visit them at their country home in Kelso, Missouri. He came about once a year and loved playing with their seven kids. When Father Martin retired, Charles and Flickers visited him in New York. They loved and appreciated him as much as I did and only realized how much he'd done for me as a young man when I told them my part of the story about the fifth grade. They said I should go see Father Martin because his health was failing.

It was a cold blustery day as I boarded the train in Grand Central Station bound for Ossining, New York. It had been a long time since my last visit with Father Martin. As I got off the train, I saw three men who were easy to identify as priests even though they were not in black suits. Black shoes, no ties and no jewelry tipped me off. I asked if I could share a cab with them to the Maryknoll House on the hill just a few miles away.

"Of course, get in, we've plenty of room and it's always good to have visitors. Now who are you going to see?"

"My old spiritual director and the man responsible for my calling to the priesthood," I said with great confidence. Immediately I saw the eyes of two of the men go down and their enthusiasm for my visit waned.

The third said in a low voice, "Oh, I guess you didn't hear. Father Martin passed away in the infirmary a couple of months ago. He's buried in the cemetery in back of the building."

Snow began to fall lightly as I made my way down the narrow path to the holy ground where so many Maryknoll priests had been laid to rest. Many of them were famous and many were just guys who, as missionaries around the world, gave their lives to announce the good news of Jesus Christ to people they didn't know. I knelt in the wet snow and as I felt my clothes getting soaked from the melting flakes, I shivered. My sorrow turned bitter and I began to pray. I felt Father Martin's warm smile coming over me as I thanked him for the love and guidance he gave me in the short time we were able to share in this life.

When all the saints are called for their eternal reward, I'll hope to be in that number and meet up with him again. Even though he always joshed about it, I know Father Martin will be much more than *in petto* to more than one pope and probably to all of them who knew him from his work in Rome and the Vatican. He's as close to God as anyone I have ever known. May he rest in peace!

I had worked seven years in New York when the USCC announced its office was going to be relocated to Washington, D.C. at new facilities near Catholic University. They had an office for me with my name engraved on the door. I went there to check it out but told my superior, Bishop Robert Lynch (now in Florida), that I did not want to leave New York and if I did would probably return to my home diocese. Jokingly, I said I didn't like the Redskins football team.

Archbishop Quinn and I had spoken and he felt it was time for me to come back to San Francisco. He warned me about the estrangement of men who were away for too long and then would have a hard time making an adjustment upon re-entry. It made sense and so after the New York office closed, I returned home.

17. Gemini Rising

I WAS BACK in California working for Santa Fe Communications in Burbank when the Loma Prieta earthquake halted the
1989 World Series at Candlestick Park between the Oakland
Athletics and the San Francisco Giants. It was among the few
times I was happy to be in LA.

I had not completely finished with my New York
connections. I had gotten to know Santa Fe through the Catholic
Communications Campaign and I was working as their Director
of Special Projects. I was in charge of religious programming.

I worked in Los Angeles but my home was in South San
Francisco at St. Veronica parish, which was close to the airport.
I also had a very nice place in Burbank with a pool in back and a
sauna. I did not like LA. I only lived a mile and a half from the
studio and sometimes it took forty minutes to get home. Then
when I was there, I would walk around the neighborhood. The
only family I knew was Bill Stewart's and his daughter was just
seventeen and too young to pal around with.

The Heart of the Nation production company in Burbank
was trying to develop a national teen show. They hired me as a
talent producer for *The Tina Yothers Show,* hosted by the young
actress from the hit TV comedy *Family Ties.* She was the star
and I only supported her with commentary and introductions to
music videos. I was Ed McMahon, but she was no Johnny
Carson. We had a live audience and it was a bummer. This
young lady was wonderful on the sitcom but just could not
converse with kids. Unless it was scripted and memorized, she
had little to say.

They used to edit the game show *Jeopardy* in our studio. It
was created and produced by my old friend Merv Griffin. On
Tuesdays, I played handball with my friend Jim Cotter, whom I
knew from the New York Athletic Club, and afterward we'd go
out for beers and pizzas. We'd go down to this little bar and
Jeopardy was usually on the TV and of course I knew all the

answers. Patrons were blown away by my brains. One guy two stools over got excited. "Man, you're really good. You should try out for that show. You'd win!"

There were a lot of young people who were producers at Santa Fe and they'd join the fun. Most of them looked up to me as I had worked nationally in a position with ABC. We weren't friends, exactly. Part of the problem was I'd be there Monday, Tuesday and Wednesday evenings and return to San Francisco Thursday.

Back at St. Veronica's on Friday, I would do my laundry, answer my mail, play handball and have cocktails with Michael Clark who never strayed outside 94123 and always saved me a stool at Mulhern's on Buchanan Street. Mike and I met when I lived at St. Vincent de Paul. I made lots of friends there and many of them are close to me to this day including Mr. Mulhern.

Saturday would be quiet preparation for my weekly homily, confessions and Mass. Sunday Masses and talking to people melted into Monday and I was back on a plane heading south for more Catholic TV production.

For fifteen months, I flew back and forth between the two Californias. I recorded a weekly TV Mass that covered the country as part of Heart of the Nation. (Twenty years later *My Sunday Mass* would be moved to Milwaukee at the behest of the archbishop, Tim Dolan.) I also co-hosted a thirteen-part series with Kathy Lennon of the Lennon Sisters. It was syrupy programming and both of us gushed with goodness, but that was not what the market was buying. A woman with a cooking show that was produced in our studio never made it to the big time either. She would flirt with me a little and she was a good talent but nobody ever bought her show.

I was still very much connected across the country with television producers and creative people who were all hoping I would make it to national prominence with a show that could influence and spiritually saturate the nation for good and God. Tina Yothers' show was a bust. Kathy Lennon was good and the show was pitched at programmers' conventions (television not software), but we never got a bite on either show. Production soon came to a screeching halt. I felt bad for Tina but it was not meant to be.

After months of commuting from San Francisco to Burbank each week, it was time to wave bye-bye to my TV persona and say to myself, "You just don't have it." But I'm still doing the TV Mass, so maybe the offices "upstairs" were training me for that part.

My work with young people led to my next assignment as the director of the Campus Ministry at San Francisco State University. It was reinvigorating being around students again and I felt great being back home in the City. My new residence at Holy Name parish was close enough to Ocean Beach that I could go running there mornings. Even with the frigid Pacific waters and treacherous riptides it was paradise regained.

I went by the old Bridge studios on Van Ness. After nearly ten years, the building still had not been sold. I returned to find things intact, with all the old lights, cameras, sets, cables and wires covered in mold.

One Sunday morning, I was hit with another blast from the past. Mary Ann White came back into my life, regularly attending Mass at Holy Name with her three small children. The family lived quietly in the parish, in the same house where they'd always been. I never met her husband. He died when I was living in New York.

In May of 1979, Dan White had been sentenced to a seven-year term for voluntary manslaughter after an unbelievable "Twinkie defense" that made headlines around the world. Depression had led to a diet of junk food, resulting in "diminished capacity," making pre-meditation impossible, or so went the successful defense argument! White's paltry punishment for the double murders shocked and outraged the City. The spring after George Moscone and Harvey Milk were assassinated, the "White Night" riots rocked San Francisco. The mood was awful. Anger flared and people were ready to explode. City Hall was heavily damaged and police cars were torched.

Dan White served just five years in state prison and was paroled to southern California for his protection. By the time he returned to the City, the haters who had lauded him for "killing the fag and the fag-loving mayor" were nowhere to be found. White, who had been a paratrooper in Vietnam, a policeman, a fireman, and a San Francisco supervisor, found himself lonely and alone. He was a pariah. No one wanted to hire him and no one wanted to associate with him.

He attempted to resume his life with Mary Ann and the children. Their family had grown with the addition of a second son, afflicted with Down Syndrome and born while his father was in prison, and a baby daughter born after his release. Dan White imagined a new life for them in Ireland. But eventually Mary Ann moved out, taking the children with her. In the fall of 1985, Dan White committed suicide in the family home. Officer Dan appeared to be wound too tight for ordinary life. So he took his own, with the car running and the garage door tightly closed, and photographs of his family clutched in his hand.

Police bulletins never fascinated me as much as fire truck sirens, but my room at Holy Name was next door to a retired chaplain of the police department who couldn't take himself away from the regular and exciting announcements that would come over the scanner in his room. And because of his poor hearing he blasted the bulletins in high volume so that it was a distraction to me while I was reading or watching TV.

One night a bulletin of emergency was heralded about a gas explosion on Sutter Street. It was serious and there might have been great loss of life. I heard the announcement before I heard the knock on my door from this tall stately monsignor who asked me to put on my black suit and collar and accompany him to the disaster zone. We were off in haste and I was treated to him pulling out a red flashing light from his glove box to alert those already within the yellow caution tape area that someone important was here to help. Even I was beginning to feel the thrill.

We both prayed on the way as we continued to monitor the police radio for updated bulletins about the explosion. Deep down we were hoping not to see blood and blanketed bodies strewn about the streets. But we didn't know.

Of course, the men watching the perimeter saw the flashing light and quickly recognized the driver as the police chaplain. They allowed us to pass and directed us to a safe place to leave the car. We both jumped out and were led to the captain in charge of the operation. He informed us that the fire chaplain was already on hand and there didn't seem to be any serious personal injuries nor blown up bodies.

Much of the neighborhood was shaken and multiple windows were blown out. Glass covered both the sidewalks and the street like during the Loma Prieta. Here's the good part. The rugged monsignor and I were instructed to walk to the scene hand in hand so as not to lose our balance and slip. We were literally walking on glass and listening to the crunches and eerie squeaks as we made our way closer to the site of the explosion.

It must have been quite a sight for the neighbors, because this particular street was occupied by a number of transgenders and transvestites. They were hanging out the windows making catcalls at the two men in black suits and Roman collars mincing gingerly through the glass holding hands. It wasn't until we arrived and greeted the fire chaplain that we were reminded of the neighborhood and who occupied most of the apartments on the street. They all got a good laugh at our expense but we really didn't mind since no one was hurt. Thanks be to God!

Everything seemed to be in order and we were able to retreat to the car, yes, still hand in hand for fear of falling. There was much property damage and a couple of bruised egos as we made our way back to the safe surroundings of our rectory.

If you asked me how I felt about my two older brothers, I would have to say that God gave me the best He had and the best for me. We loved each other and it was a privilege to grow up with them by my side.

Johnny was the first of my two older brothers to die. It was just a short time before his sixtieth birthday. His life was 59 years, 8 months and 2 days long and much of it was spent in the General Garage. He had many ailments and now that I look back, he probably met his Maker without a smile. His last years on earth were not pleasant. I always looked up to Johnny as he was everything that I wanted to be when I grew up. In his latter years he was not anyone I wanted to be. His body had paid the price for all the bourbons and Cokes and the thousands of beers he consumed. Johnny was heavy and he had cancer and diabetes.

I recall when he had one of his legs amputated. It was

rotting from the toes on up. I bought house slippers for the whole family. They were those big floppy kind with different animals. I got him a bear slipper. I only bought one. I put it on and got up on crutches and started for the door, which led out to a patio covered with snow. He said no one would ever believe there was a one-footed bear in his back yard.

Reminds me of a guy I knew who was bragging about how much he used to drink. I asked him if he was an alcoholic. "Hell no, Father, I was a drunk." I guess there's a difference. We didn't use the word alcoholism in our family. It was a sickness and no one seemed to be sick. Lots got ill from the drink, but nobody was sick.

At the time Johnny died, his family was all grown up and everyone had married and all but one had children. There was a lot of emotion at the funeral and I was glad to get back home to sort it out for myself. The tales his boys wove of him were legion. While the facts might have been exaggerated, all of his kids were devoted, loyal, loving and respectful. While his mode of discipline might have been a bit old fashioned, his heart was in the right place. For his part, he could never have been more proud of all his children.

Shortly after the rosary service and a wonderful presentation by the Order of Elks to which Johnny belonged, I drove a mile or two to see my eldest brother, Charlie, who was in the hospital dying of cancer. He wanted to know all about our brother's funeral and who was there and what they did. I know in the back of his mind he was thinking his days were numbered and he could probably count on the same cast of characters coming out to view his remains. He was right. There wasn't a lot of difference.

The two oldest Schlitt boys passed in the same year. For me it was almost natural. I was so young when both Mom and Dad passed and now I seemed almost calloused to death. Of course, I mourned with both my brothers' widows and their children, but I was the priest and I was in charge of the services. I gave the homily, blessed the burial ground and I did the spiritual stuff expected of me. My heart was with the survivors, with the living. I already felt pretty close to death. I wasn't hard about it, but I was inured to it. I was in the priest mode of celebrating funerals and it was part of the job.

I had talked Charlie and Mary into giving their bodies to medical science because they both had so many problems in later life. I regret that now. When I visit the family plot in Cape Girardeau I wish their remains were there so that their children and children's children might have a place to go and talk about their parents and grandparents. It seems a natural thing to do. I say my prayers and talk to them but it's not the same as if I put the body in the ground on that spot.

I never got to see Charlie again after Johnny's funeral and I didn't get to say good-by. I was in Rome for a three-month sabbatical, a type of continuing education course in theology. There were thirty guys. Because I had been in Rome and spoke a little Italian, I was like the head of the class.

I had a keen interest in scripture and was revitalized by the study. I couldn't preach the theology like a lot of priests do, because most of my congregations didn't study theology and didn't have a familiarity with the language or the ideas. But a story we can all follow, and so I told stories. Rather than just give off theological nosegays, I wanted to impart the word of God. I had a

Father Harry and the Holy Father,
Saint John Paul II

Eurail pass and after the course was over in late November, I planned to travel all over Europe until the end of December. That didn't pan out for me. I never finished the full sabbatical. Instead I had to leave the course two weeks before it ended to go home because Charlie was going to die.

I have married and buried generations from the same family. In a parish a pastor gets close to a lot of people, poor or rich. But in my life I have been associated with families who knew me as the handball player, or the broadcaster, who happened to be a priest. I don't play any favorites and I don't sponge off them. There are priests who spend holidays with the wealthy and know the family will bail them out if ever needed. They are an extension of the family (like Mrs. Ohrman wanted when she tried to adopt me). Maybe the wealthy add them to their collection of Catholic things that "not just anyone" has. I'll have to ask Floyd about this the next time we meet.

My encounters with San Francisco high society were infrequent but notable. One of my fans from the radio years ago was no less than Mrs. Barbara Tobin Thieriot. Her family founded the de Young Museum and the *San Francisco Chronicle*. They also owned KRON-TV where I worked. Baby Thieriot was the first ultra-wealthy person I knew. That's probably how she got away with calling herself Baby when she was anything but. She heard me on the radio one time.

"Oh that's a lot of b.s.," I was saying to a caller. She had never heard a priest say "b.s." before and decided she wanted to meet me. I dined with her across a table and she said, "This won't work. We can't talk." I used to go down to Atherton and hear her confession and then we'd watch a football game on TV. Her sons Kip and Dick liked the fact that their mother had a priest friend. She was a widow and made regular trips to a "fat farm" and they worried about her drinking.

Anybody who was anybody in the social world was invited to Baby Thieriot's for Christmas. I was invited too and ended up watching TV in a sitting room off a bedroom. The bed was full of fur coats. Jimmy Stewart's wife, Gloria, came looking for hers. I got the one she wanted and handed it to her. She left and came back; it was the wrong coat. They all looked alike. When Baby died, I was in her will. I got $10,000, but then the cook also got $10,000. Actually, Baby left me her Jaguar. It was a beautiful automobile. I told Kip I couldn't afford the car. I couldn't pay the insurance on a Jaguar. So he wrote me a check for $10,000. That was the first major gift I'd ever received because of my media ministry.

When I worked for ABC radio, I got tickets to the Super Bowl for seven straight years. The network invited all the big clients to the game. It was an advertisers' junket. Sunday morning Mass was held at the hotel rather than busing all of them to church. I was the celebrant. I had them out by 11:45 a.m. so they could make brunch before the kickoff.

After I had returned to the West Coast, I still flew back to New York four times a year to produce my sixty-second spots at ABC. Radio station budgets were suffering in part because of increased competition from cable TV, but demand for the *Father Harry: God Squad* spots was growing, especially in the smaller markets. My distributor, Oblate Media, was sending out twenty-five spots four times a year to over 600 stations across the country. All together with ABC and AFRTS (where I had just begun my twentieth year), I was airing on 1,400 stations. At the same time, the demand for compact discs was on the rise and Oblate wanted to transition away from audio tape and start providing my work on CD.

The first time I had tried fishing for Alaskan halibut, I caught a granddaddy. The fish weighed in at ninety-two pounds and filled the coolers my friends and I had brought to transport our catch back to San Francisco. When sobriety returned in the waning hours of our excellent fishing trip, I started to wonder what I would do with all that halibut.

I had developed a mailing list of about 200 God Squad supporters and I decided to invite them all over for a fish dinner. Part fund-raiser, part friend-raiser, "Just for the Halibut" was an opportunity to turn fish into bread that would pay for the God Squad productions. The event became a hot ticket in town.

Friends donated wine, loaves of San Francisco sourdough bread and produce for salad. They donated their time to decorate, cook, serve food and tend bar. The dinner became an annual event, growing from about fifty people the first year to 350 when we did the last one in the undercroft of St. Mary's Cathedral. That was fourteen years later.

The *San Francisco Chronicle* called it a soap opera and it had all the elements—a beautiful woman, her ambitious boyfriend, the chief of police, sex and politics.

I first met Joanne when she was a student at Presentation High School where I gave retreats. Like many teens, she also knew me from the radio and the youth Mass at the Cathedral in the 1970s. Years later, she joined the God Squad board of directors where she applied the public relations skills she had developed in her job as spokeswoman for the San Francisco Police Department. She used to drop by the chancery office with her firearm on her hip causing a flurry of excitement and curiosity among my co-workers.

The mayor of the City, Frank Jordan, was a devout Catholic. I'd been asked to help him become a better speaker during his campaign and more contemporaneous. He had just appointed a new chief of police, the first Hispanic in San Francisco history. Tony Ribera was Catholic too and Joanne's boss. She and her boyfriend, a San Francisco supervisor, had lobbied Mayor Jordan to appoint Chief Ribera who then promoted Joanne from beat cop to the PR post.

When plans were made for the second "Just for the Halibut," Joanne recruited her Catholic colleagues to attend. RSVPs came pouring in from the mayor and his wife, the chief of police, members of the Board of Supervisors and other local notables.

Halibut II was being held at a restaurant on Taraval Street called the Fog Bank. The owner was fond of tropical fish and a giant aquarium filled the lobby. The Halibut decorating committee decided to put goldfish in bowls on each table as centerpieces. When the Friday night of the event rolled around, the City's finest rolled in to the Fog Bank.

The place was electric, the crowd eclectic. My handball buddies from the Olympic Club and their wives were dressed to the nines. My barfly friends donned jackets and musician friends combed their hair. One bald biker in leather chaps stood out. He had a supporting role in the soap opera having just stepped into Joanne's PR job. None of us knew about it that night, but it was all on the front page of the *Chronicle* the next morning.

"Inside Story of S.F. Police Uproar," the headline screamed. "Chief accused of harassment—woman officer to stay on." And there were their photographs with the gist in the captions. The beautiful woman: "still believes she can do her job," the ambitious boyfriend: "backed Ribera for chief," and the Chief: "denies the charge."

Just hours before the fish dinner, Joanne had held a news conference announcing she was filing local, state and federal charges of sexual harassment against her boss. This was a bombshell in 1993. Nothing of that magnitude had happened in San Francisco before. And yet there they all were at the Fog Bank that night, the mayor smiling alongside his statuesque wife, the biker sticking close to the chief, the boyfriend sticking close to the bar and the lady cop moving graciously through the crowd making introductions and small talk about the God Squad. Some of the guests knew about the charges. I didn't. I had been talked into swallowing a goldfish.

The girl from Presentation High had grown up to be smart and tough but she underestimated the cost of her actions. The story was huge and made national news. She was demoted to a "less stressful job" (the biker got her old one) and was ostracized by many of her colleagues. Some key evidence in her case was blocked because of the statute of limitations. The trial wore on, taking a toll on her relationship with Bill the Supe. After nearly three years the Chief of Police was exonerated of the harassment charges.

I know soap operas are so entitled because they are usually sponsored by home products for cleaning. In this opera, there were several cleansings. I think everyone, including myself, learned a difficult lesson. Going public with private matters usually requires more than a pound of flesh. I always felt that if both parties had come to someone in private, there could have been a solution that would have spared everyone so much grief. Remember when the woman was about to be stoned by the angry crowd? Jesus bent down and wrote in the sand. All the accusers began to leave one by one beginning with the oldest.

The Catholic bishops of the U.S. periodically issued letters, or white papers, addressing pressing social issues. Their letter scolding capitalism for not including the poor, along with the Campaign for Human Development whose funds went directly to the poorest, were among the better things the organization ever did. The same is true for the 1992 pastoral letter, *Stewardship: A Disciple's Response.*

I had just been named the Director of Stewardship for the Archdiocese and was assigned the task of promulgating this letter and collecting the annual assessment, or tax, on parishes. *Stewardship* gave us something to shout about, gave people in the pews something to crow about. "We're part of the Church too!"

For years, participation had meant just the obligatory Mass on Sundays and holy days. Despite the sweeping changes of Vatican II, there was no real mechanism for people to become more involved. They had to join on their own. Stewardship encouraged a lot of people to donate time and talent to church and the best thing was, we could stop talking so much about money and start talking about gifts.

> *As each one has received a gift, use it to serve one*
> *another as good stewards of God's varied grace.*
>
> 1 Peter 4:10

The first class that I taught at St. Patrick's Seminary was ordained in the spring. After I had returned to San Francisco from New York, Archbishop Quinn had asked me to teach homiletics to the seminarians. I was pleased to be recognized for my gifts as a homilist and worked hard to pass along everything I'd learned about giving a good sermon. There were so few ordinations to the priesthood in 1993 it gave us all a special reason to rejoice. Most of my students had had other careers before they entered the seminary. Some had been bankers, lawyers, store managers, musicians and others had served in the military before hearing the call. It brings a smile to my face that I was able to help them sharpen their skills at presenting the Gospel message from pulpits all over the western U.S. and Guam.

The Loma Prieta earthquake woke people up to the dangers of unreinforced masonry buildings (UMBs) and San Francisco enacted mandatory seismic retrofit laws for public gathering places. The Archdiocese had dozens of these buildings and the financial challenge pitted ministries and pastoral needs against brick and mortar. At the same time, the Church had entered an era of declining Catholic population previously unknown in the City of Saint Francis. Many neighborhoods had churches within blocks of each other. A lot of them had Catholic schools that had become almost totally reliant on lay teachers and the increasing costs, combined with shrinking enrollments, meant excess classroom space.

Some of the structurally vulnerable churches were architecturally the most beautiful. St. Paul's with its twin copper spires and magnificent interior was the backdrop for Hollywood's *Sister Act*. St. Joseph's on Howard Street south of Market was identifiable from high points all over town because of its unmistakable "salt and pepper shaker" towers. Even the church that bore Saint Francis' name, with its twin rook towers and soaring archways, was on the list. Big, stolid Sacred Heart, my first home in the City, had a stories-high brick bell tower (and a half full school). St. Dominic's had been immortalized in song by Van Morrison. They got out of the fund-raising gate early and its Gothic flying buttress solution made the church an instant landmark. Parishioners and preservationists rallied to save their churches where generations of San Franciscans had gone from cradle to grave.

Archbishop Quinn was not a bricks-and-mortar kind of guy. He was a theologian. At the time he was made a bishop, he was thirty-eight years old and the youngest in the country. He came to prominence early as a thinker and a writer. But his real-world skills were lacking.

In his first job as a priest, he was the secretary to the Archbishop of San Diego. Quinn was barely ordained, had celebrated Mass back at home just the once and he was jet-lagged. They gave him a desk. He had never seen a multi-line phone and the lights went on. A pastor and his associate were there waiting for an appointment and the pastor had a dog. Quinn was either allergic or afraid and they had a fight. He was the archbishop's secretary and he didn't know how to answer the phone.

When he would go on vacation to Carmel, Archbishop Quinn would rent a place with a piano and invite me and Miles, back in our ACC days, to come down for dinner. Afterward, we would walk on the beach without saying much, then go inside where he would play the piano. He didn't know anything about sports and joked about it, but he was a real spiritual person with a very deep spiritual life. He didn't skip prayers or meditation to watch TV or football.

My Roman scripture teacher Warren Holleran, who impressed me profoundly with his oratory, had a lot in common with John Quinn. So did Father Milt Walsh, the associate who years before tattled about Coca-Cola in the Cathedral during the youth Mass. And so did Miles, for that matter, except he had worked in parishes and he knew the world. We all were North American Martyrs and that fraternity was our bond.

Archbishop Quinn's secret to administrative success was getting Monsignor Jim McKay, the police chaplain and Vicar General, to recruit lay people to organize the Archdiocese. Earnest and charming, Jim asked accountants to overlook the books, he asked human resources folks to interview me before I came to the stewardship office. These people were well respected and for the most part prominent Catholics. They volunteered as consultants and worked in collaboration with the chancery administrators. The deacons from Immaculate Heart of Mary, Our Lady of the Pillar, and St. Stephen really came in and took charge.

In response to the problem of the UMBs, Archbishop Quinn perhaps followed the same approach. Archdiocesan leaders and stakeholders under the direction of Father Robert McElroy worked to develop a Pastoral Plan. Quinn approved the first phase, and after months of meetings and anguished protests from the UMB parishes, the Archdiocese shuttered twelve San Francisco churches. Many schools were closed and buildings sold. The convent for Saint Mother Teresa's sisters in Noe Valley was turned into condos, as was the former St. Paul's high school. Most of the parishes had been deemed spiritually viable and survived, but many of the faithful were deeply shaken.

Shaken can be upset or nervousness or to the bones. Sometimes all you can do is laugh and enjoy the moment. Such was the case when my friend Leo bailed me out of the airport in St. Louis. Leo was the kind of guy who would leave the keys to his apartment at the local pub nearby in case any of his friends had too much to drink and couldn't drive home, or who had just arrived in town and didn't have time to book a hotel. He was a pilot for TWA based in San Francisco and was working most of the time. I knew him from the Chestnut Street bars.

I was in St. Louis waiting for my return flight to San Francisco. My niece Renda drove me to the airport and waited with me until the flight left. We got to talking in the bar and did not hear the call announcing the last chance to board. By the time we realized it, we had to race for the gate and just as we arrived the door to the jetway closed. I pleaded with the lady there to let me on, or to at least let me run down the ramp to see if the door to the plane was still open. She took pity on me and let me through. I flew down the walkway toward the aircraft.

The plane was just being backed up by the jet cart when the pilot looked out his little window and spotted me. It was my friend Leo. Behind me—with her long blond hair blowing in the breeze—was my beautiful niece. Without any fanfare, the jumbo jet came to a stop. In minutes, I saw the door open and I was aboard.

No sooner had I sat down when the captain announced to the passengers, "Folks, sorry for the delay, but my friend Father Harry needed to be on this flight home. I just couldn't leave him in St. Louis with that gorgeous blonde he left standing on the boarding ramp."

You can imagine the stares and the laughter and the questioning that I had to endure for the entire four and a half hours of the flight to San Francisco.

"Are you really a priest?"

Not only had I been a priest for almost thirty years, I was finally a pastor. After dreaming of that role since I was a boy, I at last had my own flock, all 1,800 families of St. Gabriel parish in the Sunset district by the ocean. It was established in the early 1940s, built among the sand dunes "west of the Boulevard." I had my own rectory with a cook on Mondays and Wednesdays and my own associate pastors. I would be administering the full complement of sacraments (that pastors often tired of and grew to take for granted). There was even a grade school with 500 middle-class San Franciscans back when there was such a thing.

The sacrament of penance over the years became confession and then after Vatican II became reconciliation. They all pretty much mean the same thing. The *matter* is the confessing of sins. The *form* is the words of absolution given by the priest. As the pastor at St. Gabriel, I heard the first confessions of the second-graders in our parish. It was a wonderful celebration for the whole family. The second-grade teacher and the religious education instructor did a fantastic job preparing these little penitents for their first. A family—mom, dad, brothers, sisters—would all approach me in the front of the church. The second-grader would introduce his or her family to me by name and then ask for the sacrament. The family would return to the pew and watch (out of earshot) as I faced the child for their first confession.

One time after sins had been confessed and a blessing given, this little boy just sat there.

"Go in peace!" I said, but he didn't budge. Finally I said, "Is there anything else?"

"Yes, Father. I told you mine aren't you going to tell me yours?"

"Son, we don't have enough time for me to tell you all of mine."

There are too many stories of reconciliation and almost all of them are of redeeming value. Because of the sacredness of the confessional seal I can't relate them to you here. Let it simply be said that confession, penance, reconciliation, forgiveness, whatever you might want to call it is the greatest gift that God gave through his Son Jesus Christ to all of us.

There were still rumblings of discontent over the church closures when the pastor of St. Cecilia's was revealed to be a serial child molester. I can recall the day it was discovered that Monsignor Pat O'Shea had been arrested on sixteen felony counts of lewd acts with children. He was accused of taking boys on weekend ski trips and overnight trips to Lake Berryessa, teaching them drinking games and taking them to bed. I had served with him on the national board of Holy Childhood. He was the Director of Missions and that group fell under his purview. He was accused of embezzling more than a quarter of a million dollars from the Archdiocese while in that position and eventually pleaded guilty.

As I heard his crimes described, all I could feel was that he was done as a priest (a man of God). He would no longer be the same guy who pastored the largest, most successful parish in the Archdiocese. He would have to give up his black suits for orange ones and figure out a way to excuse his wrongdoing. He never did. He ended up serving time in San Quentin and to this day he doesn't know what harm he caused.

William Levada, my fellow seminarian at the North American College, replaced John R. Quinn as the Ordinary of the Archdiocese of San Francisco. Archbishop Quinn's eighteen-year tenure had imploded under the weight of the parish closures, embezzlement and pedophilia scandals. At the same time, the City was working on an ordinance requiring San Francisco employers to provide benefits for domestic partners. Quinn sought early retirement to pursue writing, teaching and theological research and the more conservative Levada was installed.

Patrick Bailey was an unexpected friend, someone I encountered during my time as pastor at St. Gabriel. The Bailey family was typical of many in the parish—a mom, a dad and a couple of kids. Pat worked hard for his living, for his family and for his Church. Because he was one of the parish leaders I got to know him early on. Pat was a devoted husband and father, a devout Catholic, and a decent fisherman. No, he was an excellent fisherman.

Fishing is something I have enjoyed since I was a boy. I spent many hours on the Mississippi coaxing catfish out of the murky water and into a sizzling pan of fat. When I moved west to California, I discovered an entirely new kind of fishing—on the open ocean. Pat and I fished together on a charter boat owned and operated by our good friend Jimmy Robertson that would have been the envy of the Honkers Club. It was named the *Ginnie C II* and more than a few times I was wishing I was back on dry land instead of staring over the rail at the not-so-Pacific with *mal de mer* and not knowing how to spell it.

We fished beyond the Farallon Islands, barely visible from

SF as crumbs on the horizon, where the continental shelf drops off abruptly to more than 800 fathoms. We went in search of salmon or albacore or swordfish or whatever was in season. The open waters of the Pacific were our backyard. What an upgrade from the Mississloppy!

One day there was a knock on the door of the rectory and there stood Pat on the other side with a check for $10,000. St. Gabriel's had just begun a capital campaign for what was called Plant Improvement. It meant the place needed new paint and windows. With a gymnasium, school, church and rectory, this was no small task and would require hundreds of

Pat Bailey and Father Harry on San Francisco Bay

thousands of dollars. I gratefully accepted the Baileys' donation and asked Pat to chair the committee in charge of the project. Not long after that, he joined my God Squad board of directors and became its president.

In the spring, I received the honor of Doctor of Humane Letters from Waynesburg College in Pennsylvania. The Presbyterian school, founded the same year as San Francisco's Gold Rush, had asked me to deliver the baccalaureate sermon to the Class of 1996. Following my homily, the college conferred the honorary doctorate upon me with these words:

> *FATHER HARRY G. SCHLITT, Pastor of St. Gabriel Parish of San Francisco, California, builder of bridges and steward of God's work on earth, you have a distinguished career in Christian service. You have served the Archdiocese of San Francisco, the Armed Forces*

Radio Network through the series "Love on the Rock," San Francisco State University, the United States Catholic Conference, New York City, and other avenues for Christian communication. Your innovative approach to delivering a message of love, good will, and service, including the production of Emmy award-winning programs on television, has travelled beyond the electronic media of our time and touched the hearts of viewers, listeners, and readers throughout the nation. A skilled and contemporary communicator with a story of eternal importance, you have made a distinctive contribution to the experience of joy and grace that comes with knowing the goodness of God.

Two weeks later, my picture was on the front cover of the newspaper back to back with one of Rush Limbaugh. I was on the left. We were both giving commencement addresses in our hometown of Cape Girardeau, he to the public high school and I to the Catholic. My great-nephew had proposed me as the speaker and issued the invitation. His parents never married but his uncle Father Harry was post-Vatican II. He was the class president, in the National Honor Society, a member of Students Against Drunk Driving and had won five academic scholarships. He played soccer and was going to St. Louis University to study law. I had a Friday night wedding and Sunday services in San Francisco, so the trip was a quick turnaround. I was so proud of my nephew and wanted to be there for him when his grandpa could not.

TWA Flight 800 took off from JFK in New York City just after 8:30 the evening of July 17, 1996. I had two close friends on board, one a pilot the other his wife, a flight attendant. Twelve minutes later the 747 exploded and crashed into the Atlantic Ocean off Long Island. Don and Anneli Gough perished along with 228 others. The cause has never been determined.

I officiated at the Goughs' memorial service on a hot Saturday morning a couple of weeks later. I recall how meaningful it was as we went first to have the religious ceremony at the Greek Orthodox Church where the couple had been married and then on to a hangar in Sonoma County for the memorial service at the airport where Don had kept the biplane he flew for fun.

In Greek churches the image of the *Theotokos*—mother of God—enjoys the place of prominence. Whereas in most Catholic churches we have a crucifix as the center of attention, high and behind the altar, the Greeks have the woman Mary, the mother of God, with a small child on her lap.

At the Schellville Airport, there were hundreds of mourners including a large contingent that had worked for TWA and other airlines, most of whom knew each other. These "fly boys" and "fly girls" who called the world home were often like family, sharing apartments and living in the same communities convenient to airports during their off-hours on the ground. Together this crowd had flown millions of miles—many of them had worked the same New York to Paris route of the doomed flight—and here they were honoring two of their close friends who were on the wrong plane at the wrong time. The loss was intense and personal.

I'm not sure what I said but I know how I said it, with great emotion and feeling. The Marin county newspaper had the story on the front page of the next day's Sunday edition and reported me saying that everybody dies, but not everybody lives, but that Don and Anneli had. "They enjoyed the precious time they had in this life," I said. And then I told everyone to remember the energy both the Goughs put into their lives. I do recall singing a verse from *On Eagle's Wings* as we wept:

> *And He will raise you up on eagle's wings*
> *Bear you on the breath of dawn*
> *Make you to shine like the sun*
> *And hold you in the palm of His hand.*

18. Vicar Schlitt

I HAD KNOWN BILL LEVADA since my Roman days at the North American College. A number of years later as a new bishop, he was appointed to serve on the communications committee of the National Catholic Conference of Bishops. I was the national director for the Catholic Communications Campaign at the time and we saw each other often and visited at meetings. So I felt perfectly comfortable in making an appointment to see him to ask for a change in my status from Director of Stewardship and pastor, to working full time at St. Gabriel.

It was my fourth year at the parish and as a pastor. I was really liking it a lot. I knew most people by name, knew their families, their kids, and it was beginning to feel like home. It was starting to be too comfortable. I was still going to the chancery office twice a week to serve as Director of Stewardship and there were weekend and evening meetings. That was a job. Being pastor was a privilege.

I went to see him with a giant smile on my face quite certain that he would honor my request. We had just completed a very successful fund-raising effort at the parish for replacement of windows, painting and a number of other things that had to be done and we had gone over our goal.

He greeted me by saying, "Oh Harry, I'm so glad you made this appointment. I wanted to speak to you about a new assignment I have for you."

Before I could make my request he said he would like me to assume even greater responsibilities at the chancery and become the Vicar for Administration. I wasn't sure what that meant but I knew it was the end of my pastoral life in a parish. I had worked only four years in a ministry that I had dreamt about and planned for during all my formative years of study. Now I'm asked to come to the office nine to five, five days a week, with no time off for good behavior.

"I'll give you a couple of days to think about it but I would really like you to serve in this new capacity. It's Monday. Can you come and see me again on Wednesday? I'm leaving for Rome in the early afternoon and would like to wrap this up."

I was the one being wrapped up. I was encouraged by my predecessor, the future bishop Robert McElroy, to take the job. I think because of the success I'd had in administering the stewardship office, McElroy recommended to Levada that I become the vicar. Archbishop Quinn had not been interested in administration and deferred to Bob's direction. Levada had his own style, you could call it hands-on, and McElroy wanted out. Like me, Bob had a parish and a job in the chancery. Only he was the one being released to become a pastor full time.

"Oh," added the Archbishop, "I would like very much if you would move in with me to the residence behind the Cathedral."

Now I'm not only leaving the rectory where I was king of the castle, I was returning to the Archbishop's Residence where I would once again have intimate knowledge of that passage from Matthew's gospel where it says that Jesus came not to be served but to serve. It was a double whammy, vicar and roommate at the same time. I did not want it.

It was July 1, 1998, when I turned the key to the new residence for the first time. They were still working on the last of the renovations. The structure had once been a convent. I spent three nights there before Bill Levada moved in and we became housemates for nearly ten years. When it came to living in the same space, once again I found him to be a very kind and thoughtful man. Of course, we had plenty of room.

You might think that living with a man of Bill's talents and abilities would tend to make one feel inadequate or, at best, like a second-class citizen. But that was not the case. In fact, I flourished as a priest and administrator because there was never a feeling of being lorded over and I knew I had my talents (and failings), which were different than his.

I would go to the opera or the symphony with him once a year and he would go to the ballpark with me. I'm sure he enjoyed sports more than I enjoyed dressing up and falling asleep at the opera hoping for halftime so I could get something for my throat. It didn't take long for us to realize the differences in our tastes and our druthers. But that never prevented Bill from inviting me to every dinner and every function that took place in the residence, even though I was only the vicar.

We never traveled on vacation together nor did we go out a lot for dinner. Our food at home was the best prepared by the archbishop's chef. She had been a pastry chef at a luxury hotel when she was discovered to have managerial ability as well as cooking talents. She is still in service to the current Archbishop of San Francisco.

A businessman? I don't think so. But there I was at a desk with an administrative assistant and all the electronic and IT tools necessary to manage a multi-million dollar operation. Of course I was the pastoral minister who suddenly became the temporal minister or director of temporalities as it's called in Canon Law. It simply means I really don't have anything to do with the soul or Jesus but rather the body and Mammon or whoever else is looking for the funds to make it all work.

There were five major things I was supposed to direct and I was none of those professionally. I wasn't a lawyer, a banker, a property manager, a fund-raiser, nor a human resources expert but there I sat with all these offices answering to me. The director of each office was a layperson and well qualified to do their job. My part was to make sure everything they did complied with our mission and our goals as the Roman Catholic Archdiocese of San Francisco. It was an education for me.

In New York I had managed the $7 Million Catholic Communications Campaign for several years, but there was more collecting and giving from a purely spiritual capacity rather than just dealing with money, power, property, personalities, law and growth. We were able to put large sums of money together from different donors and networks and develop programming for radio, TV and print that would serve the Church directly.

In my office it was day-to-day activity centered around making decisions about temporal affairs without much reference to the gospel. In my early years, I did this work for sixteen years, I missed regular prayers and invocations to God for help. So I began every meeting with a prayer even if it was a dispute or a report on things and matters foreign to faith and prayer. It helped every situation.

One year, I figured out that I attended 247 meetings and those were all scheduled. They did not count the various ad hoc gatherings that took place in my office or the hallway or a conference room that dealt with emergency matters that needed an instant decision, like someone screaming obscenities at another employee or discovering that someone had been dipping into the archdiocesan till without permission and lining their personal pockets with extra cash. I was not the best at temporalities, but I was pretty good because of my communication skills and my ability to deal with different personalities. After all, when you get right down to it, it's people in positions of power that make the difference. If they are happy and working, a great deal can be accomplished.

I sought the help of a trusted friend when I felt like I was in over my head or needed an impartial viewpoint. Pat Bailey had proved adept at the helm of the God Squad and steadfast as a pillar of St. Gabriel. He was also an insurance lawyer who knew a lot about business matters. I could rely on him for help with that side of my job. I suggested Pat for inclusion on the archdiocesan Finance Council and he was appointed.

I was promoted from Vicar for Administration to Vicar General by Archbishop Levada. It was more prestigious and meant you answer only to the archbishop and have rank over the other department heads in his cabinet. Later that same year, I was put in charge of the North American College reunion of 150 guys from all over the United States. Alumnus Bill Levada called me into his office the day it began and told me the pope had made me a monsignor. Right! I was secretly thrilled to be named a Prelate of Honor because of my sister Della. She had expected me to be a bishop so monsignor gave her encouragement that I was doing good work somewhere in the Church.

A close priest friend, who was also my confessor for some years before I went to New York, had made it his life mission to welcome and encourage those who had left active ministry opting for another mode of transportation on the road to eternal life. He gathered them together on a regular basis and introduced new ones to the community, always making sure that their children were included too. Monsignor Jim Flynn had been the pastor at St. Gabriel when I went to him for spiritual direction, confession and, of course, one of his famous Manhattans. He died of lung cancer too early in life as his cigarette habit could not be broken until it was too late.

Jim's obituary in the *Chronicle* said he "developed his own family of priests and laity throughout his many years of service." The mourners who filled the Cathedral for his funeral bore testimony to his extraordinary ministry to ex-priests and ex-sisters who chose love and marriage. I was fortunate to have been there to experience what he had been able to accomplish.

A copy of a letter written by one of our paid consultants to his boss back East had surfaced at the chancery office. It said not to be concerned about Reverend Harry G. Schlitt as he was "feckless" and renewal of the contract for services to the Archdiocese of San Francisco would be sought from a higher and more suitable source. You, too? I had to go to the dictionary to discover the meaning of feckless.

> *feckless*
> *1. Lacking purpose or vitality: feeble: ineffective.*
> *(Scottish feck, efficacy, short for effect + less)*

I had never heard it used in ordinary conversation and the attribution came out of nowhere. The same man who wrote it about me was probably a good swimmer.

One of my spiritual directors in my early days of preparing for the priesthood used to tell me that if I could not say anything good about another person, say that they were probably a good swimmer. You see, in the minor seminary, we arrived in September and went home in June. We didn't have a swimming pool so none of us really knew who could swim and who couldn't swim. So the escape from giving another guy a bad rap was to refer to their natatorium skills which we knew nothing about.

The good swimmer I was referring to finally bit the dust as a consultant to the Archdiocese when I simply refused to pay the exorbitant contract amount that he wanted. It also followed a very poor if not completely unsuccessful effort to raise money for our Catholic schools. Most of the pastors were now fed up with the services rendered and it was no secret among them—nor in my office—that this particular firm would have to wait a long time before being offered a Catholic contract in this part of California. Needless to say, I was on this man's Schlitt list of priests who were not only feckless but unfair and hurtful.

When our new offices were opened on Peter Yorke Way in 2001, he was invited to visit and tour the space. He made sure that his response reached me by letting one of my co-workers know that he would not set foot in the building until that "son of a so and so Schlitt" was gone. That didn't happen. Within a year he wanted something, another favor, and he was back making nice and kissing up in order to introduce a new business scheme. Funny, I didn't seem so feckless now that I was the Vicar General. The assignment afforded me the opportunity to weigh in pretty heavily on decisions regarding finances in the Archdiocese. Even good swimmers should think twice before they burn bridges.

Feckless was no longer applicable to the name or the man Monsignor Harry G. Schlitt.

I returned to broadcasting with a weekly televised Sunday Mass. I had done the same thing for Heart of the Nation and of course Miles was the original, but producing my own "show" with volunteer staff I'd known for a lifetime was a fulfilling ministry for me. It has been the most fulfilling as a priest.

At the same time I came back to TV, I was saying good-by to my God Squad spots that I'd been doing since 1968. Why quit? There were two main things.

1) I didn't know the music anymore. In my fifties, Tower Records current hits were still keeping me plugged in to what people were listening to, but by the time I reached my sixties, I didn't have the interest to keep up.

2) The other reason was the God Squad had begun offering scholarships to kids around the country with the intention of having them write the scripts. Instead it turned into a full-time job keeping up with the kids. While it was a success, it was only

a success while I had time to deal with it.

So after thirty-four years, more than half my life, and 6,000 scripts it was bye-bye Father Harry and the God Squad.

I had a close friend who helped me when I was thinking about writing this book years ago by asking a lot of questions. One of them was, "What are the sounds you hear when you are with other people?"

I borrowed my answer from Saint John of God who wrote, "When laughter is shared, it binds people together and increases happiness and intimacy."

The sounds that cut through the din for me are laughter and conversation that is upbeat and encouraging. My hope is that people echo happiness from within. It's a bit Pollyanna-ish on my part, but that's what I like to hear. My favorite expression from all the Catholic spiritual writers comes from 19th century French poet and convert Léon Bloy who embraced a life of abject poverty yet was able to write, "Joy is the infallible sign of God's presence."

When you are with happy people who are pleased with their lives and those in it, you can be pretty sure that God plays a role in their feature film, if not in the screenplay.

Don Novello, the comedian who as Father Guido Sarducci spoofed the Vatican and the Catholic Church in general, said we should have a positive icon like the jolly Pillsbury Doughboy. Instead, we have a crucifix.

Admittedly, it's not easy to understand the cross. As Christian people we have to take it up now and again, but we don't have to stretch ourselves out on it every day and just hang there. Religious guilt often provides the excuse to do so. We have to come to our senses and realize that all the saints didn't suffer like we think they did. There are just as many saints present in our lives as there are who are canonized by the Church. We just don't always recognize them and give them credit.

There are families where saints not only survive but thrive. Goodness comes from people who have a positive attitude. As the expression goes, "paying it forward" can do more than all the time spent on our knees doing penance for something we did wrong.

Being positive is also the more difficult task. There is a constant fear of things not turning out the way we planned. I wonder, if John XXIII returned today to find the windows not only closing one by one, but being locked and shuttered, as if the end was near, what would he do? WWJD?

What the sainted John wouldn't do is live in a cloud of fear and guilt. That will keep you indoors and afraid. I don't know who came up with this, but it rings true in many of my homilies, "When fear knocks and faith answers, fear goes away!" Listen for that response of faith. You might be surprised what you hear.

19. On the Bench

A FEW OF MY PRIEST FRIENDS are "on the bench."

It all began with great gusto in 2002 when the Bishops of America gathered in Texas to examine the sexual abuse scandal among priests in the United States. The hearings occurred as a result of the pandemic abuse of children by clergy in the Archdiocese of Boston, whose leader at the time was my former bishop from Springfield, Bernard Law.

While the world watched on live TV, the Bishops got down to business, crafting a document entitled *The Charter for the Protection of Children and Young People*. It detailed procedures for handling allegations of sexual abuse of minors by clergy and established a zero tolerance policy for those who were accused.

I knew we were not all perfect when I first went to the seminary. It was no great surprise that a few turned out the way they did. I believe that pedophilia is a bit like alcoholism in that it is a sickness that is within and cannot be cured (as proven) by taking a man out of a school situation and placing him in the desert where there are no children. It worked while they were there but didn't take hold and cure the individuals.

You already know about my experiences with Bernard Law. The man I knew was not a monster nor feckless. But I do think that coming from Springfield, Missouri, where there were dozens not hundreds of priests, he was ill-prepared to watch over the many priests of the Archdiocese of Boston, the fourth largest in the country at the time. He was in over his head in the job. That's happened to me once or twice. This time the consequences were shattering. You may recall Law's civil rights work in the South. He entertained the notion that he had even greater work to do and started spending too much time in Cuba, away from his archdiocese. Law wanted to convert Fidel Castro.

I am not saying these things in his defense. It is simply what I know of the man.

As the General Meeting of the full body of bishops wore on,

I watched closely on television and then witnessed death blows to a number of guys around me who were accused, yet nothing was proven. It didn't seem to matter. Once the accusation came, the priest was sent to the bench without as much as a hearing. Canon law does not afford the same right to due process that the constitution does.

I knew at least a dozen priests who were asked to retire or go to the bench during my time as Vicar General with Cardinal Levada but I was never privy to the details of individual cases. Since I had oversight over the Archdiocesan budget, I knew what was expected to be paid out to settle cases and also the kind of numbers we were encountering. But there were no confessions to me, no clandestine individual meetings, no tears shed on clerical shoulders in private, no strong feelings from me one way or the other, just the disappointment that we had a new sickness among the clergy.

That said, I know two of the cases very well as I have heard from both sides in both instances because the priests involved were my friends.

One of my favorite priests, and a very helpful mentor to me when I was dealing with Archdiocesan finances, had been accused by one of his nephews. He has since passed away. He was asked to leave his rectory residence the same day the accusation was heard by the Archbishop. Life as he knew it was over in a moment. I suppose the same could be said for the victims of abuse. There was a closed parish in Marin county where we did some alterations to the rectory so we could house three or four of these men who were on the bench. The Monsignor was at least ten years my senior and I had the miserable task of telling him where he was to live and what rooms he was to take. I did it. The usually affable, jocular and very popular parish pastor moaned and cursed and then he cried. "Harry," he said, "you know me, you know the profile painted by my nephew is not me." I nodded in affirmation but then had to complete my task of acquainting him with his new living quarters. It was difficult and until I meet my Maker, I guess I'll never really know what happened.

In the other case, the alleged abuse involved a priest I consider to be a close friend. His accuser claimed he had seduced her thirty years earlier. Again, only they and God know the truth, but in all our years of friendship there was nothing that I ever witnessed him do or say that convinces me it's true.

It's really none of my business to comment on either case or either side of the process, but it's not out of line to say how disappointed I was when the infamous Dallas Charter was promulgated, with no room for even a hint of mercy, reconciliation or Catholic charity.

Priests who might not have been guilty of anything were told to remove their collars and relinquish their black suits. They were only to offer Mass in private and forbidden to officiate at funerals or weddings, or administer the other sacraments—even for family or close friends.

This is a crusher for guys from big families with nephews and nieces who were having first communions, graduations and other celebrations where the priest usually plays a significant role. The saddest occasion is the death and funeral of a parent. The benched priest is not allowed to say Mass in public. It simply doesn't make sense to me. Just another reason why I'm not bishop material. I feel sorry for the bishop of the diocese who has to make the phone call and inform the guy "grabbing some pine" that he cannot baptize a baby nephew, or assist at the marriage of his sister or, honest to Pete, not be able to celebrate the funeral Mass of a parent.

Father George had a younger sister who was to be married in the fall. He pleaded with the Archbishop to be the officiant at the ceremony. No can do, it's a public ceremony and the statutes are very clear. You can imagine how his mom and dad and his little brother felt seeing him walk in in his black suit with a tie and slide into the pew with them rather than walking out of the sacristy with the groom and the groomsmen to the altar to offer the Mass and bind his little sister in matrimony.

Other men that I know readily admitted to what they did, even though what they did was much less severe in nature than pedophilia, and would not merit complete abandonment by the Church if they were taken to court, or if the Church in this country had not adopted a policy that even an accusation would put you on the bench and you would be relieved of your duties. A few of these men still gather regularly to pray the Mass and talk about their issues. It's a support group that gives them some consolation. They are still not allowed to wear the Roman collar or perform sacramental ceremonies in public. I'm not talking about criminals here, but men who might have been accused and the Archdiocese chose to settle in court rather than go to trial because of the punitive damages that might ensue if they lost the case.

It seemed to bear a lot on economics, not unlike priestly celibacy, which too often has been linked to money by the Church—they don't think a parish could afford both a priest, his wife and children. While it would not be easy, it could be done. Many of our new brothers from the Episcopal church congregations can attest to it.

I am not an expert in this field and I have NOT been privy to most of the behind the scenes activities that went on in the Archdiocese of San Francisco. My musings are all personal and much of what I based my opinion on was from sources that I would not classify as "very" reliable. But in my humble opinion, it was all precipitated by the legal beagles of the Church who were doing everything in their power to prevent lawsuits and, more to the point, suits that would end up with the diocese paying punitive damages. The prevailing wisdom in the U.S. was such that most legal opinions were given to bishops in order to avoid trials at all cost, or suffer diocesan bankruptcy and the accompanying opprobrium.

In the case of the Archdiocese of San Francisco, our learned counsel knew how much money was in the bank and he knew the real estate. The numbers went to the Finance Council and they devised three plans for settlements. All the money was to come from the sale of property and austerity measures at the chancery were to be implemented.

Life at the office was very sensitive after 2002 and the Bishops' stance on abusive priests. I heard the term "walking on eggs" from Cardinal Egan in Rome. Most of the chancery employees felt like they were doing just that. It seemed like the daily dose of news from the paper and the TV stations would never end. Whispering turned to open discussion and individuals were both scourged and defended, praised and forgiven. A pastor would be in the tribunal office (where annulments are processed) inquiring about a marriage case one day and gone the next.

The knowledge that I had was limited but I know we did everything possible to eliminate any future abuse. Now that we've gone this far, it seems unreal to see how a priest could minister for so many years and not be caught and reported. But that seemed to be the case with parents who were embarrassed and of course the victims who were frightened and in some cases affected mentally for most of their lives. The slightest hint of an impropriety is now immediately investigated and dealt with in a matter of days. The Archdiocese of San Francisco went through all the tests of the Catholic Conference, which included fingerprinting anyone working for the Church whether it be bishop, priest, teacher, coach, assistant coach or anyone who was around the children of the church or the church school. I truly believe that we had the problem under control by the time I was out of the office. However, one never knows. When dealing with this challenge, there is never a sure thing.

The mood at the chancery was one of extreme unhappiness. We would have the news media to address as well as going for depositions and arbitrations. It went on for about five years before the proper and rightful tools were in place to deal with it.

After the Bishop's declaration on clergy abuse, almost every diocese set up a review board to go over individual complaints and to make recommendations to the Bishop of the Diocese. The Board was made up of a lay chair, usually a physician or a psychiatrist, an expert in youth counseling, along with a legal expert (attorney or judge) and in our case the Archbishop and two senior priests. That Board still exists here in San Francisco and even though their caseload can't be very heavy (I have not heard of any new cases for almost ten years) they still meet on a regular basis.

My role as Vicar General for the Archdiocese of San Francisco made it my job to handle the financial and pay-off part of the process, but I had no voice with the committee that was set up to deal with accused priests. My input was inappropriate, my feelings irrelevant.

While it might be true that I was left out of decisions formally, it might be pointed out that I lived for ten years with

Levada and would go on to live six more with his successor, Archbishop George Niederauer. That meant I prayed the Mass with them in the morning, had breakfast with them and dinner in the evening, and usually a drink during the news before dinner. It also meant that I had complete and full access to the most powerful men in the Archdiocese. They told counsel what to do and when to do it. I would like to think that I had some strong influence in their thinking, if not for original ideas, at least as a protection against what they might not do that would make things worse. Both of them listened to me and took me seriously. I was not the great mind of McElroy, nor a legal wizard, nor many other things, but I did have great influence in what was done and said from the top.

As to my spiritual influence, I am not one to judge, but I believe that my insistence on beginning every meeting with a prayer made a difference as to how individuals purported themselves in those meetings.

The Carmelite sisters of Springfield prayed for many years that I would remain faithful to my calling as a Catholic priest. It was a little embarrassing after my 25th anniversary when a good priest friend informed me that the sisters were still praying that I would persevere in my vocation. I do believe their prayers were responsible for getting me through many a ticklish situation that could have easily turned into a major problem.

Today, I rejoice in my priesthood and rarely do anything ministerial or sacramental without thinking of my brother priests who have been removed from active ministry. There are many good men who have succumbed to the circumstances of our times and the day and age in which we live. My words here are not an excuse for criminal acts perpetrated by priests, but rather to point out that one stroke of the brush colored an entire profession and many a good guy with tar and feathers that they did not deserve.

Archbishop Levada had given me another promotion within the chancery. I added the title Moderator of the Curia, which gave me rank over all the offices in the chancery. Bill and I enjoyed a good working relationship and even at home there were almost no disagreements. Well, I remember this one.

It was shortly after the sexual abuse accusations against priests began, maybe 2003, when we were disturbed by a protester in front of the residence. He was shouting obscenities as we were heading to the chapel for our morning prayers and Mass. It was loud and graphic.

"God will not forgive you #@&%ing priests for what you've done to children!!"

"Archbishop," I asked, "do you want to go out and calm this man?"

"Harry, he's talking about priests. I'm an archbishop. Why don't you go?"

I thought about it for a minute. I could see the anger and rage as I peeked through the curtains and then I checked the closed circuit TV monitor by the door. I decided not to go out.

Bill looked and me and said, "Well . . . ?"

I shook my head and proceeded to the chapel.

"He is bashing priests and I'm a monsignor."

That didn't sit too well but it was the end of it.

I think Archbishop Levada and I were the closest when we said prayers and had Mass together. But there was one other occasion, when we went to the Presidio of San Francisco to attend a "ceremony of apology" for victims of clergy sexual abuse.

The group refused to use one of our many parish facilities for the meeting, choosing instead the former military base turned national park. The room was packed with TV cameras and news people eager to witness what was a major story at the time. Because shoes dropped all over the world—not just in the Archdiocese of San Francisco or in California—the press was eager to jump on any one as if it were the only one.

About 135 people were there. Archbishop Levada took a seat in the rear of the room while I wandered closer to the front and sat next to another priest. There were only about a dozen priests in attendance.

The fireworks began with a number of women complaining about not being compensated for what had happened to them twenty or thirty years before. The ranting and raving interspersed with fu---- and other expletives was mostly aimed at the Archbishop. At one point, as he was being derided and chided, they called for him to come up front so he wouldn't miss any of the tired old alley language being thrown at him. He did. He came forward and took it all.

It was a long nine hours of premeditated, calculated frustration that was dished out. Half way through, most of the media departed. When the crowd called for the archbishop's resignation, and for Auxiliary Bishop John Wester to replace him and admit that this would be the only way to save the Church in San Francisco, I was ready to go. But no, it went on for a couple more hours.

In all that time, there were at least three men and two women who spoke who had been brutally abused and one could only feel for them and what they had gone through. It was sad and brought me to tears. It certainly was worth the beating that we all took to realize how horrible their youth had been at the hands of sick priests. I didn't feel very much at all for those who dominated the afternoon and evening meeting. It was difficult to distinguish between who was really abused and who was there to get money and/or be on television.

The two men who were abused by Pat O'Shea were the only two who were credible and deserved millions and constant apologies from the Church. O'Shea was sick. Of all the priests who were accused, and I know them all and dealt with all of them, this was for real and for the sake of his own weakness, but sinful and criminal. The men who had been altar boys were victims from the beginning to the end and were respectable and sensible in their complaints. Had others followed suit, it could have been a whole different story. But they didn't. It became more noisy and blustery and one by one the news media headed for the doors.

The moderator was a smart and supportive religious woman who tried to keep order. The crowd kept telling her to sit down and listen like the rest of us. She finally did.

When it was his turn to speak, the archbishop said, "The whole Church has been shocked and scandalized by the abuse done by a few of her priests to children and young people. The Church is slowly learning how deep this wound is, how slow to heal, and how diligent must be our effort to ensure that it will not happen again."

It was almost dark when Bill and I got home, went to the kitchen, boiled some water and had pasta and a sandwich, both of us agreeing that the afternoon had to have been the low point in our lives. It was a day I'll never forget and one that upped my admiration for the future Cardinal William Levada.

After much had been said and done and the media had blasted the Archbishop and the Church in general, I did happen upon one of my confreres at a dinner place and he was wearing the black suit and the collar. This man was guilty. It was decided in the courts. He did time in prison and had been released because of age and illness. I knew he had been "defrocked" and so was a bit surprised by his manner of dress. I was cordial and said hello but it gave me the shivers, as I did know about him from the men he had abused as boys and knew he was a sick individual. One of the men spoke up when Levada and I went to that open mike session for the benefit of the abused (and I might add the media) at the Presidio. When he told his story, it made me cringe. I could not imagine anyone with the same training and commitment that I had in the priesthood doing such terrible things to a little boy.

20. Silver Penny Farm

THE SILVER PENNY FARM was seventeen acres near Petaluma owned by the Archdiocese of San Francisco. It was established in 1840 and the original house still stands but on neighboring property. The main house at Silver Penny was built in 1899. Descendants of publishing giant William Randolph Hearst had given the property to the Archdiocese in 1985. It had become a retreat house where a person could pause from the rush of life and open himself or herself to a more beautiful creation that God had put right in front of them. It had roses and trees and shrubs and lots of birds to chirp you up in the morning and swallow the mosquitoes at night. It was a place where you could find peace in the land and the landscape.

I first discovered it in the early 1990s after I returned from New York and began going there for personal retreats or one-day getaways to read, swim and enjoy the quiet and the sunshine of the country. It was pretty much a sheep farm and the surrounding fields were full of wooly characters that didn't make much noise and didn't smell like farm animals. I used to watch them in the rain and wonder why they didn't shrink. Everything wool that I ever owned did.

Silver Penny was run by a retired priest who had served in the Navy and had worked as a hospital chaplain most of his priestly life. He was assisted by two women religious, one of whom lived there full-time and another who commuted from hospital work in San Francisco. They worked hard and maintained the place to the best of their ability. They cleaned and washed, did the gardening, dumped the trash and when the place finally closed all of them were eighty or older. It was sad for me as the Vicar General to tell them that the Archdiocese intended to sell the property because they had no more use for it. But that's another story.

When I first moved to San Francisco, I used to spend the

Fourth of July in front of the television either watching baseball or tennis. A number of times, I ended the day in a Marina Green saloon toasting the holiday with friends before walking to the waterfront to watch the fireworks (when you could see them through the fog). The holiday passed and it always seemed such a waste.

The Chestnut Street bars were where I first encountered some of my closest friends. They spent the Fourth of July in those safe confines where they knew the barkeeps and were guaranteed to meet others with the same holiday objectives. I had the idea of getting them out of their zip codes and into the sunshine where they could breathe fresh air, away from cigarette smoke and the strawberry smell of bathrooms and the constant blare of the TV letting them know who would make the Wimbledon finals or where the Giants were in the standings.

Let's see, where to start . . . I spoke to two charming and attractive flight attendants and asked them if they would help me move the male masses off the bar stools for a new venture. Nothing like a good-looking hostess to turn their heads to listen to what Father Harry had to say.

"I'm inviting you to a small retreat place," I began. "It only accommodates twenty-six people. There is a pool and lots of space to play cards and also a large television to watch the games and the matches. It's only a forty-five-minute drive from the City and it is very inexpensive. You can bring your beverage of choice and I'll provide all the food and snacks. It will cost you less than $30 a day."

It was my solution to getting several chronic drinkers and a few alcoholics into a new venue where they could see something different, breathe something different, eat something different but be with their friends and drink the same adult beverages that drew them to the Marina watering holes. It worked. I still have the invitation from the first year and it went like this:

WHO IS INVITED?
No sore heads, no religious freaks (save one), no political analysts, no one who has an ax to grind or who desires anything more than relaxation, companionship and good food and drink.

It wasn't unusual to note that they followed my rules and behaved beautifully. That's not always the case where drink flows freely. I only had a couple of rules. The most important was that they not get back in their cars once they arrived and unpacked until it was time to depart. Of course, we had to make ice runs and go out for extra food. For the most part, no one took advantage of being in a new area that they might want to explore after alcohol persuaded them there was "more" beyond the Farm. In all of our holidays there, I recall only one person who left angry and that was because the man who had raised her expectations for the holiday getaway ended up jilting her. Fortunately, she left in the early evening before any major imbibing had begun. After I heard the tires of her car spit up the gravel in the driveway, I thought to myself, "Well, there's one we won't have to worry about next year."

Fourth of July at Silver Penny Farm
Seated from left: Sister Hope, Father Ray, Sister Joanne and Father Harry

One of the key organizers always had games for the different tables to play after dinner and before dessert. There were prizes and lots of laughs over competition that amounted to more laughs. We'd adjourn to the parking lot for our own display of fireworks. They turned out to be treacherous for us in the dark and dangerous for the property. Dry summer fields surrounded us and the idea of roasted lamb so long after Easter was not appealing.

Eventually, we scrapped the fireworks and headed to the nearby pond for a fishing derby. There were lots of little bass and hardly ever one worth keeping but it was fun to see them bite and stretch the lines. I think in all the years there were never more than four or five fish worth cleaning and eating.

Of all the ministerial efforts that I had made over the years, I believe this was one of the best. It lasted twelve years from 1992 to 2004 when the Archdiocese had to sell the property. It brought people together who cooked and cleaned and respected one another for who they were and not who they might be. Most were over fifty and had pretty much run the gauntlet of life. Strong bonds of friendship were built over the years at the Silver Penny and our closing Mass brought many a newfound intimacy with God.

Anneli and Don Gough at Silver Penny

In observance of Independence Day, we prayed for our country and especially all the men and women who had served in the Armed Forces to keep us a free nation. We lost several of the group to old age or early demise during those twelve short years and the closing prayers were always for them and all who had attended over the years.

The director of the Silver Penny, Father Ray, always said it was important that people know they would have the freedom there to find what they were looking for. It was certainly true with the group I put together with one or two exceptions.

It was pretty much the same group who greeted the new millennium at the Penny in 2000. We dressed up and drank champagne, toasting the arrival of the New Year around the world with the help of a giant TV we rented so we could watch the celebrations as they occurred. We catered dinner for the first time and swapped our shorts and overalls for gowns and tuxes to welcome the 21st century. Little did we know then that our days at the Farm were numbered.

When the Archdiocese made the announcement that they were going to sell the property, it was met with great turmoil by the sisters and the father who had managed it for so many years. They were getting up in years and the work was too hard. There was not enough income to hire people to do the work and so it went on the auction block. There was immediate interest and it was snapped up by a couple who had recently sold another nearby parcel of land to the government for $19 Million. The Silver Penny price was peanuts to them. They had all the good intentions in the world of continuing the work for which the Penny was famous, excellent hospitality and a simple bed and breakfast.

But alas, nothing is simple when it comes to money, property, and people who tell you one thing then follow another personal agenda. Today the main house sits majestically on the small hill surrounded by the same flock of sheep and the same nearby farmhouse. But most of the flora and fauna that graced the outside have disappeared including huge trees and shrubbery that kept the noise in and out. An iron gate with a password lock spans the entrance and even an old onlooker from days past is not allowed up the driveway to reminisce about all the great times he had there.

I had known from Kae that Dr. Don had been battling pneumonia but his death came as such a shock. He was seventy years old. I gave the homily although it was not a Catholic funeral. Don's son-in-law, who is a Protestant minister, conducted the service. The little church was bulging with radio and media types. It was a sincere audio blast from the past. Don would have been the first to yell "Amen."

A month after Dr. Don died so did Pope John Paul II. To the surprise of almost no one, Cardinal Ratzinger stepped into the shoes of the fisherman, except they were red slippers. Benedict XVI was virtually an extension of his predecessor and probably too old, but he was elected because he wouldn't change anything John Paul II had done.

The change in Rome shifted the sands in San Francisco. My boss and roommate, Bill, was summoned to the Vatican, elevated to William Cardinal Levada and appointed to succeed Ratzinger as the Prefect of the Congregation for the Doctrine of the Faith. The man who had impressed me as a theologian in my seminary days had risen to the top job defending the Catholic faith. He had also become the highest ranking American in the Vatican.

My new Ordinary was Archbishop George H. Niederauer, who had gone to high school with Bill Levada where they were in band together. George was Teutonic by name but filled with the spirit of a Renaissance Man. He generously extended an invitation to me to remain living at the residence. I was happy to oblige. The two of us proved compatible and I was glad for the status quo.

Wayne and I flew to Florida in 2008 to see Roy, two weeks before he died. He'd known about the ALS for less than a year and his decline had been rapid. He was unable to speak but wrote on a tablet. His days were numbered and he thought he would spend them in a home and had made all the arrangements to live out the rest of his days there. There was no family other than some out-of-state cousins, so he'd been left to deal with his illness alone. Lou Gehrig's disease can be an awful torture for the person, and the people who know and love that person. A close friend of mine had recommended that Wayne and I go visit Rufus before he died as it would mean more to him then than if we attended his funeral. We did, like Gideon's "flowers while you live," only in our case it was sauvignon blanc.

True to Roy's character, there were several bottles of Orvieto Bigi in his fridge so we could properly celebrate his beautiful life. We gathered in his living room and had sandwiches and vino bianco. Wimpy and I left quietly knowing that Rufus would soon be in heaven with JFK.

Roy was eulogized as kind and generous with a jovial laugh and in my view that is a life well lived. Teacher to the end, he had asked for donations in lieu of flowers for two young people from his parish who would be traveling to Australia that summer for World Youth Day.

I was making that same trip. After all the hoopla of my prior visits Down Under, I was grateful this time to be accompanying Archbishop George Niederauer and playing a supporting role.

World Youth Day occurs every two to three years and is the Vatican's way of reaching out to young people in different parts of the globe. Similar to athletes gathering for the Olympics to demonstrate what they have trained for and lived for most of their lives, young people from all over the world would come to greet the pope in a public display of their Catholic faith and spirituality. It's such a large event that it normally takes place on the outskirts of a major city where there is room for the kids to camp, mix, mingle and feel the significance of their commitment to their own faith. They also get to experience the power of community and learn that they're not in this alone. The event was held in Rio de Janeiro in 2013 and marked the first encounter that South Americans had with one of their own, Pope Francis.

I had been to World Youth Day two other times, once in Denver and once in Toronto. On both of those occasions, I was producing a program for young people sponsored by Covenant House, a New York shelter for runaways, featuring a good friend and comedian Michael Pritchard. He has an unusual talent for bringing out the best in kids who have gone astray or perhaps have not had the chance to flourish like kids with families and support from relatives, teachers and pals who could show them the way.

John Paul II had been a unique personality and a tireless public figure. In the presence of young people he had radiated joy and love, showing all of us by example how to act and comport ourselves. I recall lying in a sleeping bag in the dirt at Cherry Creek State Park outside Denver. The Holy Father was less than a mile away still talking and singing with the young people while the rest of us were trying to get some shut-eye. We couldn't see him nor hear what he was saying but we knew from the lights and the crowd that he was still there.

His departure later that night was not all that gratifying, as the rotating blades on his military chopper provided by the U.S. government whipped up a cloud of dust that I can still taste. Mixed with saliva, it formed kind of a mud-like substance that left a dirty taste in your mouth. The pope ascended above the vast throng of humanity while the young people waved flags, played guitars and danced the night away praising God and showing the world that youth are not all bad. I could carry on with other highlights from my first Youth Day, but back to Australia.

Archbishop Niederauer and I first had spent a week on vacation in New Zealand traveling from the North Island to the South Island by ferry, then by rail. Train rides are fun, but like sheep, once you've experienced a million grazing in the fields you've been there, done that. Hours and hours peering out the window and not really knowing if or when we would arrive is not my idea of a vacation.

Eating mutton in new and usual forms was an unexpected adventure the two of us shared one evening in Christchurch when the archbishop spotted an Italian restaurant and wheeled me through the front door without even checking the menu posted beside it. We could smell the garlic and knew that the ultimate in New Zealand cuisine was at hand. Both of us ordered spaghetti and meatballs. Right, you guessed it, meatballs made from mutton. We both whispered a short prayer of gratitude to the Good Shepherd just for being able to enjoy a bountiful dinner in a wonderful country.

Upon arrival at the hotel in Sydney, I discovered that my credentials for Youth Day had not been issued. The archbishop could come and go to the events as he pleased and attended almost everything. I had to remain on my own and, left to my own discretion, had a great time doing what I wanted, when I wanted, only joining Himself for the evening meal.

The final day and the public Mass with the pope at the Royal Randwick Racecourse were incredible. By that time, I had a pass that said, yes, I was indeed a Catholic priest, a monsignor, in good standing and of no immediate danger to the Holy Father.

The city of Sydney put on its Sunday best for the papal visit and once again the young people themselves were the highlight and the gift of grace to the rest of us who attended as part of our duty and ecclesial office. God still works best through young people and the many good parents who inspire them to dig deeper into their lives to discover God and his gifts.

I departed Sydney and flew to Melbourne to visit my old pals who were so generous during those years when I came for the Royal Children's Hospital Appeal. Then I flew to Brisbane where Ric Melbourne was waiting at the gate, which you could still do then in Australia. My bags were there and the fun began.

Ric and his wife had a home on Tamborine Mountain. It was surrounded by wineries and the balcony overlooked the ocean and the Gold Coast, which is the Miami Beach of Australia. It's about forty minutes down to the beach. We were looking forward to some great fishing, but it rained all night, so instead there was great sleeping. We watched the rain fall all day and Ric played the guitar. He reminded me of Dr. Don who frequently would quote to me the record label of a particular song. I was always amazed at the memory. I could not remember the lyrics.

We went down the mountain, bought some fish and prawns and then went out for a long fish lunch. We sat on the wharf, drank two bottles of sauvignon blanc and enjoyed oysters and chips and more fish. It was delightful. He was and still is a good friend. Mike O'Leary was the subject of much of our conversation as Ric remembered him from the last trip and pointing out to him a tea called 19. Mike drank it and never was able to get up to work the next morning. We never found out what was in it.

By the way, the papers and the television were still filled with Pope Benedict. It had been quite an impressive visit. I watched the departure on TV for over two hours. They paraded the 747 around the runways for Qantas for a long time. I guess they gave the pope a free ride in exchange for the publicity. They got more than they deserved. The pope sat in seat 3A First Class. I was in 2A on the same plane returning to San Francisco. It was like having your own bedroom. It had everything including pajamas, cocktails and movies. I could get used to it but I would never be able to afford it.

Ric and I had reminisced about our times together and for a couple of days fooled ourselves into thinking we were still young, vibrant and ready to conquer the world. Woe is me when I start thinking that way. It leaves very little room for humility and docility and all the other lessons I was supposed to learn from the Shepherd and his numerous references in sacred Scripture.

"Harry, do you love me?"

"Lord, you know that I love you!"

"Feed my sheep."

My favorite one about the Shepherd is this:

1. Find them
2. Feed them
3. Don't fleece them

It's my lesson to pastors when they are over-zealous about second collections.

Angela Alioto is one of the most active people in North Beach. She was a one-woman building crew in reconstructing the oldest parish church in the City. The church that shared its patron saint with San Francisco had been one of the UMB parishes closed late last century. Before moving on to greener pastures in Rome, Archbishop Levada met with former Mayor Joseph Alioto and his daughter Angela to implement plans for the creation there of a national shrine to Saint Francis. A replica of the chapel in Italy was painstakingly constructed inside the gymnasium alongside the retrofitted St. Francis of Assisi church.

Angela took it on as a personal devotion to see that it was done. I was able to assist in a small way by joisting with several of the Fathers who felt it was a waste of money. I raised over $110,000 toward the project from my personal friends and supporters of the God Squad. The cardinal returned to the City of Saint Francis in the fall and blessed the National Shrine of Saint Francis of Assisi opening its tiny doors to the public.

That Christmas, I was back in front of the cameras hosting a national TV special that was filmed in the little chapel. The one-hour program was produced by my old network ABC and aired on their television stations across the country.

The broadcasting work was invigorating as it always had been. The administrative work was grinding me down and I started thinking about retirement. Catholic priests are eligible once they reach the age of seventy. I wrote a respectful query to my archbishop and was looking forward to focusing all my energy on the TV Mass, a little fishing and some handball. Things move slowly in an institution as old as the Church and just after my 71st birthday I was released from my chancery duties. Almost.

I was asked to stay on and help my successor learn the Vicar ropes. Then what the Dallas Charter calls a "boundary violation" occurred at St. Raymond parish. The pastor had put himself in the situation of leering at a young boy. His father reported it to the Archdiocese and the priest was gone by the afternoon. I was asked by the Archbishop to fill in as interim administrator until someone full time could be appointed. I packed my bag and had my first meeting with the parish council and interested school parents. It was not fun. I listened and assured them that this would be the end of that particular priest in any parish, in any state, in any country of the world.

I recall going through the ousted pastor's files and picking up a few odds and ends of his that were left behind. I studied the photographs of his mom and dad, of others in the family whom I did not know. I felt so blessed not to have a pedophile's mind nor make up. What a curse! How could you enjoy life? What would your thoughts be as you went about your daily duties as a priest—and a priest with a large grammar school? Oh my!

After six months of parochial shepherding, the parish returned to normal and now prospers as one of the finest in the Archdiocese. The most important lesson was for me. It was a grace of God to be able to assume that priest's duties and discover the love and fidelity that the people of that parish had for their Church and their immediate Church family. It was six months that I dreaded when I was asked to go, but six months of spiritual nourishment that I could never have gotten from a retreat. Thank you Jesus!

21. Lost Generation

IT WAS THE FIRST WEEK after I retired from my normal duties in the office from nine to five, five days a week. It was called a job. I used to brag about being a priest because I never had to go to work, I was always there (ba dum bum bum). That was pretty much the case as I did the routine office job and then helped out at parishes over the weekend or had some other fund-raising activity that took up my free time. Once I finally did retire at seventy-two, I promised myself that I would never again get in a hurry about anything or anyone.

That first weekend, I had a wedding in Redwood City at two o'clock and an evening Mass at five in Fairfield. I suspect the distance is about sixty miles. I had paved the way with the newlyweds, letting them know I could not stay for the reception and dinner. I hit the highway almost before the groom kissed the bride. I was bound and determined to make it. I was doing great until there was an accident on the Golden Gate Bridge. There was such a backup that I would never make it by five. My nerves were on edge and I was sweating profusely as I knew I wouldn't be on time. My vision was of people getting up and leaving thinking the priest would never arrive and who does he think he is, wasting my time like this? I tried to call but only got the parish answering service.

I broke the speed limit (yeah, right, not in a hurry) but made it about fifteen minutes after the hour. People were in their pews singing hymns. I apologized more than once only to hear one of the pillars of the church belt out, "No hurry, Harry, we'll just sing a few more tunes and go home." I was forced to limit the homily to a wing and a prayer.

It's been awhile since I retired, but I'm still anxious about a lot of things. Some of us are built that way. I'm not worried about getting old but I don't get excited about things as I used to. The same sermon twice. That is one of the worst things I can imagine at this time in my life. I return to the same themes. But with a different story to highlight what happened.

I had more time in retirement and got to catch up on current events. I was watching CNN one morning and there before my eyes was Justin Monaghan, still living and very active as a pastor in Joplin, Missouri. I listened in stunned amazement. Justin was talking about how he had spotted a tornado coming and got two blankets and jumped into the bathtub on the first floor of his rectory and covered his head. The funnel cloud had roared past as he lay face down in the tub, taking the rectory from over his head, along with his church, his school and a good portion of the town where he lived. When he pulled back the covers and peered out from the tub it was all gone. He was trapped for an hour before his parishioners found him and dug him out. This man has had more lives than the proverbial cat.

His story has a happy ending, waking up as a pastor when the building had been blown away around him and knowing that the Lord had spared his life one more time. He even got to meet President Obama who came to survey the devastation of the catastrophic EF5 tornado that killed 158 people and injured eleven hundred more. There must be something important ahead for my dear pal Justin Monaghan.

This was a sure sign of his conversion and the need to be ever vigilant against temptation and never touch another drop. I'm so proud of this man and the grace that God has given him to go through what he did and get up again and again after the falls from grace. It's a minor miracle and a blessing to the many people who listen to him preach, attend his Eucharistic celebrations, go to him for confession, and have their children baptized and married and their elders buried by him. I'm left with the words, "Yea, God. Thank you for reconciliation."

That same month I celebrated at a memorial in the Cathedral of St. Mary in San Francisco for Joan Ohanneson who died of Parkinson's disease at eighty-seven. She had been my mentor and guide through the priesthood and my early years in California. We had worked on a number of projects together. *Tread Softly* was a slide show presentation done in the late '70s about the elderly, how they were being cared for and just how many more of them there were going to be in the near future.

Part of the show featured an elderly priest and his volunteers helping people onto a bus to take them out of the retirement home and into the City. The group was called the FreeWheelers. Joan sang their praises and gave kudos to those responsible in that show. They are still active today. What a pleasant surprise as I walked into the Cathedral on that Saturday to celebrate her life with her friends and family to see two large buses painted with the FreeWheelers logo. The seniors were there coincidentally, enjoying Mass, a lunch and entertainment in the undercroft while Joan was being praised, saluted and mourned in the Cathedral upstairs.

Joan had written nine books in her lifetime. Her most famous work was *Scarlet Music*, a novel about Saint Hildegard of Bingen. She wrote inside the cover of my copy, "To Harry with affection and gratitude. Still love you in the same old way. Joan."

As I said, she meant a lot to me. She counseled me through my neck surgery and a number of fortunate maturation points with the opposite sex. She was my "saviouress" during many difficult times, when I needed a woman who could relate to me and knew who I was.

At one time in my life I thought I was the most honest person I knew. I didn't care about the topic or the people around me. I was convinced that I would tell the truth the rest of my life. I worked with someone who hyperbolized a lot. It made me even more honest.

I thought that as long as I told the truth I wouldn't have to remember what I said. That was usually the case when you made things up or embellished them or simply lied. It always got you into trouble. So it was going to be my quest in life to become the most honest person I knew.

If someone said to me, "Describe yourself to a stranger," I'd say that I like to think I'm easygoing, genuine, the most honest person I know. I read somewhere that honesty is supposed to be your servant not your master. I'm not all together sure what that means, but I'll take a stab at it with the example of having a five- or a ten-year plan. That would require a vision and a dream.

When I left Rome in 1965, I sincerely believed that priests would be allowed to marry. No matter how beautiful the sight or how good the feeling, without someone to share it, the experience is glazed and numbing, one dimensional. There is no pleasure, no goosebumps that complete the cycle. Whatever the experience, it loses its flavor on the bedpost overnight.

In the course of my career, I spent hours and hours sitting in dark studios putting my words together with words that had already been put together with music, trying to make something work. I felt that the round peg of the song would never fit the square hole of the story I had to tell. But every now and then, something clicked. What the lyricist had to say matched what I was thinking and the sounds and the beat and the magic of music brought my message to life.

More than once, I felt myself shouting in the loneliness of quiet after hours, when I could afford to use radio and production equipment that were reserved for commercial use during the day. It all came to a crescendo for me when the piece hit the airwaves and someone would call and say, "I heard you talking about me last night and you don't even know me." What a high that is when you hit a nerve, a vein, a person's soul and you had no idea.

I have had lots of mail over the years and I must say the best came from people I've never known. Here is a letter from a teacher in Japan who used to listen to me on Armed Forces Radio. All of these years have gone by and I still get warm and fuzzy feelings from someone like Makoto.

> *Dear Monsignor Harry Schlitt;*
> *Greetings from Japan!*
> *Hello! Thank you very much for e-mail reply quickly. It's been a very long time since I wrote to you in 1984. Do you remember me? I arrange the letter and I found your letter sending from New York or San Francisco.*
> *I happened to find your topic of Catholic San Francisco online edition. I've listened to your show "Love on the Rock" of the God Squad 27 years ago. I was a junior high school student at then. And I studied English through your radio*

programs in Japan. Also I've correspondence with you. I long for then.

    I'm now teaching English at the high school in Tokyo, Japan. I support my family. Please tell me about your current life if you like.

    Thanks again for your e-mail and thank you for your continued kindness. Please feel free to write or e-mail me anytime if you have a time. I look forward to hearing from you!!

    Best regards,
    Makoto K.
    Kasukabe, Saitama
    Japan

God bless him for taking the time to write. I guess that's the gist of this story. We never know how important it might be to someone else to let them know that what they said or did meant so much to you in your little part of the blue marble we call Earth.

Over the years, I've found women to have the sensitivity to appreciate and enjoy when something special was going on with the other party and they were eager to talk about it. Maybe it all goes back to that lack of communication that I attributed to teens when I called my first show *I'll Never Tell.*

I've spent many wonderful days and evenings with married couples. When we go our separate ways it always leaves an empty place in my heart. Oh how much more meaningful would it be to reminisce with a loved one about what just happened and plan for something in the future. People have dinner parties and often the guests are thinking of how they will reciprocate and one-up them on everything from soup to nuts. I guess it's a natural thing to do.

When you get lonely and there is that deadly silence that creeps into the cranium and renders the earholes useless, it is the sound of other people that I long to hear. Loneliness still comes into play when I can't share myself, my desires, my dreams, my thoughts with someone else. There are different kinds of groups that people join or belong to that afford them this privilege. Alcoholics Anonymous is probably the most well known. "Hello my name is Harry and I've been sober and talking about it all of my life."

I belong to a group called Jesus Caritas, which was inspired by priest and martyr Charles de Foucauld who died back in 1912. It has been useful to me for the past thirty years as a sounding board and a place to go for advice from people you love and respect. Sure it's a support group and it's only five priests. We meet nine times a year. We spend a quiet hour in the chapel with the Blessed Sacrament. Then we say the daily prayer of the Church followed by a review of life. This last part is the most meaningful as it affords each of us an opportunity to give an account, or not, of our spiritual journey, our health issues and our day-to-day lives. After we let go, then each of us might have a question about the promise we have made in the past to ourselves without distraction in order to allow God and the gift of God's grace to come into our hearts and minds.

It's the hardest thing to do because it requires putting everything else aside and turning off the cell phone, the iPad, the computer and everyone else around who wants to talk or be with you. It's supposed to take you away from your work, but it turns out to be work when you try to find the time and the space to desert your life for the desert. Solitude is not the same as loneliness.

The group I have been meeting with has been together more than thirty-six years. I'm a rookie and got to join when one of the guys died. Of all the meetings, conferences and gatherings that I've gone to in the past twenty years, this is one that I look forward to. I use the time in prayer to prepare my review of life. Oh, and it does include the good, the bad, the ugly and whatever (the indifferent).

The brain tumor came on quickly and the battle didn't last very long. Pat Bailey was just fifty-seven years old when he died. His obituary said he was "a man of tremendous talent, warmth, kindness, and most importantly unquestioned character and integrity." He had asked that memorial donations be made to the God Squad. Once again, cancer ended the life of a good man.

I boarded the 38 Geary bus. It was piloted by a rather heavy-set woman with "hurry" in her head. I bobbed and weaved my way to the back of the bus then the herky-jerky movement whipped me and almost threw me to the ground. I finally secured myself by grabbing a strap and a pole and was anxiously awaiting the next major movement in that avalanche of public transport. Much to my surprise a young lady looked up at me, after removing the cell phone from her ear, and kindly offered me her seat. Off went the old-age alarm in my brain. I stood staring into space thinking this might be the beginning of the end.

It was just ten days after my colon cancer surgery and I was upbeat and positive. After all, my surgeon had told me only a day or two earlier, "You're cancer-free, no need to see me again."

In 1954 when they cut open my father, they simply sewed him up again and said you have six weeks to live. In 1960 when they finally found the cancer in my mother, they did pretty much the same thing. Having experienced their deaths and then watching all three of my siblings get the disease, I'd always expected it would strike me as well. Yet I felt that even though I'm retired from the chancery office and my duties as Vicar General, God still had much more work for me to do.

I have yet to make it to the cover of *Sports Illustrated*, but, like my sister, Della, I'm an official cancer survivor. Cancer is a good teacher. It certainly makes you pay attention and I learned a lot. Every day is a learning experience. Experience is what you get when you don't always get what you want. The good and bad people that come in and out of life are my teachers. It's a pedagogy that I would endorse for any human who loves humanity and wants to help. It's also good for the soul.

"Excuse me, sir," the young woman repeated breaking my reverie. "Could I offer you my seat?"

No thanks young lady. I can't sit down now. Thanks to prayer, I've got much more work to do. I'll have to hang on and make the best of the rest of the trip.

But, THANK YOU!

My old friend John Mahoney did not fare as well as I had. He died in a St. Louis nursing home from lung cancer at seventy.

He had lived for three years after the diagnosis. Like Charlie and Mary, he had donated his body to a medical school. A woman described as a long-time companion was listed among his survivors. He was mourned citywide.

John had always attracted women. In high school he'd pitched for his baseball team, been the captain of the soccer team, quarterback of the football team and a straight A student. Parents exhorted their children to emulate him. His mother wanted one of her sons to be a priest and he turned down a football scholarship and entered the seminary.

He and I had been friends almost our whole lives yet he never told me his secrets. A young woman contacted me once saying it was important for her to talk with me about John. She had met him, as had I, through soccer and was in love with him. I saw her briefly at the St. Louis airport and she asked me to pressure John to marry her. This happened not long after Lizzie had ended our relationship. I knew there was nothing anyone could do. She married someone else.

John drank a lot after that and ended up leaving the priesthood. He went back to school and got a doctorate in education and counseling, then served eighteen years on the St. Louis School Board with what his obituary called "a missionary zeal to help children." In an era of white flight from the city, he fought against renewed attempts at segregation much like Cardinal Ritter had before him.

Another friend from our days at Cardinal Glennon was successful in the business world beyond his wildest dreams. When I first saw his name on television during the college basketball season, I wondered if it was the same guy who could out-rebound me and pushed me to become a better basketball player. It was. Charlie was the roundball buddy who had left the seminary when I left for Rome. He married Mary Beth and they had three boys and a girl. Now the children have children and Charlie is retired. His kids are running his company.

I've renewed our friendship via e-mail and in person to ask for his support with the TV Mass ministry that I'm doing in Northern California.

"Of course, I'll help you Fuzzy. My family and I have been blessed in the world of business. We have a family foundation and I would be delighted to be a part of your ministry. After all those years of blocking your jump shot in the gym, I don't think I can stand in your way when it comes to doing good for God. Count me in!"

You all know that old adage about burning bridges and moving on. The longer I live the more important it seems to hang on to friends and family as long as you can. You never know when you can be helpful to each other in a completely different way than you imagined. Who would have thought that two nineteen-year-old boys pushing each other around in the gym would come to serving God in such unusual and unique ways, that is, one providing the means, the other meaning to help.

My mail is stacked on my desk with a little note on each envelope as to what was contained and whether or not I should respond personally. It's the mail from the TV Mass. I receive about ten pieces a day. My producer continues to make me look good by delivering it once a week so that I can continue responding to my mailing list, well over 1,200 today, who want a special blessing or a prayer for a family member or friend who has come on hard times.

People who don't know the communication business often wonder what a producer does. This lady does everything for me including making me look good as I get older and wrinkled and set in my ways. She produces the daily reminders that I must continue to grow inside and out giving me the motivation to strive even more to better my skills in whatever I do.

This producer is the same lady who has twice saved my life by forcing me to go to the doctor to have spots checked. One was a malignant melanoma. The second was a continuous prodding to go for the colonoscopy that demonstrated my colon cancer which eventually was surgically removed followed by chemotherapy for six months. My "producer" was at every session driving me to and fro and making sure I was able to get up the forty-seven steps to my room in the old rectory where I lived. She is of Swedish descent and sometimes half carried me.

Two years away from that terrible experience, I can now see how difficult it was. I also now understand how inside I didn't want to accept that I was about to meet my Maker or have my life in a sling for someone else to do everything for me. But hey, that's what a producer does—everything.

That's the story behind the story. When a routine colonoscopy revealed that I had colon cancer, I fretted for a short time and then I prayed. My prayer was to let family and friends know that I was begging for their prayers. You really don't have to ask. People volunteer when they hear the dreaded word cancer. I could never thank all who did pray. There were cards and letters, telephone calls, e-mails and personal greetings. The heavens were heard. The "power of prayer" has once again come to the fore. I for one am grateful.

I can now return to the TV Mass re-energized to pray for all the sick, the suffering, the incarcerated and those in elder care who are unable to go to their parish church and experience the blessings of the communion of faith firsthand.

22. Men in Red

CARDINALS, I've known a few.

Make no mistake, I'm a huge fan of this distinguished group of men. One does not become a cardinal without great sacrifice and the gift of grace from the Holy Spirit assisting them in their own spiritual growth and development. They wear scarlet as a sign of devotion to the Church, symbolizing willingness even to shed their blood for the faith. It may look like it's for show, but when push comes to shove, the cardinals are the ones in the forefront with their lives on the line. Oh wait, yes, there are exceptions. But among those that I know, I know these would go the distance and think it's worthwhile to pass along a tidbit or two about them.

Bernard Cardinal Law

I will always be grateful for the decision Bernard Law made that allowed me to remain in the media world half-way across the country. Of course, most would remember Cardinal Law for his fall from the lofty position as Archbishop of Boston to a post inside the Vatican where he would be for the remainder of his active ministry. It is not for me to pass judgment about his decisions in Boston that precipitated a nationwide investigation into clergy sexual abuse, but I do know that he loves the Church and is one of those who would sacrifice his life for it. Fortunately I was able to tell him this when visiting in Rome many years later.

He always called me the "great communicator" and while I relish such a title, I would never have been able to minister to so many without the use of radio and television. Even at this writing, I reach over 35,000 people a week with my Sunday TV Mass. Some readers might be taken aback at my gratitude for a churchman like Law, but I know he was trying to do good and like many of us, made mistakes along the way.

Edwin Cardinal O'Brien

Cardinal O'Brien preceded Tim Dolan as rector of the North American College in Rome. It was always good to visit the college and know the person in charge. Later he became the military ordinariate for Catholics in the Armed Forces. The cardinal now serves as the Grand Master of the Equestrian Order of the Holy Sepulchre of Jerusalem, of which I am a member. I haven't seen him in a few years, but if I do I'll thank him for his unselfish dedication to the Church and remind him about my handball game.

William Cardinal Levada

I have told much of what there is to tell about my friend Bill but there are still a number of stories tucked away for another time. I conclude by thanking him personally for the assignment that gave me a thoughtful housemate and the opportunity to assist a very hard-working clergyman.

Joseph Cardinal Ratzinger

After Cardinal Levada was assigned to Rome, his successor and classmate, Archbishop George Niederauer, kindly invited me to stay on at the Archbishop's Residence. Over the twelve years I lived there, a number of distinguished people came through, either for a visit or dinner or to spend a few days. When my friends came over I'd get a kick out of asking them to take the seat at the end of the couch, then watch their reactions when I pointed out that the man destined to be Pope Benedict XVI had sat in the very same spot.

I was first introduced to Cardinal Ratzinger when I arrived home fresh from a meeting of the local Kolping Society. It was a German organization founded to help early immigrants in the San Francisco Bay Area. Their president was a member of St. Gabriel parish and nominated me as an honorary member. They had asked me to give a short talk on my own German heritage and then pinned me with a sign of membership.

I entered the living room knowing I was going to meet the man I'd learned to distrust from reading about him in the *National Catholic Reporter* for years. He was always doing or saying something that appeared to have no connection with the pastoral side of ministry. At the time he was head of the Congregation for the Doctrine of Faith and was depicted as the "Vatican Watchdog" when dealing with men and women all over the world who were not conforming strictly to the teachings of the Catholic Church.

I was completely disarmed by his firm handshake and piercing eyes that looked at me directly as I was introduced. He immediately recognized my pin and noted that I must be a member of the Kolping Society. I told him I had just come from a meeting. It's the old story of hearing about someone for years and reading what they had done and then being in their presence and realizing that you didn't know them at all.

Joseph Cardinal Ratzinger, the future Pope Benedict XVI, with Father Harry

The next day, I had the privilege of escorting him to our beautiful cathedral and showing him around. As we peered off the east balcony, I pointed out that the red brick building in the distance was a Lutheran kirche and was undergoing some renovation. He asked about the pastor and I reluctantly told him it was a woman. He again looked me in the eye and again said nothing. It was obvious to me that he did not approve, but he knew that churches in the U.S. were different.

Cardinal Ratzinger spent the week at the residence. I never saw him again until Archbishop Levada was elevated to cardinal and I went to Rome for the ceremony. Once again, Bill introduced me as having been his vicar in San Francisco and Joseph Ratzinger acknowledged me as the monsignor who was kind to him when he visited the City. I had my picture taken with Pope Benedict during that papal visit and gave a copy of it to my favorite restaurant for their wall.

I will always admire and respect him, but most of all for his recent decision to retire from the papacy and live the rest of his days in quiet and prayer. After 600 years without change, it took great courage for him to make this announcement and disappear within the gardens of the Vatican to live out the rest of his life. As a close friend and working cohort of the late Pope John Paul II, I'm sure he was affected by the difficult time the pope had in his waning days as leader of the Catholic Church and thought to himself, it must change. It did when he stepped down quietly and without great pomp and circumstance.

To conclude all this cardinal stuff, it is not to impress anyone with those I know or why I might be connected anymore than anyone else. But I do believe I enjoyed a privileged place among some of the great ecclesial leaders of modern times. As I said initially, to become a cardinal, to be in the conclave, is no small privilege. It comes at a steep price and from a depth of knowledge and spiritual principles realized in a short lifetime. Most cardinals are advanced in age. I think, with good reason. They have had more experience, are closer to God, and have withstood some martyr-like trials during their priestly lives.

I would not have written about cardinals, among them my personal friends, if I did not have a love and a respect for the individual and the office. More than once a priest would inquire why I had not become a bishop. Well, thanks be to God, it wasn't my choice.

As a famous bartender once told me about his bar, the only things that change in this place are the shoe size and the smoke. Now even the smoke is gone.

I didn't know I snored. I was snoring while sharing a room with a sick person like myself in Lourdes. I told him that except for the dorms in high school, I had lived sixty-three of my seventy-five years on earth sleeping pretty much in a single room and I really hoped I wouldn't keep him awake. I told him to call my name out loud if that was the case. He did, over and over again. I never heard a thing. Next day I asked for a single room because I felt so guilty disturbing his rest.

Father Harry *la malade* in Lourdes

I was in Lourdes on a pilgrimage with the Knights of Malta. It was a large group, about 150 people counting the staff, the companions and the *malades*, or the sick, who were making the trip as a gift from the Order of Malta. At the same time there was also a group there from New York being led by the Cardinal Archbishop Timothy Dolan. He offered a Mass at the grotto where the Blessed Virgin Mary had appeared to Bernadette Soubirous. The next day in the underground church, he led the service for the blessing of the sick. There were 25,000 people in attendance. I was so proud of him and what he has accomplished in the Church. I wanted to see him in person and tell him that. One of the hospitality leaders said he would find out where the cardinal was staying and ask if there were any public functions that I might attend.

It was late on Sunday afternoon and all I wanted to do was eat and go to bed. I was still recovering from chemotherapy and the trip to Europe had taxed my strength. I received a call letting me know there was a cocktail party at the American Association and I was invited. I had no idea where that was or who would be in attendance. I just wanted to take a shower, put on my old clothes and relax. But there was something pulling me to clean up, put on my clerical suit and try to find the American Association hotel. So I did!

I was hot and tiring out when a couple I knew flagged me down and said they had just left the reception and that they had told the cardinal I was looking for him. In fact, they had his personal card where he had written a note to me.

Just then, he came out of the hotel. I walked right up to him and he turned and said, "Harry, my man, how's life?"

After a short conversation about the old days and times in St. Louis, he told me and my two friends that he would not be here as a priest today if it had not been for the retreat I had given forty-five years earlier. He said he had been ready to leave the seminary and abandon the whole idea of priesthood when I had talked to him about giving it some more time. After all, he was only a freshman in college.

Well, that made my day. My chest went out and my head began to swell. If I were a peacock, I would have been in full bloom.

Oh, I forgot to say while I was walking those narrow streets trying to find where I was supposed to be going, I whispered a prayer to Mary letting her know that I really would like to see him but if it wasn't meant to be, that would be OK too. It happened! I'm sure both of us experienced some of the spiritual growth for which that little village in southern France is famed.

23. Two Islands

I LOOKED AT THE GLOW-IN-THE-DARK Timex on my wrist only to discover it was 2:20 a.m.. I couldn't sleep but I had been in this dreamstate for such a long time. It was almost like Joseph in the Scriptures when he had a dream to do this and a dream to do that, only it was really an angel telling him to do something very significant. But this didn't dawn on me until almost daybreak.

I rubbed the sleep out of my eyes and stared out the little square window of the 15th century structure where I was sleeping (or not). Suddenly I was wide awake and realized that the dream was really the homily for a funeral service I would likely be giving one day for Warren Joseph Holleran. Warren had been the Scripture teacher in Rome who brought Bible stories to life with his vivid depictions and opened my eyes to a dynamic style of preaching. He was the Scripture professor at St. Patrick's Seminary for many years. An international scriptural scholar, he is also part of my Jesus Caritas prayer group.

The building where my bed was had been constructed so many centuries ago that I felt like I might be among the many others who had lived there before. It's called Fort Shannon and is located just a mile up the road from the township of Glin. It was being renovated by a close friend of mine who invited me to come for a visit. I made it a vacation. There was no TV, no radio, no telephone, just this beautiful old house with such a marvelous history surrounded by the countryside and overlooking the lovely River Shannon as it made its way from Limerick to the sea. The gardens were well kept and filled with flora and teeming with fauna.

There were old fruit trees and young ones. I plucked an apple with some red from one but as it covered my palate I knew it was not quite ready to eat. My mouth puckered and the sourness of the apple made me think how Adam might have felt after he took his first bite.

There was a slight stream running across the property only to disappear into a rock wall that was about ten feet high and separated one man's land from another's. Two small planks spanned the stream so that it was possible to make your way easily from side to side. A good strong whiff of the country air left no doubt that there were animals on the other side of the wall and with or without a bleat or a moo you could tell by the smell of manure that they were near.

Warren had asked me a couple of years ago to preach at his funeral. It was a complete surprise and a great honor to have been invited.

"Why me, Warren?"

"Harry," he said, "My classmates would be so old they wouldn't want the pressure of the preparation it would take to do the job."

Not everyone knows what it's like to preach at a preacher's funeral. There are always the preaching critics and they are not to be toyed with. They fill the front pews alongside the bishops and archbishops just waiting to see whether or not you hit the mark. God only knows what that mark might be.

"I would love to Warren," I told him, "But I hope that you will select the Scriptures and let me know if there is something special you want me to say."

He laughed in his inimitable way and assured me as God did with so many in the Scriptures that the Spirit would provide.

So here I am in the middle of the night in Ireland, unable to sleep, preparing a eulogy for a man who is still very much among the living.

We each have our own gifts so it's not possible for us all to be scripture scholars. As I've said before, after twelve years of study I only knew how much I didn't know and would never know because of my inability to read and study the original documents. That would require a facility in Latin, Greek, Aramaic, as well as a lifetime of studying the minute details of each and every letter and phrase. Some scholars spend the better part of their lives on a chapter or two of the Bible. Those on fire with their meaning have been given a special gift by the Spirit and the responsibility to share their insights and knowledge with the rest of us. Such was the case with Warren who spent his life teaching in a seminary and taking the scriptures apart phrase by phrase.

Once as a young priest I telephoned him and asked if he could suggest a "homily help" that I could use to bring the words of Scripture to life on Sunday. People didn't have the time nor the gift to delve into the life and depth of God's Word. Once again he coached me to speak from the heart of what I knew and make sure that my everyday life was included in the words from Scripture. At the time I wasn't sure what he meant, but little by little the Word began to have more meaning.

As I grew older I could relate the story that I read with the story that I was living. It was the story that was all important. There would never be enough spirituality in my own life to convince others to follow the Word, but with it as a guide and basis for my own story someone might be moved.

So what might I do in the homily for Warren's funeral to move the many clergy who had been taught sacred Scripture by this venerable giant of the field? By the grace of the Spirit I had been privileged to get to know him better through our mutual support group, Jesus Caritas. At the conclusion of each meeting we read the Gospel that would be used at Mass that coming Sunday. Then we would each give our interpretation and what we might pursue as that week's lesson for the faithful.

Warren always had the best take on the reading, but never gave his rendition in a way that diminished our own conclusions. It was such a blessing for us. We went forth eager to preach the Word and impress the flock with how much it held and what they might do with it to build up their own lives.

I'm back to the Scripture that I would use at Warren's funeral, presuming he outlives me. His mother was over 100 when she passed and he might follow in her footsteps. I, on the other hand, had survived colon cancer but might get hit by a bus at the roundabout in Glin because they still drive on the other side of the road.

So if it's God's will, the basic idea that I would pursue is from II Samuel:11 describing the life of King David. My initial influence comes from a book that I read many years ago entitled *That Man is You* by Louis Évely. He was born in Brussels in 1910 and taught at the University of Louvain. He established secular fraternities inspired by Charles de Foucauld which were the forerunners of the Jesus Caritas groups. In the jacket of that book, Yves M.J. Congar, O.P., says that Évely had:

"... a knack of making us perceive the full import, spiritual and human of the truths we thought we understood and of making us see them from a different angle, under irrecusable light . . . he makes the Gospels come to life, so that we often seem to be reading them for the first time."

That's for me!

So back to the homily. David was "a ruddy youth, handsome and delightful to behold." He had just about anything and everything he wanted. After all, he had slain the giant and with the help of God there was nothing he could not do. He had amassed a fortune in flocks and fields and most every other thing of value, including several wives and an army that would die for him.

Knowing the human condition, it's not surprising that upon spying Bathsheba bathing on the roof of her home, David would swell up with such desire that he must have her. So he did. And to make things worse, he summoned her husband home from battle presuming Uriah would hasten to the bed of his wife. But Uriah was so faithful a soldier that he spent the night in the barracks so as not to offend his king. It gets worse as now David sends Uriah into battle and gives orders that he should be placed in the front lines where he is killed. Relieved and absolved of his guilt about sleeping with Bathsheba, David then takes her in and she bears his child.

Onto the scene steps the prophet Nathan, who relates the story of a poor man with only one sheep, a little lamb that he was raising almost as a child. When his neighbor with great herds and flocks had visitors, he stole his neighbor's lamb and slaughtered it for his feast instead of killing one from his own flock.

David reacted furiously at the conclusion of this story demanding to know if it was true.

"Who is this man?" shouted the King. "I'll hunt him down and kill him."

Nathan whispered to him softly, "That man is you."

Thus the title of Abbé Évely's book of poetry and the forceful meaning it still holds for me today.

Back to the human condition. I have realized that blessings have come to me in almost everything I have attempted in life. So these blessings often color my judgment, then I make decisions that do not conform with the blessings. I can blame myself and my lack of good judgment or I can blame it on the human condition and move on. The Gospels tell us this in so many different ways. They are a mirror where each of us could see ourselves . . . not merely reflected but exposed and denounced. The trouble comes when we use the Gospels to look at others and turn away incensed at their blindness, their ignorance, their hate.

I walked into the kitchen from the shower (outdoors, one of my favorites) and said to my sister, "Do you know what I like best about visiting the East Coast?"

"Sure," she said. "The outdoor shower you love so much."

"No, that's not it. It's the fact that cocktail time comes three hours before you expect it."

I had stopped over in Martha's Vineyard on the way home from Ireland to San Francisco. I'd just looked at my watch and it said quarter to five. My sister and brother-in-law had enjoyed "Martha time" at 5:00 p.m. as long as I'd known them. In sickness and in health, they treat the time like it's sacred and mix the hour before dinner with good conversation and memories of days gone by.

Della was seventy-nine and her husband was eighty-four and they had been together almost sixty years. He was grappling with lung cancer and she was struggling to answer his every need. He would hardly let her leave his sight. But the two of them loved each other and humbled me with the depth of their commitment. Marriage is the only sacrament that a priest, bishop, or deacon does not administer but rather comes through the couple themselves. They give the sacrament to each other with their commitment to love and cherish until death. I was witness to this living gift between Della and Pete. In my experience, when two people make these promises and vows to each other with God being part of the deal, it will be much easier to deal with all the drama that might follow with God on your side.

The Vineyard has been compared to the tiny town of Mendocino on the Redwood Coast which is "arty" by California standards with one of the most beautiful coasts by God's standards. I visited there with the Darlings only to be told it doesn't hold a candle to the island's rock walls and quaint homes. I have to agree. The private secretary to archbishops Quinn and Levada used to go Mendocino to get away from things. He died at fifty-nine from a heart attack. As right-hand man to the Ordinary, he bore a burden that paled compared to mine as Vicar General. When I first saw the news about Monsignor O'Shea in the paper, I went up to his office to see if he thought it was all true. It was. His memorial in the beautiful coastal town says, "I asked God for Heaven and He gave me Mendocino."

On another summer holiday, I had invited some of my Bostonian priest friends to take the ferry over to the island for the day and enjoy a meal of fresh fish that I would catch. I did indeed and we feasted on fish and fish stories from our four years together in Rome. It was an evening that could not be repeated or staged. We spent the night sprawled in various corners of the cabin only to awake to rain and a wet trip back to the ferry for the return to Boston.

You've heard the one about the station wagon full of nuns? Archie Bunker of *All in the Family* was sure he'd win his whiplash lawsuit until the witnesses for the defense turned out to be a station wagon full of nuns. Well, I was driving the Darlings' station wagon with six Catholic priests aboard when I came over a hill and through the rain saw a car with no lights stalled in the middle of the road. I swerved to avoid the hitchhiking driver to my right and rammed into the back of the stopped car, sending it hurtling through the brush until it stopped just short of a huge tree.

After the sharp jolt, we all assured ourselves that we were in one piece and then went to the aid of the other driver. Fortunately, no one was injured except for a classmate in the back seat who broke his little finger reaching to grab a buddy in the front seat so he wouldn't strike the windshield. When the Massachusetts State Police arrived to assess the damage and the fault, it was apparent that we were not going to be cited. The trooper called an ambulance which took my broken-fingered friend to the hospital with lights flashing and sirens blasting. In the small-world department, the responding officer happened to be a childhood pal of the injured priest (who is now the bishop of Long Island). Insurance covered the damage but not the hardship it made for my sister and brother-in-law who would now be without their station wagon for the remainder of the summer.

There is a narrow lane that goes from the main road to the group of small houses where the Darlings live. It's always been rough with ruts from use when it's wet or simply from use. Pete is like the mayor of that lane. He knows all the cars, the voices, the sounds of the motors, the tires on the gravel, the distinguishing roars from various mufflers, so that no one can really come in or out or pass by Windway, the name of their home, without positive identification. It doesn't matter who you are, where you come from, or how much money you have, there are no free passes to the beach without undergoing intense scrutiny from my brother-in-law.

Several of the houses within eyeshot of Windway, like Whale and Langmuir and the real estate lady's home, are about to fall into the sea. They are all supposed to be moved inland or done away with this year. It's a little eerie thinking about owning land and suddenly it falls down onto the beach and is reclaimed by the sea. What might have been ten acres is now nine. It makes the arithmetic interesting when you begin to evaluate your land by so-much-an-acre. The deed might say ten acres but when you look around you can see that one has disappeared. It's irretrievable and just gone.

The same could be said about grace. We do all these good things in life to build up our storehouse of grace. Then we might have a fall or two and wonder what happened. The grace has disappeared. So now we have to shore up and attain more grace in order to have the full ten acres we thought we had. Best of all, unlike pricey real estate on Martha's Vineyard, grace from God is free. Just ask.

24. Shrine of Saint Francis

I RESIDE AT THE SHRINE of Saint Francis of Assisi in the center of North Beach, an area in the City noted for fine foods and an Italian atmosphere. To the early arrivals, Italy was the South Beach and the shores of San Francisco made up the North Beach. It's where Joe DiMaggio brought his bride Marilyn Monroe home to live and where the Beat movement was born. Catholic Jack Kerouac said "Beat" was an extension of his beatific philosophy.

The church was established in 1849 by a priest from Walla Walla to extend the Oregon Territory for Catholics and in particular for those who were migrating to the fields of gold. It later became a cathedral church and was used as such until 1854 when what is now called Old St. Mary's was opened. The priests at St. Francis conducted services in English, French, Spanish and Italian. Of the church's many pastors, the most noted is a Father Terence Caraher who, during all of his time there, waged war against the evils of the nearby Barbary Coast. But that's another story for a historian.

I have heard the tour guides on the corner of Vallejo and Grant point to the saloon just outside my window and say how during the great earthquake of 1906 the firemen had a choice of saving either the bar or the church. Since they spent more time in the former, they chose to put out that fire first. In the meantime, only a skeleton of the original church remained, the four walls and the two ninety-five-foot towers that still mark the corner of Vallejo and Columbus Avenue.

So I'm here in this former parish, now called a Shrine of Saint Francis, with its rich history and continual flock of pilgrims who come to visit the "Porziuncola," an exact replica of the chapel Saint Francis rebuilt and took as his home in Assisi, Italy. Francis came upon an abandoned chapel in the forest and restored it into his "little portion," or his corner of the world. It says in Latin as you enter, *Hic locus sanctus est* . . . this is a holy place.

On the converse, I've been told that my little corner of the world, the rectory next door where I reside, is haunted. It's rumored to be home to the devil's work, largely because one of the former pastors was the official exorcist of the Catholic Church in these parts. More to the point, he was the arbiter of who is and isn't possessed. He never performed an exorcism. Cases of suspected possession were kicked upstairs. He still serves in that capacity and is a bishop now (although retired). He was the first Chinese-born Catholic bishop and speaks in tongues—English, Mandarin, Cantonese, Italian and French. He missed the film *The Exorcist*, being in West India at the time, but read the best-selling book as a matter of education. Author William Peter Blatty was a comedy writer who did this serious work and no one will ever remember a joke he wrote. The re-release of the film was good for the Bishop's business, spawning a predictable uptick in self-diagnosed possessions.

My only credentials working with the devil came from a video on satanic cults I wrote and hosted some years ago about the work of the devil in rock & roll music. The documentary gave me enough notoriety to be asked to come to a house in Illinois and rid it of the remains of the devil's work there. I had asked my bishop if I could go and his reply was simple and succinct, "Father Harry, evil spirits are a serious matter. It would take a much holier priest than you to square off with the devil." No question. He was right.

I don't know if the rectory was haunted or not, all I know is what I experienced there and it wasn't good. It was in reply to a retort I made about being old enough to fend for myself in the neighborhood. In fact, the man in question once told me to my face to go (the "f" bomb) myself and that I was the rear end of a donkey, if you know what I mean. There was another priest present, a friend of his, and I thought an apology was in order and said so. It never came. In fact, the man scrambled out of the room and I never spoke to him again.

I saw him. I passed him in the halls. I watched him spend hours with the woman in question, as he was part and parcel of the furniture in her office. Now and again I saw them from my window hand in hand heading toward a local *ristorante* for lunch. Little did I know what was happening or why it was happening until I read the paper just as it has been reported.

The *San Francisco Chronicle* filled me in on the "Racy tales of kinky sex at North Beach Shrine." New York's *Daily News* took alliteration honors with "Sexy spanking scandal at San Francisco church." The alleged embezzlement and sexual harassment didn't even make the headlines.

A private investigator has informed me after a brief interview that if this goes to court I will probably be deposed and asked to appear.

"But I had nothing to do with any of this," I protested.

"You live in the residence of the Shrine," was his reply.

Maybe there is still some of the evil spirit here that lurks about and I'm too blind to see.

25. Circle of Life

THE LAST FOUR or five years I have been giving the invocation and benediction for San Francisco's renowned Academy of Art University. Commencement is held in the Bill Graham Civic Auditorium re-named posthumously for the fabled music promoter. Every time I'm there I can't help but think of him and all the great shows he produced over the years. During my brief time as a television personality, I had the privilege of interviewing a number of rock stars but no one more important than the man who helped make them. Bill Graham had lost his life in a fiery helicopter crash coming back to the City from a show at the Concord Pavillion. Heavy winds and rain whipped his chopper into a high-voltage tower where it luridly hung for more than a day. I was in Rome on the theological sabbatical when he died, a month before my brother Charlie.

Lung cancer finally took Della's husband, Pete, in the spring. We buried a small box containing his ashes on his beloved island, not far from Windway. There is a headstone both for my sister and her husband marking the site. A painting of Pete looking down at the surf illustrated the cover of *American Art Collector* magazine that same month. A talented woman who'd gotten to know Pete through their mutual love of Up Island lore had captured him forever in her painting. Heather Neill called him "the Admiral" because of the binoculars slung on his shoulder and the way he stood watch over his lane and the waters beyond. She presented a print to Della on the day of the memorial. It hangs at the bottom of the stairs near the front door where she can see it often.

I don't ever remember being alone with Della on a trip until a couple of years ago when my first cousin, Phil Bucher, celebrated his fiftieth anniversary as a priest. You might remember Phil was instrumental in Bishop Law's decision to excardinate me from Springfield. Della and I flew to Missouri together and had a wonderful time. We ate and laughed together and had quiet time in the car where we could share tales of our family and the many years gone by. Now that her husband has passed, I'm sure we'll have more time together. She and I are the last ones standing and the pleasure of a relationship with Della, when we are both old with time, is one that was worth the wait.

Wimpy and I are still plying our trade as monsignors, both retired, and doing our best to work as much as possible. This year we traveled to Ireland with a good friend from my New York Athletic Club days. I've stayed at his home in Glin on the River Shannon before but it was new to Wayne. We cooked and traveled around a bit and visited the local pubs. It wasn't until after Wayne had played nine holes of golf (without a cart) that his seventy-five-year-old body said, "Hey, you can't do this to me." He suffered a mild stroke and his one leg and side went out on him. We got him home and into bed.

He said he was fine and ate dinner and had a vodka before bed. At three in the morning, I was awakened by him brushing his teeth and shuffling around the room. Barely conscious I mumbled, "What are you doing Wayne?"

"I'm getting ready to go," was the reply.

I was more awake. "It's 3:00 a.m. Wayne. We're not leaving until nine in the morning."

"I know," he said (to my relief), "but it will take me a long time to get dressed. I'm not doing so well on one side."

I got up and helped him dress and he lay there on the bed with shoes and socks and his arms crossed over his belly as if he were laid out in a casket.

Our friend got him in first class on Aer Lingus and we flew to New York. I pushed him in the wheelchair to American Airlines and he boarded a flight to Atlanta where he changed planes to get to Dubuque. He was met there by his cousins and went directly to the hospital. He lost his driver's license for awhile but I'm happy to say is doing well and will soon join me for another outing somewhere not so far from his doctors. There is so much more that I could relate about the Four Future Fathers of America who met to save the world. Two of us are still kicking and we're not looking for the bucket.

I saw Warren today, a bit more feeble but he looks just fine. He told me he was spending his time in prayer as preparation for the final lap of life. He'll probably outlive me.

Lizzie just let me know she has breast cancer. She starts radiation next week and wrote to say she couldn't come to the party I was hosting in September for my anniversary. Her daughter had just had a baby and Liz was a grandmother. It all seemed impossible.

Michael O'Leary and Jim Swanson celebrate with Father Harry

In the autumn, a lifetime collection of family and friends came to San Francisco to help me celebrate seventy-five years on this side of the grass, fifty years this side of the collar. There was a full weekend of activities starting with a big party Friday night at the Golden Gate Yacht Club where my old friend Bob Mulhern is the general manager. They say when you're dying your life passes before your eyes. I was lucky enough to have that experience without the aftermath.

Cardinal Levada, now retired and living at St. Patrick's Seminary in Menlo Park, regaled the crowd with his presence. The only cardinals most guests had ever seen were either baseball players or birds. It was a thrill and an honor to have my longtime friend Bill participate in the festivities.

Jim Purcell was at the gala. He had been my wingman when I was ordained and he hadn't seen Della since then. They had a wonderful reunion. Jim had been a class behind me and had left the priesthood when he fell in love with the sister in charge of Religious Education at his parish. He had made a career at the Jesuit Santa Clara University where he rose to vice president. Jim had the gift that keeps on giving in the spiritual sense. He never lost touch with his Maker and applied all the early principles of goodness both from his priestly training and his family.

Della was happier than I had seen her in years. Setting down the burden of caregiving and seeing an end to Pete's pain had returned her to the land of the living. Her eldest, Susan, had come from Massachusetts with husband, Michael. It was good to celebrate with the Darlings in a year that had brought them such sorrow.

Dr. Don's widow, Kae, was accompanied by her son, David, and his wife. He was the able sailor who shot the stars with a sextant long ago on the *First Claz Miracle*. Miles was there and in fine form. Jim Swanson and Kathleen Emrey from the old ACC and Bridge days were there. Michael O'Leary, the director of my TV Mass, was the unofficial photographer. My producer was also there making sure the food trays and the wine glasses stayed full. Michael Clark, who did not have to leave his zip code, came early and stayed late.

My brothers' families showed up en masse, dressed to the Midwest nines and so happy to celebrate with Uncle Father Harry. Sister-in-law, Betty, came with her second husband, Doyle Dumas, of Tennessee. He and she had become acquainted at the nursing home where his mother had lived and Betty had worked as a nurse. Betty was mother to the "R" children.

Firstborn Ronnie, who had made me an uncle when I was twelve, was there with his striking wife, Pandora. She could carry her unusual name. I'd taught Ronnie to swim when he was a little boy, the same way his father and uncle had taught me. Today he's a pilot for FedEx and makes it a practice to stop by on his West Coast runs. Johnny and Betty's eldest daughter, my elegant niece Renda, and her husband of forty-three years, Wayne, were on hand. She still wore her blonde hair long, but now it was tied back in a ponytail with some threads of silver. Nephew Rick, looking like he'd just stepped out of a Bass Pro commercial, is my fishing buddy and the brains behind the Fronabarger award. He was there with his wife, Jane, who is a better fisher than he is. Tail-ender, John Junior, came with his wife, Beth. They are both members of my God Squad board.

Two of Charlie and Mary's children came out, one of the twins, Jim, with his family, and big sister Sheila, a county visiting nurse, who traveled with a friend. Her husband, Dave, had stayed home to care for their quadriplegic daughter.

I don't know anyone with a heart as big as Sheila's. Maybe it's because of what she experienced when she was not quite three years old and her baby brother Bobby died from the aspirin overdose. More likely it's the Holy Spirit. The story about her youngest child is worth telling, as I have done many times in my homilies.

Stepping onto the creaky front porch of the leaning farmhouse in the backwoods of Missouri, Shelia had picked up the faint sound of a baby's crying. It was coming from the nearby barn barely standing on pilings that were way too rotten to hold such a structure. Having raised her own two children, Sheila had recognized the sound and headed toward it. In the straw lay a newborn babe with twisted arms and legs. She was barely alive but breathing and strong enough to cry and catch the ear of an angel encountering another angel.

Sheila and Dave soon found a way to adopt this helpless abandoned baby. They named her Linda which means soft and tender in German and, in Spanish, beautiful. She is twenty now and still twisted and unable to take care of herself. She cannot move any part of her body except her face. She is bright and able to read, even though she can't hold a book or turn on any kind of electronic device. Linda cannot talk but she laughs and utters sounds. She speaks with her eyes and her parents are now able to interpret and understand. It's truly a miracle to behold.

I'm just fortunate enough to be the great-uncle of this marvelous young lady. Some time ago, Charles and Flickers were introduced to Linda by way of my God Squad newsletter and helped buy her a new wheelchair so that she could be transported. A couple of years later without prompting, my friends went back and gave my niece some more money to update the chair.

Sheila is still the rural nurse who drives about the county helping those who cannot get to the doctor or the hospital. Like the angel she is, she is borne up by the beauty and the beast of suffering that her daughter must endure day after day. I cannot imagine how much love is enkindled within that home in order to make the sacrifices and perform the duties essential to daily life. Mercedes-Benz had a commercial one time that talked about what is reality and what is perception. It's not unlike our relationship with God. We are eager to judge our neighbors by what we perceive. But that perception is not always reality. Linda is reality. To see her body and her person, one is

Father Harry's great-niece Linda

moved. To know her as a human being and talk to her through her eyes is real, true, good and beautiful. Our relationship with God may not always be perceived as real but you know and God knows.

The Friday night party rolled into Saturday and later that morning it kept on rolling up to wine country for a day in the vineyards tended by a longtime handball buddy and his wife, both big supporters of the God Squad. Sunday broke clear and beautiful as is often the case in September in San Francisco. The clan was gathering one last time at a Mass of thanksgiving for the part they had played in my life. I was dressed in crimson robes and greeting arrivals in the vestibule of St. Vincent de Paul church, my old Marina home. My producer stood nearby in true blue.

Friends who had missed the first parts of the party made it to the church on time. There were people from the Silver Penny Farm days and the Chestnut Street watering holes, the former TWA crowd and the God Squad board. William Cardinal Levada, who had been at the festivities all weekend long, gave a surprise tribute that made the crowd laugh and get a little teary with his take on my priesthood. After communion, niece Sheila picked up her guitar and accompanied by her friend, belted out a song about Jesus that stilled the house. Her voice was brimful of love and so big and beautiful she could have played Branson. It was the finale to a celebration filled with the Holy Spirit and the multitude of blessings from my priesthood.

26. Thanks, Cornelius

WHY I REMAIN in the priesthood is no secret to me but I did ask myself that many times over the last fifty years.

Why I remain still peeks its head over the fence now and again to question who I am and why I'm here and where I'm going. That will come later . . . You need to look over the wall and see what's on the other side. After all who was I and why didn't I relate more of my feelings in this story I had to tell. In spite of all the times I said, "I'll never tell."

I'll take another cruise down the river on that one and see if I can't set a better stage so you'll know.

I remain because of other people and their prayers for me. Like the Carmelite sisters who continued to pray for my vocation long after I left for California. People like my parents, my brothers, my aunt Armella, DJ Ryan, Sister Bertha, even Mrs. Ohrman, and my spiritual advisors and bishops. Like the friends and strangers and the faceless audience of the TV Mass who prayed for me during my colon cancer.

Why I remain is still as simple as it was when I discovered how powerful the gift of prayer is for others. It's why twice a month I get up at 5:30 in the morning and drive from North Beach to Pacifica to pray with a small group of Missionary Sisters of Charity. I frequently say Mass for them. (I have never brought them any ducks to clean.) This is Saint Mother Teresa's brood. They are simple and holy and I need their help.

They have what looks to be an old motel with a home attached for the nine sisters who live there. They run a hospice for indigent and poor men who have no place to go to die and no money to pay to get there. Most of them are AIDS patients. Their ministry is to care for these men in their final days. The sisters are the last chance for any care and kindness or even a smile before they go.

A few weeks ago Sister Joseph asked me if I would have a funeral Mass that morning at seven o'clock. Sister said to me,

"Father, this man died about three in the morning. There are no relatives and we don't even know his name. So we baptized him shortly before he died and named him Cornelius." I vested for Mass in the small chapel, opened the door to the sanctuary and tripped over the feet of the dead man who was laid out on a mattress right in front of the altar in a beautiful Filipino shirt with a white sheet covering his lower extremities. What a surprise! So I said the Mass and prayed for Cornelius and the repose of his soul.

Later that month when the fish were not biting, I yelled out to my fishing buddies that maybe Cornelius could help us. Unbelievable! We filled the cooler.

I have anointed a number of men in this charitable facility over the years. Just last week I asked Sister how those men were doing, the ones with whom I'd prayed. The ones I'd given the sacrament of the sick. Without blinking, she looked me in the eye and with a straight countenance replied, "Oh Father Harry, they're all dead."

God loves us because God is good, not because we are good. I've spent most of my life trying to be good and to do good, only to learn that it really isn't up to me. God loves us because God is good.

God came to earth to live as a man, Jesus. Human beings are wounded, imperfect and like the clay of which we are made, fragile. The Latin word *vulnus* means wounded. Remember my grad school thesis? Our word vulnerable comes from that Latin root. Catholic teaching says that a priest is an *alter christus*, another Christ. As a man and a priest I am a wounded healer. I might think I'm a pretty nice piece of pottery but I am Father Harry, I am imperfect. I am vulnerable. Carl Rahner, the great German theologian calls all humankind "an unfinished symphony."

I can't help but see on so many faces in different church spaces how important it is to know that we are all Church. I might see myself as an officer or a so-called lieutenant among the titles that go around, but I don't see myself any more nor any less than the many who have come in and out of my life as People of God.

Just yesterday at Mass, the lector who did the readings was

a former radio announcer and was so pleased to introduce himself to me. "I take it you are THE Father Harry from the radio and the man I googled before I came to church," he said. "It's an honor to meet someone from the Bay Area Radio Hall of Fame." That would be me, noted as charged. Thank you for recalling what I had forgotten. It's been a long time since I've sat in front of a mic in a closed studio and entertained myself, my audience, the producer and the engineer on the other side of the glass. I miss it. I really do. It was a learning experience that you could never get from a book or a classroom. It was unique.

My priesthood has been a life like no other. It's never been a job. Going to work and being at work are quite different when it's a privilege just to be there. It brings with it a spiritual passport that allows you to go into the lives of other people, to cross their borders, invade their privacy, step on their personal path, listen to moans and groans, and finally to be stamped and welcomed as a helpful visitor. Some yearn to be questioned and advised and even warned about the course they have chosen. Sanctity of life applies to me ad infinitum. My life is a privilege not a right and thus holy, not because of me but because of others.

I didn't know it until some time after I first came to San Francisco that most—if not all—of my brother priests dismissed me and my radio work as something to draw attention. That it did and I can't imagine any of the apostles not using the same tool if it had been available to them. Over time, a lot of time, I earned their respect. I was spared a lot of bad relations with priests because I had nothing to do with their assignments. That unhappy lot fell to the Vicar for Clergy. When I accepted my assignment from Archbishop Levada to be his Vicar for Administration, I heard more than one priest say, "I wouldn't want your job for anything in the world." This time they weren't talking through their hats. And while it felt good to finally be recognized by my brothers for who I was, it had been a solitary journey and one that was lonely.

The complexion of the priests of the Archdiocese of San Francisco has changed. Two priests who are brothers used to routinely snub me. Now they are among my best friends. They don't know anybody anymore. So many priests are dead or as good as. Every year there are more and more foreign guys here. The two guys who just moved into the Shrine, the Vicar for Administration and the Director of Development, are from Queens, New York, and both will have an uphill climb to get to know the clergy.

When conservatives gained the upper hand in Rome in the 1970s, the theology and training in seminaries did a turnaround. After many years of changes in the Vatican there appeared to be a whole new scope of thinking. More and more of the younger priests seemed so conservative wanting to return to pomp and circumstance and not really eager to roll up their sleeves and dig into the social problems of society that my training led me to believe were the most important. As a result, the new guys coming into the priesthood had made a switch from Vatican II and social justice. Their focus was their own spiritual growth and piety and fear of the Lord.

Two of the hardest working pastors I knew had associates who wouldn't answer the door in the middle of the day when parishioners came looking for a priest. One of them actually said, "I'm doing my spiritual readings now. I'm not available from two to four." For the first time I thought fondly of the rector at Sacred Heart House of Studies who wanted to know what "out" meant when I took my first day off in a year. These new guys thought the parish owed them a living and entitlement seems to be the going word these days.

I just had a call from a former colleague at the chancery saying how much I was missed and how narrow my roommates are. She cannot believe the opinions that they put forth even to the detriment of this great pope who is reaching out to the poor and the sick. In replacing ultra-conservative Cardinal Raymond Burke from his Vatican post and his warnings across the bow of the Curia, Pope Francis made it pretty certain where he stood and what his papacy was going to entail.

I grew up in the old Church and I was exposed to the new Church, the one with the open windows, to the Old Testament AND to the New Testament. The old was that of the laws and the prophets, and the way things were done was by reward and punishment. The new was no longer about what you should do by laws, but by mercy and compassion. By love.

Vatican II unleashed the most basic tool—words—when the Latin Mass was dropped. Vatican II also sanctioned media as an important ministry. Vatican II told us we were a Church of love.

As a priest, as a man of German heritage and as a gentleman, my calling card was, "I'll never tell." As a broadcaster, I was able to use those words in my media ministry and to talk for the first time about love. To shout it from the airwaves.

Yet here at the end of my working life, there was the return to pomp and rules and laws. The emphasis was no longer on love.

By the blessings of the Holy Spirit I survived cancer, unlike my parents and my brother and so many others I have loved. But the greatest blessing that I have known is, in retirement, seeing it come full circle with Pope Francis to my original inspiration for priesthood, that desire for the eternal love of God assured by helping (loving) others.

27. Martyrs Jubilee

I WAS AT THE PORZIUNCOLA making some last minute preparations. An elderly couple walked by and I said, "I bet this is one of my classmates." The surviving members of the North American College Class of 1965 were beginning to arrive in the City of Saint Francis for three days of festivities I had organized in celebration of the fiftieth anniversary of our ordination.

Wayne came in a few days early so the two of us would have some time together to visit. We raised our glasses to Jim and Roy and then, like most old people, we talked about our health. The last time I had seen Wimpy he had just had the stroke. There was my bout with cancer, so a significant part of our conversation was basically how fortunate we were to be alive and to be healthy. He told me how he was making it back after the stoke. He looked good and sounded good, but I saw that he was really weakened. He walks with a cane and can't carry a big bag. He can't walk more than a couple of blocks and he's got to rest. He shuffles and his knees are both bad. He needs to have them both replaced. Travel ops we would have together would be limited now.

We fell into the easy conversation of age-old friends. We said how lucky we were to have been priests for fifty years and for all the people we've met and the opportunity we'd had to do the work we do. When we were ordained we had this great love for the Vatican and the Mother Church and Rome. That's kind of dissipated even though we find a new treasure in Pope Francis. What he's done in his short papacy is mind boggling and lifts you on a great wave of hope.

In October of 1961, seventy-two of us were Vatican-bound on the *Cristoforo Columbo*. You already know that ten, Roy among them, left before ordination. Eighteen have since died. A third of those forty-four still living are married and about half of them made the trip to San Francisco. Four of the wives were ex-nuns or working in religious education. Classmate Dakin Matthews arguably could be called the greatest commercial success. He's enjoyed a long acting career, his most recent triumph coming in the Tony-winning *Rocky, The Musical*. His wife didn't go to the awards ceremony, saying that she was not interested in any of that stuff he does. "I play golf," she said. Melvin, as I knew him in Rome, had been the classmate who was ready to rat me out over my day at the beach with Ranny Riley. Funny how things turned out. Our class was long on talent, but did not fare so well as executives. Five guys became bishops. Two even got as far as archbishop. They were the cream. With nary a cardinal our class would never have a say about who was pope, although Dakin did play Cardinal Wolsey on Broadway.

The wind and the rain did little to dampen the occasion; if anything it was reminiscent of the December day in 1964 when we became priests. The Fisherman's Wharf motel where everyone but Wimpy stayed is a short walk from the Shrine. I booked a bus for them the day we con-celebrated our anniversary Mass at the Porziuncola. We looked funny enough without walking through North Beach in the rain with our albs and stoles. Afterward, the bus took us to the Golden Gate Yacht Club for cocktails. With the ice broken and tinkling in glasses, conversation began to flow as freely as the liquor. True to our demographic, there was a lot of talk about surgeries, my wife almost died, what ever happened to so-and-so, those kinds of things. Of the Roman group there were only about two or three we had lost track of. Nobody knows what happened to them. There were some well spoken toasts at dinner later that evening, first to our alma mater the North American College, then to the United States. Dakin delivered that one. He was really into it. The final toast paid tribute to the Holy Father.

On the third day we rose early for a Mass in memory of our deceased classmates. I thought about the gifts JFK and Rufus had brought to their ministries and how they both were rejected by the Church for being who they were. It happens in many dioceses even in San Francisco where the Ordinary feels one way about something and a whole group—like our teachers in Catholic schools—feels another way. It becomes a major challenge. In the long run nobody wins. Negative thoughts and feelings fill the air and it takes years to get back to normal.

Afterward, we gathered for what I billed as an open forum. Our upperclassman, Miles, served as facilitator making sure no one would hog the limelight. We each had three minutes to fill in the others on what we'd been doing for the last fifty years. One guy, or rather one archbishop, talked about working in a mental institution. It appeared to many of us that he was at home there. Some remarks were meaningful and deep. I didn't have much to say except, "I'm working on a book and when it comes out I expect you all to read it so I don't have to waste your time here."

50th anniversary of ordination, the North American College class of 1965

The time capsule speeches evoked inevitable comparisons between then and now. Then there would have been excitement and high-strung emotion for two reasons. We went over as young men and returned as ordained priests with the expectation of coming back to the states and changing the world. And after living four years in Rome away from family, all of a sudden you have a car, your own place to live, your own telephone. When we talked about now, the State of the Church was on everyone's mind. My good buddy Wayne kept asking about the present Archbishop. I really didn't know him well enough to have an educated opinion, only a response from the promise of obedience.

Likewise, I don't need to talk about the guy who cursed me to my face in my own home, nor his relationship with the priest who witnessed that incident yet remained silent. It still hurts when I think about what they were able to undo in such a short time. Now here I sit cringing every time I hear another decision being made in the office that I ran. It's really hard to understand that I'm no longer in charge. I had my chance. It's time for someone else to bear the burden. Like it or not, I'm out of it.

All the money I saved and worked for to balance the budget flowed down the pipes with a few good flushes. It was not only the new group at the chancery, but hires from the top that made the bottom so apparent. I couldn't help but think of *Modern Youth and Plumbing* from my days at the minor seminary and how that little pink pamphlet was nothing more than a bundle of briars piled on little people by Saint Augustine because of his own sinful life.

28. In Sync

BOXES FILLED THE MAIN ROOM of the suite in the St. Francis of Assisi rectory that had been my home for the last two years. The back room office was already stripped, computers and printer packed, shelves empty. My Fronabarger award was tucked in a box next to little plastic bottles of water in the shape of Our Lady that I'd brought from Lourdes, along with a photograph of my dad as a young man, and a red-white-and-gold 49ers blanket that cushioned the lot. There were two items still on the wall, the photograph of me with Pope Benedict and the full page *Billboard* magazine ad with me in headphones from 1978, framed, that promoted my God Squad spots to the industry. A friend told me recently that you can buy the ad on eBay. Who knew I was collectable? If you want to see the photograph of me and the pope emeritus, look for a copy on the wall in the bar of Capurro's at Fisherman's Wharf. Tell Paul Father Harry sent you.

I packed the *Theologica* in a crate that used to hold LPs (originally milk) and prayed it would be the last time I'd ever have to move those books. The mini-fridge would ride in the back of my RAV4 so as soon as I got to my new home I could re-stock it with cranberry juice, Corona, Bud Light and Diet Pepsi. Important items like my chalice, bible and iPhone were with my keys on the hall table. A print of Saint Priscilla in the catacombs was still on the wall there. I bought it in Rome when I returned to celebrate my anniversary Mass. It was where I said my first Mass and is meaningful to me. It would ride with me in the passenger seat. The big furniture was tagged and ready for the Delancey Street movers, all except the large glass and chrome bar that had been in the quarters when I arrived. It was staying. It wasn't my style.

Now I have a peaceful home miles from the cadence of chancery activity and future plans for the Church, while the historical Archdiocese which I knew continues to suffer ridicule and dismay because of those who now seek a balance and a beauty in a way of doing and thinking, a plan that will restore the Church to the thirteenth century. Father Harry of the God Squad will not be part of it except for the theology of Paul which makes us all part of the Body of Christ and worth our feathers even if we're not flying.

Think I'll watch some TV.

Epilogue

Water Across the Road

I'VE BEEN FORTUNATE to have a close friend since 1961 who owns a home on the beach not far from San Francisco. When I told him about wanting to leave the Shrine, he invited me to live in the apartment adjoining his house.

Who would have thunk it that at age seventy-five I would be both retired and still working, and living by the sea?

And so by God's grace here I sit like someone who has already died and gone to heaven. Watching the waves crash against the rocks and counting the hours before the tide goes out and I can walk on the beach and relish the golden red sky off the horizon. It's a taste of the heaven that I've been working all my life to attain. It's almost too good to be true. I always said that if I had it any better, I'd be twins.

Even as I age, it becomes more and more certain that I will die knowing that through the gifts of God I was given unique talents and opportunities that very few ordained priests have or ever will have.

The Lone Ranger, Roy Rogers, Gene Autry and many others in the Old West rode off into sunsets after a hard day's work at facing their foes and making things right. I can just put on a wetsuit, grab my boogie board and ride the waves until I'm ready to plunge into a hot shower, pour myself a whiskey and think about all the things that I did and said and the lifetime of stories that all began with those three little words. I'll never tell.

Acknowledgments

The author gratefully acknowledges Jeff Arch, the late Patrick Bailey, Della Darling, Madeline Hopkins, Cardinal William Levada, Diane & Tony Martorana, Archbishop George Niederauer, James Normile, Michael O'Leary, Teresa & Michael Ohleyer, Wayne Ressler, Jeananne Milhon Schachern, and also the God Squad Board of Advisors.

About the Author

Father Harry has been telling stories most of his life. Precocious as a child, Harry George Schlitt was the youngest in a blue collar German Catholic family, raised in southern Missouri along the Mississippi River among myriad aunts and uncles and cousins. A natural athlete, thespian and all around good guy, he lacked academic prowess. In a remarkable twist of fate, he found himself transported from rural America on a full scholarship to study in Rome, where he was ordained a priest in 1964. Short on theology but long on charisma, he began a ministry that moved from the high school classroom, to the pulpit, to the airwaves. His first broadcasting gig was as a disc jockey on AM radio in the Ozarks. An improbable series of encounters led him to work at Chicago's legendary WLS-TV, FM radio in Las Vegas, every leading radio and TV station in San Francisco, twenty years on the Armed Forces Radio and Television network, and ultimately the ABC radio network—as Father Harry of the God Squad. He has written thousands of radio scripts and television monologues, more sermons than he can count, and numerous official letters to the many institutions of the Roman Catholic Church. This is his first attempt at a memoir. Retired as Vicar General and Moderator of the Curia from the Archdiocese of San Francisco after fifty years of priesthood, Monsignor Schlitt lives in San Francisco where he plays handball and continues work as a broadcaster presenting the Sunday Mass on TV each week.

CPSIA information can be obtained
at www.ICGtesting.com
Printed in the USA
LVHW051136231219
641443LV00014B/999/P